89 - 0379

THE ANTHROPOLOGY OF
WAR & PEACE

THE ANTHROPOLOGY
OF
WAR & PEACE

Perspectives on the
Nuclear Age

Paul R. Turner, David Pitt
& Contributors

Bergin & Garvey Publishers, Inc.
Massachusetts

First published in 1989 by
Bergin & Garvey Publishers, Inc.
670 Amherst Road
Granby, Massachusetts 01033

9   987654321

Printed in the United States of America

Library of Congress Cataloging-in-Publication Data

The anthropology of war & peace: perspectives on the nuclear age/
Paul R. Turner. David Pitt [editors] & contributors.
p.   cm.
Bibliography: p.
Includes index.
ISBN 0–89789–142–2 (alk. paper) : $44.95
ISBN 0–89789–143–0 (alk. paper) pbk : $18.95
1. War and society. 2. International relations and culture.
3. Nuclear disarmament. I. Turner, Paul R., 1929–   . II. Pitt,
David C. III. Title: The anthropology of war & peace.
U21.5.C65   1989
303.6'6—dc19   89-6925
CIP

To Robert A. Rubinstein
For his tireless efforts in anthropology to help the cause of world peace

CONTENTS

ACKNOWLEDGMENT

It is only in retrospect that we can see how this volume had its inception. It started with a paper that I presented at the 83d annual meeting of the American Anthropological association in Denver, Colorado, November of 1984. The paper was entitled, "Witchcraft and the Cold War," and an expanded version of it appears in this volume. I submitted the original version to Robert A. Rubinstein, editor of the *Newsletter of the International Union of Anthropological and Ethnological Sciences*. He published the article in 1985 and it was read by my coeditor-to-be, David Pitt, of the Geneva International Peace Research Institute. David was unknown to me at the time, but he wrote and suggested we work together on a volume on anthropology and the cold war. I agreed, and this volume is the result of our long-distance correspondence and the work of our contributors.

Appreciation is due to Marcia Lang for typing the manuscript on computer disks in her "spare" time as administrative assistant in the Department of Anthropology, University of Arizona. Barbara Fregoso, departmental secretary, did an outstanding job of preparing the final copy of our manuscript for the publisher. Ann Gross has been our book editor at Bergin & Garvey, and she has gone beyond the mechanics of editing to make suggestions that have had a significant impact on our book and for which we are grateful. Finally, we, the editors, have found Bergin & Garvey to be good publishers to work with. We recommend them to anyone looking for a publisher.

Paul R. Turner

FOREWORD

It is pleasing to see that anthropologists are turning their attention to the cold war and nuclear questions. The social aspects of international conflicts, and particularly the best ways of resolving them, have not been well understood. It is a most urgent task to uncover these deep-lying dynamics since this knowledge will help both those who negotiate and the general public who are so often confused and disappointed. The Geneva International Peace Research Institute (GIPRI) is especially interested to encourage the kind of innovative work that Professor Turner and David Pitt and their colleagues have started.

Alexandre Berenstein
President,
Geneva International Peace Research Institute

FOREWORD

INTRODUCTION
David Pitt

This book might be considered unusual in several ways. First, the anthropologist contributors write not about magic or kinship in exotic climes but about the chilling reality of the world around us, perpetually threatened by what has come to be called the cold war and its arsenal of destruction. Second, with one exception, the book is written by American scientists, some of whom have been intimately involved in the cold war processes and all disillusioned, in one sense or another, with contemporary *realpolitik*. Third, there is a consensus in the book that the differences between the great power blocs are more apparent than real. What divides the world may be essentially cultural and ritual factors which have little relationship to any rational political or social doctrine. Fourth, since the nuclear explosions of Hiroshima and Nagasaki and the quantum leap in the deadliness of weapons, there is a new urgency to find a global solution to war. All this requires innovative negotiating and research, in which anthropology could take the lead and move out from its traditional focus to combine research with action.

This anthropological concern is not new, even if the cold war itself has attracted little attention. There is, in fact, a long tradition of anthropological interest in war and peace as social phenomena in world affairs and in applying the insights of anthropology to solving the problems of war. Certainly some of this experience was derived from being the servants of colonial governments who wanted to pacify bellicose natives, or in participating in war relocation schemes, or even in suggesting that the Japanese emperor should be retained after World

War II (Foster 1969). Before World War II, however, there were few specialized studies of war. Otterbein (1973) explains this in terms of the pacifist and humanitarian views of anthropologists, as well as the suppression of war at the sites of their fieldwork. War was not a fundamental theoretical interest at this period of time (Ferguson 1984a). Since World War II, there has been a much greater interest in peace and disarmament, especially as the nuclear arms race escalated and Americans became involved in Vietnam. By 1964 the American Anthropological Association could adopt resolutions seeking world peace and disarmament (Bunzel and Parsons 1964). Margaret Mead became a champion of this and other good causes. Elsewhere in other countries, in anthropology or whatever name the discipline went under, there were similar movements, so that by the time of the Ninth International Congress of the Anthropological and Ethnological Sciences, a whole volume could be devoted to the anthropology of war (Nettleship 1975). Now there are many books and much controversy as anthropologists have joined hands (or shaken fists) with other disciplines. Indeed, a new synthetic discipline had emerged called Peace Studies. And all the time political scientists, if not historians, have been directing their attention at great length to the cold war.

Yet in all this there are very significant gaps which stimululated the writing of this book. Anthropologists, though interested in war and ultimately disarmament, have said little more than any well-meaning peace activists. There is little effort to get inside the culture of the cold war, East and West. This is partly because the Soviet Union is largely an unknown territory for Westerners. Some ethnographies have been written by emigrés from the Soviet Union, trying to reconstruct a lost world for them. Mead's followers, unfortunately, have emphasized psychological themes and thus produced work that is little more than stereotype, as in Gorer and Rickman (1962). If there is little Western anthropology on the Soviet Union, there is even less contact with the considerable body of Soviet social science (including anthropology), some of it concerned with the problems of war and peace. Only recently, with the formation of the Subcommission of Peace in the International Union for Anthropology and Ethnological Sciences, has there been a focus on the problems of peace and fruitful dialogue between socialist and Western anthropologists.

Deficiencies exist on the Soviet side, too. According to the Dunns (1967), ethnography was slow in starting in the Soviet Union, and they claim that some branches of sociology were barred until the 1960s, though this does not seem to have prevented them from using this material to write their book. More significantly, perhaps, ethnographers, as they are usually called in the Soviet Union, or sociologists do not write a great deal on problems of war and peace, and certainly not on the cold war; this is left rather to international and military experts (Scientific Research Council 1985).

Somewhat similar comments may even be made about those disciplines that have focused on the cold war. The dominant perspective is one of simplistic political analysis, if not propaganda. To paraphrase Berlin (1979), the hedgehogs who see only a small number of big things have overwhelmed the foxes, for whom life lies in complexity. The anthropological contribution is, however, not just to point out this complexity but also to emphasize the possibility that qualitative cultural explorations are more important than the quantitative arithmetic of power politics, economic gain, or prestige.

The question is often asked: why is an anthropological contribution different from, or better than, any other analysis? The answer may be that human action depends most, not on some stated attitude (this is why opinion polls and advertising campaigns alike are so often wide of the mark) but on frames of mind which are deeply embedded in cultural traits, in language, and, particularly, in ritual. These social facts are often collective mentalities, stereotypes, and myths which lead on to a war psychology, not just among elites, but also throughout the public, which in the last analysis supports them.

To prevent war, then, or to promote peace, these frames of mind have to be understood. Typically, anthropologists have studied such phenomena at length and at firsthand through intimate contact. Although there are some examples of such intimacy in this book, the cold war still prevents a great deal being done in the field.

The chapters in the book fall into three categories. We begin with a section on the social and ritual activities specifically underlying the cold war. My own chapter attempts to portray the contemporary elites, East and West, North and South, as sharing the same behavior, not so far removed from the kinship and social structure that anthropologists have traditionally studied in tribal settings. That behavior, as exhibited in tribal societies, Walter Goldschmidt concludes, is not inherently aggressive but leads into conflict when pride or in-group pressures push people to fight. Donna Brasset's point is that the views of military or educational elites in the contemporary United States are shaped by cultural factors, with too little importance attached by the elites to major contemporary ethical values. William O. Beeman argues that the whole of United States foreign policy is based on erroneous and outmoded beliefs, while Paul Turner sees malevolence in contemporary international relations as akin to witchcraft.

The second section is concerned with the greatest threat of our time, nuclear war, which would annihilate the human race or reduce it to Stone Age subsistence. Laura Nader and Albert Bergesen both examine the seemingly inexorable drift to war, pushed on by what can only be called a collective psychosis, part of a rhythm in human history where war and peace come and go in cycles. The special horror of nuclear war, however, is that even minor nuclear skirmishes might reduce the world to a desperate and desolate subsistence in a cold and dying environment, as described by Elizabeth Schueler and George J. Armelagos. But no move to unwind the nuclear time bomb is simple. Keith F. Otterbein shows that disarmament has many dilemmas as long as there is an atmosphere of distrust, where prejudices and stereotypes abound and where deterrents are kept in the cupboard instead of thrown into the rubbish bin of history. On the contrary, as Robert M. Bowman relates from long personal experience, there is a climate for escalation and for moving to even more lethal deterrents and modes of destruction like "Star Wars."

But although this book highlights problems, it does offer solutions. Anthropologists in their research, as R. Brian Ferguson, and Steven L. Sampson and David A. Kideckel demonstrate, can bring to public notice the absurdities and obscenities of what is aptly called "MAD," mutually assured destruction. More important, perhaps, there are hints on how to break the vicious cycle. If war is made in the minds of men, to paraphrase a famous clause in UNESCO's constitution, it can also be broken by ideas. The so-called new thinking which David Pitt finds in the Soviet Union and elsewhere may be a means to more peaceful existence in a Nuclear Age. Whatever else Mr. Gorbachev has done in his two years in the Kremlin, he has made an enormous impression on informed world opinion by his almost weekly concessions affecting the arms race. Americans, led by a tired and aged president, seem much more reluctant to open up their defensive mentalities. But this book is evidence that *glasnost* is not only happening in the Soviet Union; there is a new thinking in the West as well. This book does not have any contributors from any socialist country, so it must be regarded as neither comprehensive nor inclusive. The next step is surely a thoroughgoing anthropological dialogue between East and West in which peace and disarmament will be prime focuses.

I

TRIBAL MENTALITY AND THE COLD WAR

1

THE INTERNATIONAL TRIBE AND THE COLD WAR

David Pitt

Peter Worsley has recently urged social scientists, and anthropologists in particular, to become more involved in the study of, and debates on, international conflict (1985:1,2). Otherwise he fears the ideas that inform defense policies will be dominated by natural scientists and technologists whose thinking is based on defective assumptions about the workings of social institutions and about "human nature." He sees a significant role for anthropologists who specialize in studying "other cultures." They can dissolve the unfortunate stereotypes that exist, especially between the Soviet Union and the United States.

The purpose of this chapter is to take up Worsley's challenge, to see what theories and ideas derived from anthropology may be applicable. We start with classification—the ways in which societies determine the relationships between social categories and groups—because classification has been relatively ignored. Needham, in his introduction to the English translation of Durkheim and Mauss's *De quelques formes primitives de classification*, said he selected this essay because of its theoretical significance and academic neglect (Durkheim and Mauss 1963). This neglect, we argue, is not only of academic significance. Analysis of the cold war and international relations would benefit from the application of notions of classification.

Further, the customs which anthropologists have noticed in the small-scale societies they have studied, customs which some other social scientists have dismissed as "tribal" or "traditional," may indeed be appropriate to the study of the cold war and international relations.

Some indeed have been noticed. Turner, in this volume, sees witchcraft in superpower relations. Elsewhere, we have described the role of myth (Pitt 1976). Competitive gift exchange models may, as Goldschmidt and Cohen (1985) have noted, represent or replace the arms race. But there is much more to be done, especially in the fields of ritual and symbolism.

There are a number of reasons which can be put forward for explaining why anthropologists have neglected international relations, for they are empiricists observing what they take to be objective facts and constructing categories from their observations. Many of the situations we are talking about, however, are not observable; there is little or no chance for participant observation in the Kremlin or the Pentagon. There are admittedly other types of anthropologists than empiricists. Leach (1976:5) has contrasted the empiricists with what he calls the rationalists, represented by Levi-Strauss and the later writings of Evans-Pritchard, where the interest is in ideas rather than objective facts. Categories then may be imposed on the data, especially in the form of opposition (in our case East and West). In rationalist analysis particular attention is paid to language and other symbolic representations. Here the anthropologist of the cold war has a field day. If behavior cannot be easily observed, there are many cold war words written or spoken, including rhetoric, propaganda, and misinformation. There are many other symbols, for example, of the kind studied by the so-called Kremlinologists, who particularly note the changing face of the power structure (Binns 1979). Then, there are all the literature and films, much of them containing the stereotypes that Worsley has talked about. Recently there has emerged a special type which Yevtushenko (1986) calls "warnography," in which there is an ideological justification for personal violence (for example, *Rambo* or *The Boxers*).

But there may be additional neglected sources or situations which lie behind the range of both empiricism and rationalism. Social values may be tacit rather than stated or acted. Again, what may be significant, like Sherlock Holmes's "dog in the night," is what is not, rather than what is, done or said. Also, both behavior and symbols may at times be characterized by volatility, if not confusion, when the structure that anthropologists normally see is absent. Theory and fieldwork alike have had trouble with such occasions, and they tend to be treated as aberrations. One can find many examples of these additional factors in the study of cold war situations. There are many tacit beliefs shared between the superpowers, like the existence of "universal values" (with a capitalist or communist label).[1] Then, there is the apparent taboo on using atomic weaponry. The "dog in the night" syndrome is everywhere in power competition, where Lukes (1973) reminds us that power derives from the ability to leave things off, rather than put them on the agenda. As for times of confusion, these are part of many collective *rites de passage* (for example, changes of leadership) or the important moments of tension (Berlin Wall, Cuban Missile Crisis).

What may be called for, then, is less the description of behavior and symbols and more of a wider situational analysis, using the skills of historical research (Pitt 1983). Many conceptual models used in the past to sort out the data are suspect and may lead to self-fulfilling conclusions. A first task is to subject existing categories and classifications to a very rigorous scrutiny.

THE COLD WAR

First, then, what is the cold war? According to Watt (1977), the phrase was coined by Bernard Baruch on April 16, 1947 and given wide currency by Walter Lippmann. It describes a state of hostility between countries expressed in economic, political, or subversive action which stops short of "hot war" or a "shooting war." It was applied to Soviet-Western relations from 1917, but more generally to the East-West situation since 1945, though some would end the cold war at 1955 and others after the 1962 Cuban Missile Crisis, after which there were attempts to control arms and nuclear proliferation with moves toward détente and peaceful coexistence.

The cold war, or whatever we call it, is hostility between countries or social systems (capitalism and communism). Such classifications immediately raise problems. Anthropologists have generally divided up the world into many more cultures (or subcultures) than the 170 or so recognized nations. The Human Relations Area Files has nearly 1000 cultures; others have suggested 2,000; while a recent linguistic atlas gives more than 5,000 (McNeely and Pitt 1985). The Soviet Union and the United States are two of the most pluralistic countries and the situation is infinitely complicated by the recent mass phenomenon of migration, which has meant that subcultural entities are now replicated in many places. Furthermore, and maybe more significantly, alongside any processes of fission have been processes of fusion, or at least volatility, where subcultures have changed their shape and form and created new structures. Most subcultures of the world are on the periphery of the power structure which directs the cold war, so that it might seem meaningless to talk of the war being between countries, let alone social systems. The concept of social systems in any case is subject to so many variations and revisions that it becomes a highly rarified ideal type of little use in analysis.

INTERNATIONAL POWER ELITES

Can we identify the subcultures which are involved in the cold war? Certainly there has been a large literature on the sociological characteristics of the power elites, both in the West and East. In the United States there is a wealthy white Anglo-Saxon Protestant tendency in both the political and bureaucratic processes. And something similar may be true of the dynasties of the Soviet Union, where much Calvinism can be found in the communism. There are similarities too in regional influences. Before Reagan, Californians were not important on Capitol Hill. Stalin brought Georgian feuds as well as Georgian wines to Moscow. The subcultural or ethnic interpretation of national politics, which tends to be frowned on in nationalistic phases, can be a valuable key to explaining what is happening in many countries from Afghanistan to Zimbabwe.

But any anthropological fieldworker from outer space studying the power elites might be excused if he or she saw similarities between the elites of different cultures rather than differences between them. Some years ago such an intrepid Francophone journalist found a remote country which he named Onuland (the UN in French is ONU) where the inhabitants all seemed to resemble one another: "They all have the same physical appearance, the same clothes and mostly the same spectacles" (Boyd 1962:42). Onuland's main export was mimeographed copies of speeches, though they hoped in the near future to produce a very rare substance called "peace."

Are the power elites of the world part of this, or at least part of the same subculture? If so, it is no new situation. The medieval monarchs of warring states were often related and settled international disputes with judicious marriages. Certainly today the power elites dress alike even if they need interpreters to talk to each other. Mrs. Gorbachev has her Gucci bag, and supposedly Soviet superiors dream of owning Volvos as well as vodka. In those neutral "watering holes" where the superpowers meet inside or outside the UN, notably Geneva, where there are virtually permanent bilateral discussions, it is not always easy to tell East from West. Indeed, the officials who conduct the talks may be seen dining together at the Perle du Lac Restaurant or chatting in the supermarket queues at the Migros. The subcultural circle is certainly not complete. There are great barriers to communication. The Soviet Union and Albania are two countries in the Geneva telephone directory that cannot be dialed direct, although telephonic difficulties may be an internal phenomenon, as can be attested by anyone who has waited through the night with the citizenry at a Soviet central telephone exchange for a call to Kiev or the Crimea. There is certainly not much intermarriage, though in both superpowers marriage may be no longer a central institution.

Too, the composition of the international power elite varies over time. Superpower membership itself is not fixed, nor is the opposition. Eighteenth century historians talk of the diplomatic revolution when the continental powers suddenly reshuffled, joining erstwhile enemies. There have been recent occasions (for example, the 3rd Review meeting in 1985 of the Nuclear Non-Proliferation Treaty) when the two giants, the Soviet Union and the United States found themselves with some other members of the nuclear club aligned against the non-nuclear powers. In the UN itself, or in the competition between specialized agencies, the North-South opposition became dominant, the latter consisting of the so-called Group of 77 (now numbering over 120 less-developed nations) against the industrialized powers.

These shifts occur despite the structural characteristics of the nations involved. Rather like Leach's analysis (1965) of Gumsa-Gumlao in Highland Burma, different political systems (communism and capitalism, democracy and authoritarianism) are covered by the same cultural trappings and may either converge towards a single type, change from one to the other, or be as irrelevant to the power structure as Lord Protector Cromwell was when he succeeded divine King Charles the First.

What is most significant to the homogeneity of the international subculture are these common ritual settings in which the power elite actors find themselves. O'Brien and Topolski (1968) call the UN a sacred drama, and it is undoubtedly a key common arena for both ritual actors and the expression of common ideas (myths). There may be nondiplomatic arenas too, notably sports, which are similar in function and increasingly politicized. Much of this ritual homogeneity is not spoiled by violent argument. Verbal violence has its own ritual rhetoric, and most speeches pass without delegates seemingly hearing or reading them. Ostracism or withdrawal need hardly affect the situation, either. When the United States withdrew from the International Labor Organization some years ago (over a Soviet appointment as an assistant director-general), the United States contribution actually increased, though through the back door. The United States still goes to UNESCO meetings as an observer and also contributes millions to some UNESCO programs, such as MAB (Man and the Biosphere). Thus, there may be a greater flow than is generally realized of people and information across the East-West divide, and not just double agents and secret papers.

NORTH-SOUTH CONFRONTATION

So much do the superpowers and their power elites share many beliefs, including the existence of "universal values," that Bertrand (1986) has said the real war is not between East and West but between North (including both superpowers) and South. He sees the question of universal values as a camouflage for imperialism.

Is the real cold war a North-South confrontation? Here social scientists, though not usually anthropologists, have done quite a lot of work. The first point is that, although the war has been cold in the North, it has been hot in the South. There are estimates that there have been as many as 400 wars in the South since World War II, with more casualties, disruption, and damage than that war (Kahnert et al. 1983). Certainly the origins of these wars are often internally derived, from power competition, including ethnic and tribal rivalries. But the war is not only hot. The North has a massive economic involvement in the South, through military sales and often related assistance and through aid and trade. Nuclear weaponry is only a small part (less than 20 percent) of military expenditure in the North.

But there may be a more fundamental relationship than the North-South confrontation which involves two types of peace development. There is *negative peace*, which is a situation of arms buildup like the cold war, and *positive peace*, where there is widespread harmony, social integration, and nonalignment (Galtung 1984). Development is also differentiated into top-down and bottom-up—the former typified by both centrally directed economies and capitalistic structures, the latter by small-scale, self-reliant cooperative endeavors. Illich (1982) argues that top-down development militates against peace not only because expenditure on armaments leaves little for relief of poverty, but also because aid and trade, which is at worst exploitative and at best creates dependencies, deprives people of their status and the chance to be self-reliant. They are not left in peace, as he puts it.

Anthropologists seem rarely to have studied these neocolonialist forms (including both the UN and the multinational corporations) which have both capitalist and socialist variants, nor have they noticed the reshuffling of categories that is involved in the South, because of the Northern presence. It has been said that development is the poor people in rich countries giving to the rich people in poor countries. The power elites of the South may have a close symbiotic relationship to, if they do not directly emulate, the power elites who arrive from the North. Together they form what has been called the development set, meeting in the local Hilton to discuss hunger and poverty, spending large portions of the budget on bureaucratic white elephants.

To say that the cold war is between the two superpowers is then something of a myth. This myth is important; it justifies the existence of military-industrial complexes on both sides of the iron curtain, and these might be said to be central to what are essentially command economies with worldwide ramifications. There may be other structural benefits familiar to anthropologists since Gluckman's (1960) study of the peace in the feud, where violence or the threat of it was enough to sustain order. The whole structure of deterrence through to MAD (mutually assured destruction) is a clear example of a Gluckman process. Sometimes the threat becomes reality, as in the United States attack on Libya in April 1986. But the widespread critical reaction even among America's allies possibly ensured that such real violence would be rare.

But the cold war, as Baruch originally said, is essentially a question of economic conflict, we would say not only, even not mainly, between East and West, but rather between North and South. How far do anthropological models and ideas help here? Marcel Mauss's (1954) seminal model of "The Gift" may well provide some significant insights, notably in seeing the relationship as a totality to be interpreted holistically. Mauss indeed saw war as one part of the process of exchange of goods and services, symbols, women, etc., by which disparate groups were joined. Indeed, there is a significant anthropological literature purporting to show how property and other exchanges become surrogates for war and also a means of conflict resolution and the maintenance of peace. The best studied examples are probably the Kwakiutl potlatch which Codere (1950) has called "fighting with poverty," and there is also Malinowski's analysis of the Kula (Uberoi Singh 1962), or the studies of *weregilt* (or *bit*), where money was exchanged in lieu of the blood feud, when somebody was killed or property damaged.

Is then the cold war, and the North-South relationship a kind of potlatch? Arms appear somewhat similar to Kwakiutl coppers or blankets. There are now enough bombs to destroy the world 50 times over, it is said. The stock of goods (including food) in the world may far exceed the needs of people to eat it, even if the milk lakes and grain mountains cannot be distributed to those who need it. Exchange rates, inflation, interest levels, may all be forms where the potlatch analogy is instructive, that is, where goods are held back from consumption or devoted to prestige activities or conspicuous consumption because of social competition. But there is a vital difference. If the North-South (or indeed, the East-West) gift exchange worked, there would not be war or underdevelopment (Thompson, Warburton, and Hatley 1986).

In the present situation it is the South which is constantly placed at a status disadvantage. The superpowers, or more exactly, the nuclear club, permit vertical proliferation, that is, the rapid accumulation of their own nuclear armaments within their countries, but prohibit horizontal proliferation, even for peaceful energy purposes. Rarely do Southern currencies appreciate. There is a constant movement away from self-reliant production in the South, notably in agriculture to cash cropping, where dependencies are created; and there is a constant movement of people away from the greater independence of the countryside to the slums of the cities, where the forces and media of change are the most intense. Even in socialist systems where self-reliance has an importance, it is often a development that is centrally directed.

The resolution of this situation may, like the potlatch, require the blankets to be burned, that is, not only disarmament, weapons destruction, but also the dismantling of Bretton Woods, decolonization, deflation, and devolution.

Perhaps this is too simple a model as well as too naive an aspiration. Is the social process simply a mechanical dialectic, détente following the cold war, independence following colonization, and so on? Clearly any new situation has something of its predecessors, whether the change is evolutionary or revolutionary, and a case can be made that sharp breaks may be more apparent than real (plus ça change, plus c'est la même chose) as in Geertz's models of agricultural involution (Geertz 1964).

There are, in fact, some other interesting anthropological models which may help explain better the dynamics of this complex situation, especially the breaks that do occur in the harmony of the gift exchange. Although Mauss included war in his schema, it was the relatively nonviolent ritualized conflict of traditional societies. Such war may have been positive in the sense of preserving or restoring social harmony. But wars, especially recent wars, have been much more negative, involving massive civilian deaths, holocausts, and ethnocide. More useful here may be Van Gennep's rites of passage model. Van Gennep (1960) saw important transitions in life (birth, puberty, marriage, death) as being marked by three phases: separation, transition, and incorporation, each with its own rituals; and he included territorial passage in his schema. The cold war may be an historical variant, that is, separation (cold war), incorporation (détente), with important periods of transition. In Van Gennep's model, this time of transition is highly dangerous, confused, and unstable. Possibly negative war, or indeed any forms of individual or collective disorder and irrationality, may be interpreted in this way. Such transitional periods are marked by a heightened attempt to impose order on such a fluid situation. Te Velde (1977), in a neglected work, shows how in ancient Egypt the god Seth was seen to bring violence and disorder into the world. Seth ignores all boundaries, he becomes homosexual, and he is also the god of the desert and foreigners. Seth is a scapegoat, explaining and ultimately re-uniting with the good god, Horus. The present tendency to vilify the enemy, as in the current United States warnography, may therefore be an expected reaction to disorder and even a positive dissipation of fear. Whatever else is said, there seems little doubt that in the dangerous transitions, every encouragement should be given to those public and secular rituals by which order and rationality can be restored (Moore and Myerhoff 1977).

The 1985 Reagan-Gorbachev talks in Geneva, for example, with their many set-pieces of smiles and hopeful words broadcast world-wide, may indeed be of great importance. The enormous publicity of this occasion is worth noticing. There were so many journalists in Geneva that the Swiss telephone company had to lay many kilometers of new telephone lines, and one Japanese news crew had to sleep on a boat on the lake. The avoidance of war, the movement from the dangerous transition phase to incorporation détente, seems in a global village created by the telecommunications revolution to depend on public acceptance. This may be another hopeful sign for the future, since it may indicate that public pressure can be influential, despite all the hierarchy and stratification of governments.

What more can the anthropologist contribute to future improvements? In the futurology of the cold war, as in its history, the anthropologist could provide models derived from small-scale self-reliant societies, including the campfire democracies of hunters and gatherers, the reciprocative or redistributive structures that were found in many parts of traditional Africa and the Pacific, or the stateless societies. The last model of segmentary lineages where there are entities without rulers or power elites (Middleton and Tait 1958) might be very useful for a wider global society. No longer would a power elite be dominant, but one subculture amongst many others, so providing the final act for the Marxist scenario where the state withers away.

Some of these ideas have been foreshadowed in Schumacher's theories (1973), *Small is Beautiful,* or the so-called Fourth World literature. Here a human dimension is discovered when the forces of production, distribution, and exchange are located within small face-to-face groups. Schumacher's Buddhist economics embrace a pacifistic approach to goods and services, to fellow humankind, and to nature, the last being an important and neglected object of exploitation in the present global economy.

But it should be recognized that Schumacher's utopia, no less than Rousseau's noble savages, may be something of a pious ideal, or at least a somewhat isolated success story. Autarky has its own limits to growth just as extreme separation creates the cold war. Separation may become apartheid, an artificial preservation of populations as endangered species in national parks, or, politically, the creation of many Albanias. Subsistence institutions, basic needs, primary health care may be excuses for richer strata to provide for a second-class, inferior development which does not reflect basic local wants and aspirations. Young people especially may not feel traditional tribal loyalties.

Vibrant grass-roots society, no less than power elites, derives vigor from the flow of ideas and people. More prosaically, it is simply impossible to stop altruistic or exploitative outsiders from labelling small, isolated communities as poor or deprived, and using any "disastrous" excuse to intervene. The telecommunications revolution has meant that there are no more unaffected islands, both because the transistor is so ubiquitous and because the younger generation seems to be particularly susceptible to its magic.

To explain and conceptualize these situations may require new kinds of models (or the revitalized models of Van Gennep or Mauss) which accommodate to the volatility and flexibility of contemporary peace and development situations. These models may find that subcultures, or, indeed all social groups, are only temporary structures to which, and through which, people come and go. There is a pluralism, then, in time as well as space. Because there is flux and also because the boundaries between structures are not usually clear lines but zones of transition, any resolution of conflicts like the cold war, whether between East and West or North and South, may first of all require not only a redistribution of power and resources, but also a recognition of the existential quality of everyday life.

POSTSCRIPT: THE MOSCOW FORUM

As we have said, it is rare for the anthropologist to be a participant-observer in much of the ritual of the international tribe, and rarer still to be present at a major event in such a secret and sacred shrine as the Kremlin. Shortly after I had finished writing this chapter, I was fortunate enough to be invited in February 1987 to the Moscow Forum, a gathering of leading scientists, intellectuals, and religious and political leaders which culminated in a meeting with Gorbachev in the Kremlin. The Western press wrote off the occasion as propaganda for the party faithful, a jaundiced view in part explained by the wide berth given most of the discussion by the press. The Forum probably contained more critics (including Sakharov) than the card-carrying cadre of fellow travelers.

The meeting was a good example of what has come to be called *glasnost* which might be roughly translated as openness or, more exactly, the widening of public knowledge and participation. Through *glasnost* a new thinking is being attempted across a wide range of subjects and practical affairs. The Moscow Forum focused specifically on the problem of nuclear weapons and the possibilities of creating a nuclear-free world.

Glasnost may mark a new phase, even a quantum leap in the cold war thaw. *Glasnost* differs from earlier phases like *détente* (the easing of tension) or later ideas like *démarche* (reduction of armaments) in that the two opposed blocs mingle and meld and the whole process is much more public. At the Moscow Forum a very considerable amount of common ground was found. Graham Greene, for example, pointed to an alliance between Catholicism and communism, and not only in Latin America.

Glasnost, in fact, may be said to have provided, or have the potential for, the ideological frame for the international tribe. Ivan Frolov, the Head of the Institute of Philosophy at Moscow State University and a member of the Politburo, as one of the architects of *glasnost*, admitted freely that the idea, and what has come to be called the new thinking, is a rather tender infant with even the parents not sure as to how the child will mature. But, some characteristics may already be distinguished. First, of course, is that of openness, the greater movement of ideas and peaceful trade to allow the basic needs of human beings to be met and to eradicate poverty. Second is pluralism, a greater tolerance of different social systems coexisting in peace between countries and within countries. A third characteristic is holism, the recognition of a healthy global interdependence in a biosphere embracing all of nature. Fourth, is conservation, not just of species but of energy, with the reduction of pollution and waste.

The significance of the Moscow Forum is that similar ideas are surfacing in the West in the ecological movements which stress holism, health, and small, self-reliant models. The major common thread is the opposition to nuclear weapons and the concerted efforts to create nuclear-weapon-free zones. Now that the South Pacific has joined Latin America and Antarctica, all the southern hemisphere, save Indonesia and Africa, are part of nuclear-weapon-free zones. India and the Balkans have plans to join the movement. The idea has spread to cities and citizen groups with even houses and cars being declared as nuclear free. The international tribe is expanding.

The Times of London (Feb. 17, 1987) saw the Moscow Forum as a partisan event, which "coupled with the traditional Soviet turgidity of the proceedings may have made a sequel unlikely." Such pessimism was certainly not present in Moscow, where the atmosphere was positive, even highly charged. The golden onion domes of the Kremlin Palace glistened on a February morning so mild that Muscovites said that the Forum had not only brought foreign guests, but also an early spring. Certainly organizational structures were established, like the Ecoforum group of scientists which are now moving rapidly towards international projects. A new international fund was established, with convertible rubles, which may support new, independent, science-based, international projects, removed from the political taint and administrative inefficiency of the UN and other international white elephants. Beyond this may be more—a quickening exchange of students and young people, a flood of tourists (perhaps even émigrés) from the East, and perhaps a peace based, as in the Middle Ages, on the common interest and kinship of a cosmopolitan elite.

NOTE

1. Contributors to the 1985 United Nations Conference on universality in Geneva came from both East and West and equally bemoaned the jeopardy they face in "universal values," that is, universal peace promoted by the UN.

2

INDUCEMENT TO MILITARY PARTICIPATION IN TRIBAL SOCIETIES

Walter Goldschmidt

Why do men fight?[1] Why do men leave the comfort and security of ordinary life to engage in an activity that has been described as long stretches of tedium interspersed with moments of terror? This is a different question from "Why warfare?"—an issue many anthropologists have addressed with indifferent success. Here we are asking: Why do individuals willingly undertake such unpleasant, life-threatening activity? This issue is important. It addresses the matter of human nature, and while anthropologists have for several decades avoided this subject, it is an issue that will not go away. The easy popular response to the problematic elements in human behavior is to blame the flaws in man's make-up.

To put the matter bluntly in the form it is frequently posed: Do men fight because it is in their nature to do so? Is war a product of man's violent character? I think the evidence that follows has something to say on this subject, and that my reading of that evidence will offer some surprises.

At one time it was felt that "primitive man" could uncover the basic humanity—the instinctive nature—that underlies all of us, since the "savage" was thought to be closer to the natural condition of the species. We have long known that this is not the case, for tribal peoples are everywhere engulfed by their own cultures, and these are just as determinant on their behavior as ours is on us. Yet, we do get a measure of man throughout the *comparative* examination of tribal peoples. This can show the range of possibilities, the diversity in the human behav-

15

ioral repertoire. It can also uncover consistencies in behavior and, above all, can establish how common circumstances can evoke similar responses.

In this chapter I report on the attitudes that tribal peoples have toward military activity and on the way young men, and occasionally women, are drawn into the business of combat. I have examined the literature on twenty-seven tribal communities and preliterate state systems drawn to represent the universe of all such communities in which military activity is salient. This sample, with a few exceptions, was taken from those societies that had high scores on military involvement as established by Ross (1983) from the Standard Ethnographic Sample (Murdock and White, 1969). This procedure assures that I am dealing with wide geographical coverage and diverse cultural backgrounds. But I have chosen to concentrate on what may be called militaristic, rather that peaceable, peoples. It does not purport to be a sample in the strict sense. I do not think this matters for in my tables I will only give frequencies of reported behavior and not indulge in any correlations.[2] The selected tribes are listed in the appendix.

DIVERSITY OF WAR IN TRIBAL SOCIETIES

The literature shows that the character of military operations varies widely among tribal societies. In those societies where there is something approaching a nation state, warfare is a matter of national policy serving expansionist ambitions, territorial protection, and possibly also the preservation of internal structure (Baganda, Fon, Kazak, Wolof, and probably Shilluk and Creek). In three of the societies, military operations, though important, were designed primarily for defense (Hopi, Papago, and Tonga). Among the Mapuche, Chuckchee, Ainu, and probably others, defensive operations were mainly against the encroachment of so-called civilized societies. Patterns of raiding and counter-raiding appear to have been characteristic of the remaining societies examined. Land was clearly at issue in some (Ainu, Haida, Maori, and Mae Enga), loot or booty (often livestock) more frequently (Abipone, Apache, Cheyenne, Chuckchee, Klamath, Mapuche, Pawnee, Rwala, and Nyakyusa).

A few societies are found that are more like the popular stereotype where raiding and counter-raiding seem to be ends in themselves and taking trophies and acquiring honor the sole apparent purpose of war. These attitudes dominated the behavior of the Igorot, the Jivaro, and the Mundurucu and to a lesser extent the Andamanese and Aranda, among whom warfare is less important. Even in these instances, economic consequences are potentially present. For instance, in the detailed description of military activities among the Tsembaga (Rappaport: 1967), who are not in my sample but who share this pattern, territorial transfers do result from wars, and there is some evidence that the military action of the Jivaro has territorial consequences.

One of the most consistent elements that emerges from the ethnography of warfare is the perception that the purpose of warfare is vengeance or retaliation. Aside from the three state-organized peoples (Baganda, Fon, and Wolof), only the Ainu, Mundurucu, and Pawnee are not described as having such motivation. The two defense-oriented people, Hopi and Papago, express this as retaliation, the others as vengeance for murder, wife stealing, or the taking of property.

While I am not analyzing these data to determine the cause of warfare, they do make it clear that the popular anthropological notion that primitive war is merely a "game" and without economic consequences is clearly not supported. Land or territorial considerations are frequently found to be salient elements (Ainu, Andamanese, Baganda, Haida, Kazak, Maori, Mae Enga, Mapuche, Rwala, Shilluk, and Wolof), acquisition of goods of some kind in nineteen instances, and in only three instances is such booty specifically denied (Igorot, Papago, Hopi). Tribal warfare is usually serious *economic* business.

FEAR

Before we examine the manner in which men in tribal societies are induced to fight, we should take note of the fact that they are not immune to fear. Indeed, inducements are necessary because men dread the fact of war. Even in those societies that place great emphasis upon military exploits and in which men are prone to exaggerate their military prowess, we find clear evidence that, such public statements to the contrary notwithstanding, men fear their own military pursuits. Consider the Yanomamo, who have come to represent the quintessential nature of tribal warfare in the modern literature, having been given the sobriquet, "the fierce people." They boast and posture on the eve of their departure to avenge a death; they brag: "I'm so fierce that when I shoot the enemy my arrow will strike with such force that blood will splash all over the material possessions of the household!" (Chagnon 1977:129).[3] But let us watch what actually happens. The leader of one expedition, though ill and in great pain, insisted on going, "*suspecting others would turn back if he did not lead it*" (Chagnon 1977:130, emphasis added). He was right:

> *The raiders had not been gone five hours when the first one came back, a boastful young man, complaining that he had a sore foot*

and could not keep up with the others. The next day a few more men returned, complaining that they had malaria and pains in the stomach. They enjoyed participating in the pomp of the Wayu Itou [the preparatory war ritual], for this impressed the women, but they were, at heart, cowards. . . . On the last evening [before the actual attack, while sleeping in the bush], the raiding party's fierce ones have difficulties with the younger men; most of them are afraid, cold, and worried about every sort of hazard, and all of them complain of sore feet and belly aches (1977:130).

Later, when Chagnon took a group of warriors part way to their battle area in his power boat, he noted that the leader

was not enthusiastic about going on the raid, despite the fact that he lectured the younger members of the raiding party about their overt reluctance and cowardice. He was older, however, and had to display the ferocity that adult men are supposed to show. In short, although Hukoshikuwa probably had very little desire as an individual to participate in the raiding, he was obliged to do so by the pressures of the entire system (1977:35–6).

So much for ferocity—whether natural or culturally induced.

Similar attitudes are found among the Abipones, described by Dobrizhoffer a century and a half ago. Though he emphasizes their military exploits and ferocity, he also says:

Should a report be spread . . . that the enemy are coming in a few days, it is enough. Numbers, dreading the loss of life more than fame, will desert their Cacique, and hasten with their families to some well-known retreats. Lest, however, they should be branded with the name of deserters and cowards, they say they are going out to hunt (1822:105).

And elsewhere, he notes that they do not "hazard an attack unless confident of victory" (1822:363).

The Creek of the southern United States, who share these public values of military prowess, also find their warriors to be reluctant. Indeed, they have *institutionalized* their readiness to abandon the war path with standardized excuses, for

if their dreams portend any ill, they always obey the supposed divine intimation and return home, without incurring the least censure. They reckon that their willingness to serve their country should not be subservient to their own knowledge or wishes, but always regulated by the divine impulse. I have known a whole company who set out for war, to return in small parties, and sometimes by single persons, and be applauded by the united voice of the people; because they acted in obedience to their Nana Ishto-hoollo, or "guardian angels," who impressed them in their visions of night, with the friendly caution (James Adair, quoted in Swanton 1909:408–9).

The description of warfare among the Mae Enga is the most detailed, intimate, and unromanticized in the ethnographic literature. These New Guinea Highland peoples also tend to express self confidence but are quite aware of fear. A youth who is afraid in combat might be excused and encouraged by his elders to raise his spirits and confidence, or will be reminded that, in any case, his death is foreordained by the sun and thus inescapable. Such a youth may also be shamed. But an older man who tries to evade his military duties—among the Mae Enga warfare is over land—will be ridiculed and told to remain among the women, who are viewed as polluting. To escape calumny, such a man will depart with his family for a period of time but even so will suffer loss of reputation and political influence.

COUNTER-FEAR

There are, the saying goes, no atheists in foxholes. The Creek use of religious belief in the support of fear, as just noted, is reflected elsewhere in the religious practices associated with war. Consider the war dance, the rituals that are designed to psych the men up for their endeavor (see Table 1), which were reported in eighteen of our twenty-seven instances. In four of these, some kind of drugs (alcohol, tobacco, or "medicines") were an important element in their rituals. Such rituals were not reported for the Fon, Kazak, and Wolof—tribes in which military pursuit is in the hands of a more or less professional soldiery.

The Apache, for instance, have religious dances for four nights preceding a raiding party. It is a dramatization of the war itself; they dance through the night with "fierce dancing," as they call it. The men are dressed as for war and appear at the ceremony to show their intention. Men who do not appear are called by name in the songs "You, So-and-so, many times you have talked bravely. Now brave people . . . are calling you." If a man doesn't come out and make good his boasts, he is not considered a man. "The dance is a profound religious experience for the man who takes part in it," according to Opler (1941:336–37), but it is religion in the service of emotional reinforcement.

In addition to such efforts to get psyched up for battle, there are other practices that help to allay fear. In eight instances a shaman, priest, or medicine man is actively involved in the preparation for warfare, often responsible for magically determining or predicting the outcome of the conflict, and sometimes accompanying the warriors. In twelve instances, amulets, fetishes, or other special devices are carried by the soldiers as magical protection and support. Clearly, tribal soldiers enter into combat with apprehension and concern, and militaristic societies regularly evoke sacred elements in their culture and counteract the negative sentiments of their citizen warriors.

WARFARE AND THE MASCULINE CAREER

It is my observation that in every society of mankind, however large or small, however independent or encapsulated in some large social order, the men and women seek acceptance and social standing in their community and will strive to achieve this through appropriate behavior to the extent they are permitted and in the degree to which they are capable. This I believe to be a human universal; what varies from one community to another is the definition of those attributes that confer status upon the individual and the culturally approved manner in which the individual is permitted to pursue such aims.[4] I perceive the pattern of activity, together with the rewards and frustrations of such individual pursuits as constituting the *careers* of men and women, respectively. In tribal societies the trajectory of such careers tend to have a standardized pattern for each sex, though of course the attainment of individuals within the society will differ as a result of circumstance, ability, energy, and the like.

In militaristic tribal societies, military activity contributes one element—often a major element—in the pursuit of career. Acceptance, prestige, material goods, and influence depend largely upon performance of men as warriors. Indeed service as a warrior is taken for granted, much as in our society men expect to work to earn a living. Even where warfare was viewed as a "necessary evil," as among the Papago (Underhill 1946:165) and Hopi, with their self-image as peaceable, this attitude appears to have prevailed. Only among political societies where the military operations are in the hands of professionalized soldiers was this not the case, though even there military accomplishments were a source of status to the soldier group.[5]

This perception of the social order leads us to an examination of the character of the military career under two major headings—preparation for service and rewards for accomplishment.

PREPARATION FOR MILITARY SERVICE

Only a few ethnographers describe in detail the training of soldiers, but many give certain specifics. In our sample, six mentioned training in skills, seven apprenticeship in warfare, and seven games and contests designed to establish military qualities (Table 2). Youth were made to endure pain in twelve societies and endurance of other hardships in nine.[6] Legends and stories designed to reinforce militaristic attitudes were mentioned in seven instances. Most societies consciously inculcate military virtues in some ways, and I am confident that if our data were more complete, they would all do so in many ways.

Where ethnographers have investigated the matter directly, we find elaborate schooling for the warriors. Among the Apache the emphasis on being brave and tough is strong and pervasive, though to be brave meant not to be afraid, but yet to be cautious. "The man who blindly ran into trouble without fear was a fool, not a brave man" (Baldwin 1965: 97). According to Opler (1941: 65), "the child and adult often listen together to accounts of the rigors of the hunt, of the hardships and glories of war, and of the cruelties of the enemy. 'As soon as I was old enough to know,' said one informant, 'I was told who were our enemies.' " The elaborate training of Apache youth included practical education to make them strong and increase their endurance and skills and religious rites to ensure their safety. Older people tell the youths that the enemy is as frightened as he is and that "if he puts on a brave front and charges, the enemy may run" (Opler 1941: 72). Boys are warned that girls will not marry a cowardly or lazy person. Youths are particularly trained in endurance and in running. One test involves running a course with a mouth full of water which may not be swallowed. If the boy swallows the water on the way, the trainer sees that he doesn't do it a second time! They match youths of the same age and have them engage in running contests and fighting. They were expected to engage in fights even with superior fighters. They also engage in mock fights with slings to learn both attack and defense. Later they fight in teams with bows and arrows and though the arrows are small, they can inflict severe damage. Later still, they are trained in handling horses, and in long cross-country journeys without food or sleep. "The boys who achieve a position of superiority during this training period rise to pre-eminence in their age group ... the foundations of status recognitions are laid in the training period ..." (Opler 1941: 74). When a boy wants to volunteer, his relatives tell him of the hardships and dangers; and only if he feels prepared is he allowed to go. He remains a novice during his first four military expeditions, and during this time he is thought to be particularly vulnerable—comparable to a girl during her puberty ritual—and receives special instruction from a relative or a shaman. Only after this lengthy training, is an Apache recognized as a warrior and as a full member of the tribe.

Jivaro indoctrination starts early. According to Stirling, when a

boy is about the age of six, he is instructed each morning on the necessity of being a warrior and incited to avenge the feuds in which his
family is involved. Such admonition "is repeated every morning regularly for more than five years, until the parent sees that the son has
been thoroughly inoculated with the warlike spirit and the idea of blood
revenge" (Stirling 1938: 51). From the age of seven, boys are regularly
taken on war expeditions with their fathers and, though they do not
actually engage in combat, they get accustomed to the methods of
warfare and learn to defend themselves and not to be afraid. At the age
of 15 or 16 the Jivaro youth undergoes an initiation during which he
must observe numerous taboos and in which he is given a narcotic
drink and tobacco to smoke in order to transfer the power of the tobacco
to him. "This power will automatically show itself in all the work and
occupations encumbent on him as a male member of society. He will
be a brave and successful warrior and be able to kill many enemies . . ."
(Karsten 1935: 242).

Among the Mae Enga (Meggitt 1977: 61–64), the training is less
formalized and intrusive but equally pervasive. At the age of eight,
boys move into their fathers' homes and spend much time in the company of men—avoiding women who are viewed as polluting and en-
ervating. Boys are expected to do useful work, but fathers watch with
approval any evidence of a son's aggressiveness in childhood scuffles.
Boys also play at warfare over imaginary houses and gardens and go
on to "negotiate settlements." Later they receive specific and detailed
instructions in the handling of weapons and tactics, and get practice
in the handling of scaled-down weapons that have been made for them.
Soon thereafter a boy will get his first sentry duty and will be beaten
if he is reluctant. No fuss is made over wounds so that the youth will
learn "what pain is all about." When a boy is about fifteen, he joins
the bachelors' association and receives a full complement of weapons.
After another two or three years he participates in the warfare but not
on the front line of fight. He is urged to participate in the battles of
neighboring friendly groups so that he can become enured to the dangers of battle.

Such descriptions make it clear that it takes a major effort to make
aggressive warriors out of tribal children. When Carol and Melvin Ember examined the social and psychological correlates to warfare in tribal
societies, the only significant relationship with intensity of warfare
they found was the socialization and training of boys for aggressiveness
(Ember and Ember 1984: 6). They rightly note that this indoctrination
is probably a consequence rather than a cause of war, for they also
found a strong tendency for such aggression training to disappear
among peoples who have been "pacified" by colonial powers.

REWARDS FOR MILITARY ACCOMPLISHMENT

In virtually every society examined, the successful warrior is rewarded with booty, slaves, women (either as concubines or wives) or the opportunity to adopt captives (see Table 3). In only four (Andamanese, Igorot, Jivaro, and Mae Enga) of the twenty-seven societies examined, was no material reward for the soldier mentioned, though in four (Aranda, Creek, Hopi, and Mundurucu) these rewards are slight or rare. It generally pays to be a warrior—if you survive.

But I believe it is the nonmaterial rewards that really induce men to fight. In almost every society examined, the returned warrior receives accolades of some kind—honor or prestige (thirteen cases), special titles or membership in special societies (twelve cases), political influence or positions of leadership (eighteen cases). Only for two societies (Ainu and Andamanese) is there no mention of any such rewards, while for the Haida the ethnographic data suggests it is the house-group rather than the individual who is rewarded. The same ambiguity applies to the Igorot, for the successful head hunter gets a special tattoo—but so does his whole group. In three of the societies listed, death in battle was recognized as a special virtue and presumably involved some postmortem status for the slain. Giving special status to the warrior is also the most effective means of socializing the new generation into military activity. Young boys see the rewards, the prestige, the strutting, and have for themselves role models which they naturally emulate.

WARFARE AND WOMEN

The role of women in the conduct of war in tribal societies varies widely. Battalions of Amazons existed among the Fon, who had a professional military group; indeed, women constituted approximately a third of the army of the king. They engaged in warfare quite like the men, emulating and even exceeding their masculine counterparts. Some Klamath women "are said to fight like the men, shouting and jumping about to add to the terrifying effect of the surprise. Armed with short spears they help to catch the women and children and to slay the aged as they run to hide" (Spier 1930: 31). Among the Ainu, women also engaged in fighting. Ainu battle was hand to hand combat between individuals and the women fought the women. Mundurucu women accompanied the military expeditions but did not engage in combat, only serving the soldiers from a safe distance. Elsewhere, women goaded men to battle (Rwala women bared their breasts and urged their men to war) while, among the Andamanese, women tried to settle quarrels and bring fighting to a conclusion. Repeatedly, women were expected to engage in ceremonial activities or to maintain extreme decorum while their men were away fighting; among the Jivaro they danced each night, among the Haida they stayed home and acted out the war, while the wives of Baganda soldiers were expected to remain chaste during their husbands' absence. Women, too, can be socialized to the demands of war; this in itself should caution us against facile generalization about human propensities.

CONCLUSIONS

War is a cultural phenomenon. As with all matters cultural, the society shapes natural human capacities and potentialities to its accepted purposes, reinforcing some and suppressing others. It does this by systematically rewarding and punishing, by indoctrinating youth, creating role models to be emulated, and honoring those who perform well with special prestige and influence. In short, it guides behavior and sentiment to the kinds of performance that define the human career. Even where we limit ourselves to societies that score high on the salience of war, we find warfare variantly perceived and differently organized. There are some, like the Apache and Abipone, for whom war is a major source of economic well-being through preying on neighbors; for others like the Plains Indians, East African cattle herders, and the Mae Enga who are caught in patterns of raiding and counter-raiding, both acquisition and protection of property are important. Among some societies, for example the Jivaro and Mundurucu, fighting seems to be an end in itself, an elaborate and deadly game in which the rewards are merely victory for its own sake. There are other societies in which not all men must undergo a military career. Maori men may honorably opt out. More frequently, however, there is no escape from military participation without opprobrium. In state-organized societies, most ordinary citizens must be conscripted, if they are needed. There are some societies in which women can join, though none I know of in which they must participate.

I saw this variance at firsthand among the Sebei (Goldschmidt 1976). On the plains, where the cattle had to be protected from marauding neighbors, militarism was honored, but on the mountain, the farming Sebei viewed fighting as foolish and looked down on the plainsmen for even living in a war-infested area.

To say that "society" "shapes" is, of course, a figure of speech. It means that those people already assembled and working together do something to those who are arriving—that is, to the youth. And what we see them doing apparently has a certain consistency—though the lack of ethnographic detail makes it impossible to prove this point. The scenario runs something as follows among war-infested tribal societies.

Youth from early onward are inculcated with the virtues of warfare and the need to be brave and aggressive. Despite the reiteration of such sentiments, they dread the actual battle, and to overcome such fear they engage in diverse religious (i.e., psychologically supportive) practices, ranging from talismans to drugs, and including the mob psychology induced by rituals of preparation for war. Even these are not always able to counteract the fear in their hearts, and many find excuses for avoiding combat, keeping as much self-respect intact as they can. Yet engage in war they do. And if they do not fall in battle, they return with booty, women, slaves, scalps, cattle, tales of their exploits, and, above all, honor. As these accumulate with each successive encounter, they find themselves increasingly attractive to the women, respected by the men, and influential in the community—providing, in passing, a model for their nephews and sons.

Such a scenario does not support the perception of man as naturally aggressive and violent. It suggests rather that the potential for aggressiveness and violence must be carefully reinforced, nurtured, and channeled.

These data suggest that the human capacity to fight rests more firmly on other—paradoxically, more social—attributes. These I will here label pride and empathy.

By pride I mean the concern with the public image of the self. This urge toward performance in accordance with the dictates of the community leads individuals to engage in those forms of behavior that society sees as admirable. The ethnographic literature indicates that this human attribute can lead people into very diverse courses of action—from celibacy to machismo; from self-abrogation to aggressive exploitation; from indolence to industriousness. It is a sentiment that is self-oriented, but significantly takes its form from other-directedness, since the qualities that enter into the behavior are set by the community.

Empathy is the obverse of this coin; the identification with others. It is this identification with the group—family, clan, tribe, or nation— that transforms individual action into community action, that transforms fighting into warfare. These two attributes manifestly are interrelated and together they make warfare possible. Personal self-image and social identification constitute the basic reasons why men fight.

IMPLICATIONS

Tribal warfare is not in itself an issue of importance; except for a few isolated spots deep in the forests of South America and in the highlands of New Guinea, it is a thing of the past, not a problem for today. We examine tribal behavior to learn the extent of human variability and to discover underlying consistencies, ultimately for the purpose of gaining insight to human motivations and proclivities as they motivate ourselves.

How do these qualities affect warfare in modern industrial societies? The sentiment of vengeance and the attitude of identification are still prominent in our international confrontations, as, for instance, in the spring 1986 action in the Gulf of Sidra, and in the popular reaction to that confrontation. However strong these sentiments and however relevant they are to the causes of military confrontation, they do not tell us why men fight.

Though the warrior has been all but eliminated from the warfare of industrial societies and, absent of conscription, is itself a career, the military career remains strong as an inducement to "cold war" confrontations (Abrahamson 1972).

But the men in combat constitute only a tiny fraction of those involved in military action. Indeed, the men in uniform and the civilians at the Pentagon are themselves but a small fraction of those whose livelihood is dependent upon the provisioning of the military arsenal. The degree to which there is a broad interest in the military enterprise is best seen in the difficulty that meets every effort to abandon obsolete activities (notably useless military bases). Each threat of such action raises a public outcry over jobs lost and local economic disaster. Careers, from those of corporate management and Pentagon personnel to workers on the assembly lines and those who service these workers, are seen as locked into the militaristic stance. Because millions of individuals see their own self-image tied to the continuity of the military presence, it is difficult to persuade them to abandon the activity.

In the pacification of tribal peoples, it is frequently found that the presence of an external authority relieves them of the necessity for continued fighting. Not infrequently they abandon the game of confrontation and counter-confrontation with a sense of relief (e.g., Barnett 1959), and they turn to more productive pursuits. For it is easy to see that, for instance, the cattle raiding among East African pastoralists does not increase the total available food supply, but in fact reduces it. The same can be said for the construction of modern arsenals, but it is difficult to persuade those whose careers depend on such an activity that this is the proper course of action.

NOTES

I wish to thank Carol and Melvin Ember, Douglas White, and Valerie Wheeler for advice in planning this chapter and Laurie Kroshus and

Michele Zack for the literature search they made. It has had the support of the Research Committee of the Academic Senate at UCLA.

1. Adapted from a paper presented at the Annual Meeting of the American Association for the Advancement of Science, Los Angeles, California, May 31, 1985.

2. The ethnography of warfare leaves much to be desired, and while, in general, one can reasonably accept at face value specific described customs and behavior, one can never be certain that the blanks in the literature represent the absence of such matters or merely the failure of the ethnographer (or his informants) to mention it.

3. In view of what follows, I find this rather enigmatic reference to property of particular interest.

4. I am not unmindful of Ralph Linton's classic differentiation between ascribed and achieved status. But I see these as ideal types; furthermore, those to whom status is ascribed must nevertheless perform in accordance with expectation, while those denied status will still seek acceptance within the limits established, or within subsets of the community, as Bailey (1968) has demonstrated for India.

5. This is, perhaps, the differentiation that Moskos (1979) makes for modern society between the military as an institution and the military as a profession.

6. While ten of the societies had initiation rites for youth and such initiation inflicted physical pain and hardship, in many the initiation rituals were often totally disassociated from any military involvement. Thus, the elaborate initiation among the Aranda, so fully described and widely discussed, has no apparent relationship to the engagement in warfare.

TABLE 1. RITUAL REINFORCEMENTS FOR WAR

ACTIVITY	TRIBES
Preparatory rites	Abipone, Andamanese, Apache, Aranda, Baganda,[1] Cheyenne, Creek, Haida, Hopi, Igorot, Jivaro, Klamath, Maori, Mapuche, Papago, Pawnee, Shilluk, Tonga
Use of drugs	Abipone (alcohol), Creek ("black medicine"), Jivaro (beer, tobacco), Tonga ("war medicine")
Shaman's services[2]	Abipone, Apache, Creek, Haida, Klamath, Mundurucu, Papago, Wolof
Amulets or talismans[3]	Apache, Aranda, Baganda, Cheyenne, Chuckchee, Creek, Hopi, Jivaro, Klamath, Maori, Pawnee, Tonga

[1]Baganda ritual consists of an oath of allegiance and therefore may serve more to assure the Kabaka that the man will not defect.
[2]In some places, shamans accompany the battle; in others they predict the outcome. Among the Wolof, it is the Griote who serves, and this may be a social rather than a magico-religious reinforcement.
[3]Occasionally, special dress "to give the men courage."

TABLE 2. ELEMENTS IN TRAINING OF WARRIORS

ACTIVITY	TRIBES
Training in skills	Abipone, Apache, Chuckchee, Maori, Mae Enga, Papago
Apprenticeship	Apache, Cheyenne, Creek, Fon, Mae Enga, Nyakyusa, Pawnee
Games and contests	Ainu, Cheyenne, Chuckchee, Hopi, Mae Enga, Mapuche, Rwala
Pain endurance tests	Apache, Abipone, Andamanese, Aranda, Cheyenne, Fon, Hopi, Mapuche, Pawnee, Rwala, Tonga, Wolof
Other endurance tests	Apache, Chuckchee, Fon, Haida, Klamath, Maori, Pawnee, Rwala, Tonga
Legends and stories	Ainu, Apache, Cheyenne, Chuckchee, Maori, Pawnee, Wolof

TABLE 3. REWARDS TO WARRIORS

REWARD	TRIBES
Booty	Abipone, Apache, Baganda, Cheyenne, Chuckchee, Fon, Klamath, Maori, Nyakyusa, Pawnee, Rwala, Shilluk, Tonga, Wolof; probably also Creek, Haida, and Hopi
Slaves	Abipone, Ainu, Apache, Chuckchee, Fon, Haida, Kazak, Klamath, Maori, Mapuche, Shilluk, the adoption of captives also among Mundurucu and Pawnee
Women[1]	Ainu, Aranda, Baganda, Creek, Maori, Rwala, Shilluk, Tonga, Wolof
Trophies[2]	Abipone, Apache, Cheyenne, Creek, Haida, Hopi, Jivaro, Klamath, Mapuche, Mundurucu, Papago, Pawnee, Tonga.
Honors or prestige	Abipone, Apache, Cheyenne, Chuckchee, Creek, Fon, Hopi, Igorot, Jivaro, Maori, Mundurucu, Pawnee, Rwala, Shilluk, Tonga
Titles or membership	Abipone, Baganda, Chuckchee, Creek, Hopi, Maori, Mundurucu, Pawnee, Tonga, Wolof
Political influence or leadership	Abipone, Apache, Cheyenne, Chuckchee, Creek, Fon, Hopi, Kazak, Klamath, Jivaro, Mae Enga, Mapuche, Mundurucu, Papago, Pawnee, Rwala, Wolof

[1]As wives or concubines
[2]Usually heads or scalps

APPENDIX: SOCIETIES EXAMINED

People	Location	Basic Economy	Sources
Abipone	Chaco, Paraguay	Mounted foragers	Dobrizhoffer 1822
Ainu	Sakhalin and Hokkaido, Japan	Foragers, fishing	Batchelor 1927 Watanabe 1973 Murdock 1934
Andamanese	Andaman Islands	Foragers	Postman 1899 Radcliffe-Brown 1933
Apache (Chiricahua)	Southeast Arizona	Foragers	Opler 1937, 1941 Baldwin 1965
Aranda	Central Australia	Foragers	Spencer and Gillen 1927
Baganda	Uganda	Horticulturists	Roscoe 1965 (1911)
Cheyenne	Northern Plains of United States	Mounted foragers	Grinnell 1962 Llewellyn and Hoebel 1941
Chuckchee	Northeast Siberia	Reindeer pastoralists	Bogaras 1904–09
Creek	Southern United States	Horticulturists	Swanton 1928
Fon	Dahomey	Horticulturists	Herskovits 1967 (1938)
Haida	British Columbia	Maritime foragers	Murdock 1934 Stearns 1981 Swanton 1909 Van Den Brink 1974
Hopi	Northeast Arizona	Horticulturists	Hough 1915 Murdock 1934 Simmons 1942 Stephen 1936 Thompson 1950 Thompson and Joseph 1944 Titiev 1944
Igorot (Bontoc)	Northern Luzon, P.I.	Terraced agriculturists	Jenks 1905
Jivaro	Eastern Ecuador and Peru	Horticulturists	Harner 1962 Karsten 1935 Stirling 1938

APPENDIX: SOCIETIES EXAMINED

People	Location	Basic Economy	Sources
Kazak	Kazakhstan, USSR	Mounted pastoralists	Hudson 1938
			Murdock 1934
Klamath	Southwest Oregon	Foragers	Gatschet 1890
			Spier 1930
Maori	New Zealand	Horticulturists	Buck 1949
			Best 1924
			Penniman 1938
Mae Enga	New Guinea highlands	Horticulturists	Meggitt 1977
Mapuche	South Central Chile	Horticulturists and	Berdichewsky 1975
		pastoralists	Faron 1961, 1968
			Titiev 1951
Mundurucu	Para, Brazil	Horticulturists	Murphy 1956
Nyakyusa	South Tanzania	Horticulturists and	G. Wilson 1938
		pastoralists	M. Wilson 1950, 1951
Papago	Southwest Arizona	Horticulturists	Thompson 1951
	Northwest Sonora		Underhill 1939, 1946
Pawnee	Central Plains,	Horticulturist	Grinnell 1889
	United States		Hyde 1951
			Weltfish 1965
Rwala Bedouin	Asia Minor	Mounted pastoralists	Musil 1928
			Raswan 1935
Shilluk	South Sudan	Pastoralists and	Westerman 1912
		horticulturists	Seligman and Seligman 1932
			Dempsey 1955
			Junod 1927
Thonga	Eastern South Africa	Horticulturists and	
		pastoralists	
Wolof	Senegal and Gambia	Horticulturists	Gamble 1957
			Charles 1977

3

U.S. MILITARY ELITES: PERCEPTIONS AND VALUES

Donna Brasset

A little over twenty-three years ago, in the wake of the Cuban missile crisis, anthropologists across the country attended regional conferences organized to consider the Western alliance strategy of nuclear deterrence.[1] The discussions which ensued included calls for greater participation of anthropologists in research relevant to problems of war and peace. Among the topics suggested as amenable to anthropological expertise was a study of the "culture" of nuclear war. In Ruth Bunzel's words, "The military establishment with its ramifying structure, its mythology, symbols, ideology, and systems of action, is an appropriate object of anthropological study, like any other sub-culture within our society" (1963:9). According to those who organized the conference, the overriding point of this kind of research would be to clarify the humanistic perceptions which anthropologists tend to have as a profession toward the threat of nuclear war (see Bunzel 1963:2).

In pursuit of this line of inquiry, I decided to explore the values and attitudes of United States military elites. The purpose was to show how social and cultural factors impinge on military perceptions of world events, as well as influence their strategic and foreign policy decisions. To this end, I spent close to a year in Washington, D. C., formally interviewing over forty active and retired senior officers at the highest levels, in each of the major service branches. Among these were former and current members (and chairmen) of the Joint Chiefs of Staff, general and flag-rank officers holding prominent positions in their services, as well as a number of colonels and captains who had experience either as commanding officers in Vietnam or as aides to high-ranking field commanders.

I talked with them in their homes, in their offices in the Pentagon, at the National Defense University, in liberal and conservative think tanks in the area, and to some who were in the employ of major or minor defense contractors. Most of those I spoke to who were promoted to the highest positions in their services were friendly, articulate, dedicated to their work, and deeply loyal to their services and academies. In short, they had the qualities of the "honorable men" depicted by C. Wright Mills in The Power Elite (1956). During many hours of conversation, I developed an appreciation of their world: their combat experiences in Vietnam, Korea, and World War II; the richness and complexity of military culture; and the complicated and demanding responsibilities which accompany their roles as commanders in the field, or as managers of the world's largest bureaucracy.

However, my research has led me to conclude that their beliefs and perceptions about world problems are at least as governed by cultural distortions of reality as by dispassionate and considered judgments of world events; that advances in weapons technology since 1945 have outpaced the ability of military bureaucracy and culture to make the necessary adaptive, institutional adjustments to them; and to conjecture that this may be the most threatening case of "culture lag" that has ever existed in human society.[2]

Many critics of today's military argue that the services have produced too many senior officers who are technocrats, bureaucratic managers, and businessmen who lack the necessary qualities to lead their troops in war. In a corrective move, the services have responded with a renewed effort to instill greater leadership qualities in their future leaders—qualities emphasizing initiative, resourcefulness, aggressiveness, and decisiveness. But nowhere are there serious plans to provide future military leaders with the opportunity to reflect on some of their cherished assumptions regarding military solutions to political and economic problems in order that their perceptions and views might be in greater accord with the implications of weapons of mass destruction in our lives.

In the last four decades, civilians in government have greatly expanded the responsibilities of the military establishment without requiring fundamental changes in the way the armed forces socialize their members to think about war in the nuclear era. One of the major dilemmas for the modern career officer is that traditional beliefs and customs having to do with achieving victory in defense of a bounded terrain have become undermined by the strategy of nuclear deterrence. As Gene Sharp put it in his recently published book on the defense of Europe: "The capacity to defend in order to deter has been replaced by the capacity to destroy massively without the ability to defend."[3]

NUCLEAR WAR

Brigadier General Robert Gard, Jr. has suggested that one measure which military leaders could take to reduce the chances of a nuclear war would be to develop whole new constructs regarding the notion of victory in battle. Senior officers need to comprehend more fully the relationship of means to ends, according to Gard, and to view deterrence of war "as 'victory' at even the lowest tactical level" (1973:574). But such changes do not come easily to military officers who have emerged from an especially inert bureaucratic culture. As Adam Yarmolinsky put it, our military is still an "island of authority and conformity rivaling only religious and educational institutions, both in established and continuous tradition, and in its impact on governmental policy"(1973:508). Despite the specter of unparalleled devastating consequences in a hypothetical nuclear—or even biological or chemical—war, military leaders continue to be socialized to plan for traditional (pre-1945), battlefield-like "victories."

There are still many generals who believe a major confrontation with the Soviet Union is inevitable.[4] Wherever it begins, they believe, it will eventually spread to Europe. The likelihood of such a confrontation "going nuclear", in their jargon, is especially high in Europe since conventional NATO forces are alleged to be inadequate to those of the Soviets. NATO commander General Bernard Rogers has said repeatedly that nuclear weapons will be used in a military engagement with the Soviet Union, as long as conventional forces in Europe "lag behind" those of the Soviets. Military leaders thus do not lack the will to use nuclear weapons. They envision numerous scenarios where nuclear weapons might be used, and many have elaborated traditional and ideological rationales for the acceptability of a potential nuclear war. A prominent three-star army general with a Ph.D. in international relations explained his criteria for using nuclear weapons in "just war" terms:

> I am not uncomfortable with our nuclear war fighting strategy. That doesn't mean I an enthusiastic about it. But I won't turn my back on the use of nuclear weapons if it meets the proper moral criteria. I don't believe the use of nuclear weapons is immoral if it fits Judeo-Christian values. I believe it is moral to fight with nuclear weapons in someone's defense, for example; in the defense of others who can't protect themselves; to fight soldiers, not civilians, and to fight in proportion to the kinds of weapons used against us. . . . Nuclear war is just a conflict extension of any kind of war. . . . True, civilians would also be killed in a nuclear war, but collateral damage goes with it, as it does in any war.

Departing somewhat from the majority of senior officers I interviewed who said they were religious, he added "[But] I don't waste a lot of time worrying about nuclear war because I have faith in the Lord. I have a strong faith that if we're on the right side, He'll be on our side [because] a life worth living is what we're fighting for." Whether or not the active duty officers I spoke to evoked the deity to legitimate United States nuclear strategy, the majority of those I spoke to were firmly committed to the idea that a hypothetical nuclear war would be fought for ideals—in particular, for what they referred to as "the American way of life."

Retired officers, free of the work strains and pressures to conform that characterize high-echelon active duty life, were more likely to question the morality of nuclear strategy. A retired Navy rear admiral, for example, questioned the deterrent value of nuclear weapons:

> It's not true that people will be too smart to start a nuclear war . . . more people are willing to win a nuclear war than prevent it. . . . We are really planning, training, and equipping for nuclear war in Europe. There is a will to use these weapons. . . . Military men honestly think they can win a nuclear war.

A retired marine corps major general, concerned about the morality of nuclear deterrence, commented:

> I love this country, and revere this uniform and what it represents. I've been in three wars and received six battle stars. I fought for peace and security. But I don't see any peace and security in the world today. The question is, does one jeopardize the survival of the human race to protect one's political interests?

Active duty officers, and particularly service academy graduates, were much less critical of Pentagon policies—the result, as one general believed, of "academy loyalty" and "tremendous pressures to conform in a highly competitive milieu." But practical constraints on their choices while on active duty also restrict the latitude of their opinions and views. In the last forty years, senior officers have been inheriting strategic and foreign policies already worked out by an array of civilian analysts in the defense and foreign policy communities. The burden of making these policies operational falls on the military establishment whose leading members are then compelled—both for personal and political reasons—to devise legitimizing rationales for what they do. Chief of Naval Operations James Watkins, a practicing Catholic, addressed the problem posed by having inherited "limited options" in an article on the morality of nuclear weapons:

> Those weapons, terrible and terrifying as they might be if used for the wrong purpose, do exist. . . . That is the reality with which I

> must deal. It is my responsibility to deal with it, in a world in
> which good and evil also both exist—a world where my options
> are anything but clear. I may not always be happy about or com-
> fortable with the usually limited options available to me. But I do
> have the responsibility for choosing between those options, and I
> must make those choices as a moral man. . . . Ultimately . . . the
> choices I make are mine alone, and I must arrive alone at whatever
> decisions I make. I must, in short, live with the consequences of
> my choices and not be afraid of them. It is at that point that I, as
> Chief of Naval Operations, as a human being, but most of all as
> a moral man, put myself humbly before God. Then, having done
> so, I simply do the best I can with the choices at hand (1982:18–20).

Expressing sympathy with the senior officer prayer group in the Pentagon, he added: "These people also have to wrestle with the threat
facing our country and must recommend proper responses to meet the
threat."

Although senior officers in all the services have dangerous nuclear
strategies and accidental mishaps to worry about, the navy has special
kinds of difficulties having to do with control of conflict escalation at
sea to warrant Admiral Watkins' concern. Naval commanders on some
submarine missions have authority to use nuclear weapons in a defensive action if they believe they are threatened by enemy forces. This
"launch autonomy" of naval commanders is potentially very dangerous, even during peacetime. Desmond Ball has documented precarious
games of "chicken" involving American and Soviet submarines, tactical military harassment (by both United States and Soviet subs) which
have involved a number of potentially dangerous episodes, as well as
collision accidents which have been occurring at a rate of "about half
a dozen a year" (1985:2). In the event of war, Ball believes that the
blurring of conventional, nuclear, and tactical distinctions, as well as
navy resistance to contingency planning regarding the control of conflict escalation are among the numerous problems associated with the
very real potential of a nuclear war beginning at sea. But all the services
face serious problems having to do with authority, command, and control during a nuclear crisis, most of which involve a complex array of
technological and human frailties.[5]

Continually beset with such kinds of plausible nuclear scenarios,
it is no wonder that military leaders resort to ideological constructs
involving the simple assurances of a black and white, "good and evil"
world, or to religious vindication of their behavior. Few individuals
are saddled with greater responsibility for the lives of great masses of
people. Like individuals in all groups, military leaders seek solace in
the supernatural to assuage their fears, to justify their decisions and

actions, or as motivation to endure in a world perceived as hazardous. Like most people, they tend to believe in the superiority of their own culture in relation to others. The problem for those who do not share their specific beliefs and values however—and that involves the majority of the world's peoples who are neither American nor Christian— is that all such people are nonetheless made potentially very vulnerable by the decisions and actions of those who would wield weapons of mass destruction in the hope of preserving an exclusively American "way of life."

ANTI-SOVIET IDEOLOGY

Consistent with the function of the military in preserving the social and political status quo, the majority of those comprising the nation's military elite tend to share the conservative values extant in American society at large. Because of reasons having to do with socialization into American culture in general, and into the armed forces in particular, most of those I spoke with were expectedly ethnocentric. They expressed a belief in the superiority of American social, political, economic, and religious institutions, an impassioned anti-Soviet ideology, and a predilection to perceive the world's other peoples as future, potential Americans.

Each of these themes has its own history, but the anti-Soviet ideology—a dominant American cultural trait—is specifically linked to the perceptions of the American political and economic leaders involved in shaping the post-World War II world. In the wake of Hitler's hegemonic goals, in a climate of rising suspicions about Soviet expansionism, and as a result of an interest in solving America's economic problem by expanding foreign trade, President Harry Truman and his advisors envisioned the entire globe as a potential economic, political, ideological, and military contest between the United States and the Soviet Union. According to Truman, the idea was for the United States to "take the lead in running the world the way the world ought to be run" (1956:2). In the cold war political environment of 1947, the National Security Act was formulated, providing the bureaucratic framework for military participation in foreign policy.

With the Korean war on the horizon, the passage of "NSC-68"[6] authorized the armed forces to acquire in peacetime unprecedented amounts of national and international resources to deal with communist threats to perceived American interests all over the world. Four massive military buildups have since occurred—during the Korean war, the "missile-gap" crisis that helped usher in the Kennedy administration, during the Vietnam war, and during the current (Reagan)

administration. A vast expansion of military responsibilities has ensued as a result: the ability to acquire and manage a wide range of
industrial and manpower resources; the development of plans to fight
nuclear, conventional, guerrilla, and "maneuver" wars—and to plan
for more than one of these at any given time; the acquisition of knowledge of the most sophisticated weapons systems and the accompanying
strategic, logistical, and command and control systems; and the assumption of a greatly expanded role in the political arena where military leaders define threats to the national security, and lobby for
capital.

Despite such greatly expanded responsibilities, and because all
institutions and cultures are slow to change, military officers continue
to spend their lives in an institution that presses for great conformity
in thought, that profoundly distrusts the dissenting opinions of "lib-
erals" and "outsiders", that encourages ideological and religious le-
gitimation of its policies, that promotes concepts of battlefield victory
which have been part of military history and culture since there have
been standing armies in the world, and that requires unquestioning
loyalty to the state. Comprehension of the great complexity of world
problems can be compromised as a result. Asked what United States
interests in Europe or elsewhere are worth the risk of a nuclear war,
the active-duty officers I spoke to asserted variations of the following
comment made by one informant:

> If Western Europe becomes absorbed by the Soviet Union, our
> survival becomes problematic. The survival of our way of life, of
> our ability to have free choice, is what is worth the risk. . . . Our
> primary responsibility is to our own people. . . . If it came down
> to a choice between ourselves as a nation, versus the survival of
> the species, I would have to say, we as a nation would have to
> look out for ourselves first, and the species second.

It is the specialized nature of their tasks combined with adherence to
traditional, patriotic values which prompts military officers to ignore
the ominous contradiction in such kinds of statements.

THE LESSONS OF VIETNAM

The content of my interviews also shows that many senior officers,
along with junior-grade officers contending for higher ranks, have rejected some of the more substantive lessons of the Vietnam war in favor
of those of a strictly tactical nature. Especially among active-duty junior
grade officers seeking promotion, the short- and long-term consequences of ethnocentrism in our militarized foreign policies are not on

their list of lessons learned from the Vietnam experience. But several of the retired commanders I spoke to believed that greater attention to the French experience in Vietnam, better understanding of the relations between the Chinese and Vietnamese, or of the attitude of a great bulk of Vietnamese toward Ho Chi Minh, would have called for a different appraisal of the plans to intervene. The rear admiral quoted previously said that he and his group went about making war plans for Vietnam "without any of us having read anything about the French experiences there." The presumption was that superior American technology and know-how were all that were necessary to win the war. Few knew much about the history and culture of the Vietnamese people, nor were they interested. As one retired army general put it, "We never, never, took into account the cultural differences."[7]

Retired army brigadier general Michael E. Lynch, who fought in the Second World War, in Korea, and in Vietnam, expressed deep disappointment over the way the United States has conducted its foreign policy in the post World War II era:

> We don't seem to appreciate the extent to which the United States can influence events for both good and evil in the world. We seldom respect the history, culture, people or opinions of other nations in reaching our positions. Too often our so-called national interests are little more than self-serving political interests of the party in power. . . . In Washington's Farewell Address he warned that the State can become too strong at the expense of the nation, the people. This could come about through foreign entanglements . . . yet every new administration since World War II has been elected more for position taken on inter- rather than intra-national issues . . . and foreign entanglements have become the rule rather than the exception for each administration. . . . We often spout history without knowing what we're talking about. Vietnam was a good example. When I saw the hate in the eyes of the Vietnamese people at the hamlet level, it told me they saw us as they did the French— mere exploiters. I said to myself: 'We have to get the hell out of here' because they would never let us achieve for them what we felt was right by our standards. . . . We're still writing our own scenarios for the world as we see it or would like it to be. To justify excessive military budgets, we view every new Soviet capability as a direct threat to our national security, and not as a response to their own political insecurity. . . . I suppose if there weren't a Soviet Union we would have to invent one, so we make a Soviet Union—make a monolithic communist movement—out of Afghanistan, Cuba, Nicaragua, Grenada. Those who seek to place the threat in perspective find their motives challenged and their

*loyalty questioned . . . and the challengers are oftentimes those
whose only concern is survival of the administration in power.
This leads us to Samuel Johnson's comment about patriotism being
the last refuge of the scoundrel.*[8]

Besides ignorance of Vietnamese culture and language, and of the mix
of communism and nationalism that had come to characterize North
Vietnamese values, American military (and civilian) planners in Vietnam also underestimated the fervent motivation of their adversaries,
as well as their skills at conducting war. The "backward" natives of
Vietnam were thought to be no match for American soldiers representing the most powerful nation on earth. However, the ethnocentric
tendency to underestimate the skills and motivation of an adversary,
while overestimating the capabilities of one's own side, has been a
factor in countless military failures throughout history.

All human societies tend to sustain traditions which bolster ethnocentric attitudes and values. In a chapter entitled "God's Country
and American Know-How" historian Loren Baritz discussed the recurring theme in American culture, originating with the Puritans, that
Americans have a mission to convert others to the truth as they understand it. This was a persistent theme in the speeches and memo-
randa of the military and political leaders during the Vietnam war. The
United States was consistently depicted as "chosen" to "lead the world
in public morality and to instruct it in political virtue" (1985:27). Beyond containing the communists, the goal of our presence in Vietnam
was to make the Vietnamese people more like ourselves, with social
and cultural institutions reflecting American concepts of morality and
progress.

There were a number of commanding officers—a minority—who
disagreed with these goals. Of those I interviewed, a small number of
retired colonels, passed over for promotion to higher ranks, expressed
sentiments similar to those represented in a 1974 survey of retired
army generals who said: "We erroneously tried to impose the American
system on a people who didn't want it, couldn't handle it, and may
lose because they tried it."[9] A few self-proclaimed "atypical" retired
admirals and generals I spoke to concurred with sociologist Morris
Janowitz's view: "The war in Vietnam is not only a tragic example of
misguided fundamental moral issues, misconceived national interests,
and profound political blunders, it is a dramatic example of the counterproductive consequence of excessive force and coercion" (1975:3).

There are numerous reasons why these particular lessons of Vietnam have not been absorbed by many in the military. First, the organizational features of an institution based on hierarchy and authority
can undermine opportunities for learning from past experience. Norman Dixon, a British officer and a psychologist, believes there is a

historical penchant for members of military bureaucracies to overlook the most important lessons associated with military failure. The apportionment of blame tends to be directed outward in order both to obtain a degree of revenge for the wrong suffered, and to minimize or expiate guilt for responsibility in the event (1976:43).

Advocates of military reform in the United States have similarly pointed to the reluctance of people in military bureaucracies to learn even the tactical and strategic lessons of defeat. In *The Pentagon and the Art of War*, Edward Luttwak claimed that because senior commanders in charge in Vietnam were subsequently promoted to the highest levels, there could be no effective reappraisal of the war:

> *Junior officers who had seen combat were often bitterly critical of what had been done, but with the senior men still in control they could do nothing to express the defects of the structure, let alone achieve reform. Instead the defeat was blamed on the civilian authorities, and American society at large (1984:39).*

The officers in my sample who were promoted to general and flag ranks in recent years are seeking ways to redress what they believe to be the real reasons for the military failure in Vietnam: too much interference from the political sector, biased media coverage, and a concomitant failure of the general population to support the war. Their sights have become directed towards achieving greater control in the political arena of a wide range of decision-making factors pertaining to military matters—toward more influence over the media by restricting journalistic coverage of military affairs, toward redoubling efforts to use TV, radio, newspaper, and other communicative means to bring the population around to military values and interests; toward curbing political interference in military matters once war has broken out; and, in the event of war, toward the longstanding "absolutist" (hard-liner) aspiration of winning military victory in a brief, but all-out war.

Short of full-scale war, current military leaders who have repudiated the policy of gradual escalation associated with the strategic failure in Vietnam, have become attracted to the merits of "maneuver warfare" involving the use of "smart" weapons—one family of which is called "fire and forget"—which can be launched from far away. The advantage of this kind of strategy, as they see it, is that these weapons are believed to involve little prospect of starting a big war, a minimal likelihood of the death or capture of Americans, and insignificant collateral damage (Wilson 1986:21).

MILITARY EDUCATION

The affection which military leaders have for technological solutions to problems of war and peace stems partly from the fact that military professionals are socialized to reject theories which press for a greater understanding of the sociocultural aspects of political and social conflict. In *The Soldier and the State*, Samuel Huntington (1957:63) explained that "the military ethic" to which military professionals subscribe, involves a comprehensive body of beliefs and values that endorse the role of the military in society. Because the existence of the military profession assumes the use of violence for political purposes, military beliefs accord with the Hobbesian notion that human nature is universal and unchanging and that violence is permanently fixed in the biological and psychological makeup of human beings. Military professionals tend to deny theories which have to do with human "progress" as a result, and instead support those which emphasize the use of force as the most viable corrective means to check political conflict.

If individuals comprising the nation's military elite tend not to demonstrate an appreciation of the wider social problems commensurate with their grave responsibilities, it is also because selection criteria favor more pragmatic abilities. Candidates for promotion to higher ranks must demonstrate abilities in planning, training, and logistics; and each of the services needs individuals with bureaucratic skills to lobby the interests of their service, as well as business "agents" for the procurement of weapons systems (see Strasser et al. 1984:34–48). As a result, education at the nation's military academies is tilted to accommodate the more parochial needs of the military establishment, rather than the wider, more complex needs of society at large.

Vice Admiral James Stockdale related to *Newsweek* journalists with disappointment that Annapolis has eighty-three engineering professors and only one philosophy professor; and Annapolis cadets were found to be no different from those at West Point or the Air Force Academy in the disdain they expressed for the academic, or "bull," majors. According to Stockdale, next to electrical engineering, the most hated subject is English.[10] In one of my own interviews, a highly placed army general said, "No, I have never taken an anthropology course in my life, and [with a chuckle] to be honest, I must say I'm rather proud of that." But as they move up in rank, officers are hampered from expanding their intellectual horizons by the great demands made on their time. "As you climb up the greasy pole," said Major General James Dozier to the *Newsweek* reporters, "there's less and less time for reading and reflection".[11]

"OUR BROTHERS ENTRAPPED"

I. F. Stone was quite right to see the military as "our brothers entrapped."[12] They are first of all entrapped by the political, economic, and ideological functions of the nation-state. Because of this, they have also become hostage to the narrow pool of ideas that emanate from our militarized foreign policies, by American cultural values and a military ethos which promote dangerously ethnocentric world views, and by gigantic bureaucracy that is not conducive to rapid or substantive change. Yet as guardians of an extensive portion of the nation's budget, and as advisors to the president and Congress on national security matters, our military leaders can—and do—have an important influence on the economic health of the nation. Their antipathy to the Soviet Union can—and does—influence their judgments on vital defense issues. Military leaders—along with strategic analysts in the civilian sector—are not the "realists" many often claim to be. Although they are continually confronted with tremendously complicated and very serious "real" problems of a military nature, the leading members of our military establishment share with all political and economic elites the propensity to bring their narrowly defined interests and culture-bound perceptions into the national and international political arena where they contend for power and advantage.

At the same time, and for very practical reasons, a great many of our military leaders exhort restraint when it comes to plans of an interventionist nature. There have always been pragmatic senior officers who have been very concerned that the United States not become involved in ventures which it cannot effectively control—to become "bogged down" in another Vietnam, for example, or have the armed forces placed in the kind of vulnerable position in which the Marines were found in Lebanon in 1983. A number of those I spoke to felt that the current civilian appointees in the Department of Defense are "hawkier" than many in the military when it comes to committing United States forces to the various "trouble spots" around the world. A similar stance for restraint characterized many military leaders after the Korean war as well, but their worry about being bogged down in "another Korea" did not prevent military personnel from being sent to Vietnam as advisors only a few years after Korea, or from remaining there in full force for ten long years. Important practical lessons learned by some in the military leadership thus have little utility if they are not also learned by their civilian superiors.

SOCIAL CONSEQUENCES

Sociologist Charles Moskos commented that "the military is undergoing a fundamental turning inward in its relations to the civilian structures and values of American society" (1973: 547). He cautioned that the defensive reaction of a traditional military to the nation's cultural elite could mean that the military "could develop anti-civilian values tearing the basic fabric of democratic ideology" (p. 549). At a time when the mood of the country was against the war in Vietnam, was anti-military, and generally "liberal" in political voice, Moskos was right to ruminate about the implications of a military at odds with American society. But the current era, characterized by a congruence of interests and values between the military and a predominantly conservative society, also has potential for challenging democratic institutions by developing the political capability to squelch alternative ideas regarding the role of the military in political affairs.

Especially problematic are military definitions and appraisals of the Soviet threat. Fear of Soviet military capabilities coupled with lack of knowledge regarding their intentions, compels our military leaders to exaggerate the nature of the threat. From a military perspective, it is far better to overestimate than underestimate the threat because it is the job of military leaders to insure that potential adversaries do not gain a military advantage. However, at a time when the military commands financial resources and manpower unparalleled by any other competing sector in society, exaggeration of the Soviet threat is no small matter. Left unchecked, the perspectives which military personnel develop through focusing their attention almost exclusively on their adversaries' weapons systems can come to weigh heavily on the social and political institutions of the state.

Militaries in highly industrialized societies are reliant on sophisticated technologies for their armaments, the resources for which are located in particular locales all over the world. As a result, they have developed a vital interest in the economic and foreign policy matters of the states in which such resources are found. In his paper "Changing Military Priorities" (1979), for example, General Maxwell Taylor listed the protection of overseas trade as an important United States military priority. As he saw it, the threat to our national security is intimately linked to threats to the national economy because of its growing dependence on foreign imports, especially oil. The military needs to make certain of these foreign markets their concern, he believes, because arms equipment and the capacity to make war are dependent on a sound economy. A sound economy in turn provides the military with the necessary material needed to protect the overseas trade and markets essential to a sound economy.

Few generals or admirals have so well articulated the complementarity of U.S. military, economic, and political interests. In advancing his view, General Taylor was demonstrating a loyal professional soldier's dedication to the viability of the United States armed forces, as well as his loyalty to the United States as an economically thriving entity. But his recommendation also reflects the legacy of a military bureaucracy grown so large and complicated that its members have become pressed to devise their own foreign policies to serve its needs. Where there is no comparable civilian sector to check against the inflation of military interests, there is always the danger that a society will drift towards militarism; or, as Ernest Becker once said, that the militarists will "bend our best ideas to their age-old practical nightmares" (1971:xi).

In his aptly titled book, *Culture Against Man*, Jules Henry wrote that in America whoever does not obsessively hate and fear the Soviet Union isolates himself because public opinion is intolerant of a more reflective attitude. The result is "unthinking acquiescence and extinction of all possibility of solving the underlying problem. When such fear is joined to the fortunes of political parties, extinction of fear becomes problematic" (1963:122). This remains a poignant caveat. By denouncing views which press for alternative understandings of Soviet military behavior—views based on in-depth examinations of Soviet intentions and motivations, for example—military leaders may be foreclosing some of the very perspectives which, in the nuclear era, could be vital to our survival.

Numerous writers in the last several decades have argued that the military threats and aggressive posturings of both sides only serve to exacerbate tensions in an already dangerous political environment; that the only serious way to reduce the likelihood of nuclear war is to work toward the relaxation of tensions between the United States and the Soviet Union. This means less military posturing and more diplomacy, negotiation, and compromise—words which are anathema to many who have lived through World War II and learned to equate such ideas with "appeasement" and, ultimately, with war. However, because of the ever present possibility that any military conflict could—by accident or design—escalate to the nuclear threshold, there is a dramatic need to do away with the application of World War II analogies to current political-military problems. There is also a need for a rapid transformation of traditional ways of pursuing political, economic, and ideological interests through military means.

Neither of these needs is in the offing among the nation's military and political elites, however. Like many people, military officers and other policy makers have a hard time adjusting their long-standing beliefs and assumptions to the demands of the nuclear age. Moreover, in a democratic society the mandate for any change in the way military leaders are socialized to view their role in society must first come from a civilian sector with sufficiently different ideas than our political leaders have had since the inception of the cold war.

CONTRIBUTIONS OF ANTHROPOLOGISTS

There are countless areas where anthropological insights can enrich and humanize the constructs of those who constitute the defense and foreign policy communities—the military and political sectors, the scientists, strategic analysts, and scholars of international relations who have laid down the ground rules for thinking about war and peace. Perhaps most obvious, is the contribution anthropologists can make in reducing the fear that propels the arms race between the United States and the Soviet Union. No other discipline is as well equipped as anthropology to address the problem of cross-cultural ethnocentrism and the "mirror imagery" political adversaries have of one another. We need to develop our own brand of Soviet experts who will describe and analyze the complexities of Soviet society in greater breadth and depth than is typical of scholars lacking a background in anthropology. In the event of a "thaw" in cold war relations, such an effort could be a product of a joint effort with behavioral scientists within the Soviet Union, the purpose of which would be to work on ways to mitigate mutually antagonistic perceptions (cf. Bunzel and Parsons 1964:438).

We need also to convey greater understanding of the limitations of some of the dominant values of American culture in the nuclear era. The penchant of many Americans and their decision makers to be confident and optimistic that "things will work out" stems from a relatively fortuitous history in which technological progress and the lack of foreign invaders in 200 years have played a part. But, as Thomas Powers pointed out in his insightful paper, "What Is It About," (1984a:206), the Soviets have a very different history and, as a result, they do not share in our optimism. According to Powers, a breakdown at Geneva is viewed by the Russians with genuine alarm. They are truly frightened by our military posturings. Many Americans, on the other hand, tend to rely rather too easily on the belief that in the final analysis, there is nothing to worry about, that our experts have everything under control, and nothing really bad will happen. But these are cultural attitudes that are ill suited to the gravity of the situation we face. Anthropologists have an important role in identifying them as such.

Anthropologists also need to bring their expertise in regional studies to the attention of the plethora of policy makers who see the world in bipolar terms. The world abounds with examples of ethnic, religious, political, and economic groups whose needs and techniques for social change transcend Soviet and American ideological or economic agendas for development. Our literature is rich with examples of the internal and international social and economic inequalities that elicit conflict among groups. We can bring these to bear on the discourse among policy makers on the causes of conflict and aggression among the world's many peoples and cultures. William Beeman, an anthropologist and Iranian specialist who was a consultant to the State Department during the Iranian hostage crisis, has been urging anthropologists for a number of years to write about their understandings of other cultures in the prominent journals and periodicals read by members of the foreign policy community.[13]

Further, there are numerous research topics related to world tensions that would benefit from the application of anthropological theory and method. Among these would be studies of the many subcultures that comprise what Senator William Proxmire dubbed the "military-industrial-bureaucratic-trade association-labor union-intellectual-technical-academic-service club-political-complex" (1970:8). Such studies would elucidate the values and assumptions which promote militarily provocative world views, as well as challenge those views which run counter to anthropological knowledge about human behavior. Floyd Hunter, the sociologist who conducted empirical research on the nation's corporate elites has set a methodological precedent for these kinds of projects (Hunter 1953, 1959, 1980).

Finally, the physical anthropologists among us need to disseminate greater understanding of the tentativeness of all living systems, including human beings. Humans are not immune to the laws of nature which to date have claimed for extinction the vast majority of all the living systems that have existed since the earth was formed over four billion years ago. There is thus a great need for wider appreciation of the physiological and sociocultural factors that have contributed to our survival as a species lest current and future policy makers inadvertently jeopardize our chances for survival through failure to understand our vulnerability.

C. Wright Mills believed that the onus of responsibility for an enlightened approach to modern social problems falls on the intellectuals in society, in particular, on the social scientist. To close on an inspirational note, I quote Mills on "saving the world":

> I do not believe that social science will "save the world" although I see nothing at all wrong with "trying to save the world"—a phrase which I take here to mean the avoidance of war and the re-arrangement of human affairs in accordance with the ideals of human freedom and reason. Such knowledge as I have leads me to embrace rather pessimistic estimates of the chances. But even if that is where we now stand, still we must ask: If there are any ways out of the crisis of our period by means of intellect, is it not up to the social scientist to state them? (1959:193).

NOTES

I am indebted to the Institute on Global Conflict and Cooperation (University of California, San Diego) for funding this research, to Floyd

Hunter for providing the motivation and necessary prodding for it, to Col. Carl Bernard and Brig. Gen. Michael E. Lynch for the many hours of thoughtful discussion about military matters, and to Col. Trevor Dupuy, both for guiding me through military history and, like Carl Bernard, for providing useful introductions to the military community in Washington, D.C.

1. The meetings were held in New York, Boston, St. Louis, Washington, Denver, and Palo Alto between February and March, 1963. They were the product of a 1981 resolution of the American Anthropological Association calling for anthropological involvement on issues pertaining to threats to human survival.

2. Culture lag refers to the idea that parts of a social system are interdependent, that changes in one part of the system require adaptive changes in others, and that the time lag between the original change and the adaptive adjustments involves maladjustments in the social system (Ogburn 1922).

3. Quoted, without citations, in Kennan (1986).

4. See Steven Strasser et al., "Can We Fight a Modern War?" *Newsweek*, July 1984, p. 48.

5. See Carter et al. *Managing Nuclear Operations* (Washington, D.C.: Brookings Institute, 1987).

6. The reference is the National Security Council paper—entitled "NSC-68"—drawn up by the Department of State and Department of Defense officials during the Truman administration. "NSC-68" called for extensive changes in United States foreign policy, including a dramatic buildup of American and Western European arsenals. For details, see "NSC-68: A Report to the National Security Council by the Executive Secretary on United States Objectives and Programs for National Security." Reprinted in the *U.S. Naval War College Review*, April 14, 1950.

7. Quoted in Kinnard (1977:92).

8. Because the general quoted had an opportunity to clarify his statement for this chapter, it differs somewhat from an earlier quote in an unpublished paper I distributed among a small number of people.

9. See Jonathan Alter et al., "Tickets to the Stars."

10. Ibid.

11. Ibid.

12. Personal communication

13. See William Beeman, "Anthropology and the Myths of American Foreign Policy," in this volume.

4

ANTHROPOLOGY AND THE MYTHS OF AMERICAN FOREIGN POLICY

William O. Beeman

Anthropology has rarely been recognized as one of the "policy sciences," yet at this point in history, anthropological skills are needed more than ever for the government officials, businessmen, and journalists who deal with an increasingly complex world.

I have had the opportunity to work with the United States State Department, with Senate and House subcommittees on foreign and military affairs, and also as a writer and commentator for newspapers and other periodicals. One of the most important lessons I have had to learn in dealing with officials and with the public in general is to confront directly an extremely powerful and pervasive American belief system about the nature of foreign policy, how it is conducted, and how it affects American life. These beliefs are troublesome because of the hold they have in shaping political strategy, even when they fall far from the mark in reflecting reality.

At best, foreign policy and military strategy based on this system of belief is ineffective. At worst, it is actively detrimental to American interests. The difficulty is compounded when one realizes that every nation is operating in the foreign policy realm from a similar base of beliefs that are equally inaccurate. I will deal with some of these other belief systems below, but I will turn first to that set of beliefs which I identify as particularly American. I will then apply it to several case studies: the Iranian hostage crisis, the Lebanese Civil War, and the Soviet occupation of Afghanistan. All of these confounded this American system, causing enormous frustration and confusion among policy makers. Finally, I will suggest some small ways in which anthropologists might play a role in aiding the policy process to become more effective in confronting the realities of foreign relations in an increasingly interdependent world.

THE FIVE PRINCIPLES OF BELIEF

In formulating five principles of belief in American foreign policy, I am not claiming that this is the only set which may be formulated. The principles do, however, constitute a cohesive whole, and they do reinforce each other.[1] Moreover, they become a set of beliefs for our age— post-World War II United States. Those who have memories of earlier periods in American history will be able to see how the current belief system differs from that of previous periods. The five principles follow:

1. *The world consists of nation-states.* The essence of this belief is that the world consists entirely of nation-states with basically homogeneous populations whose primary identity (and thus homogeneity) derives from identification with their common nationhood. It is not surprising that foreign policy makers in the United States should come to believe this. The United States was, after all, the first great nation founded on this principle, and one natural tendency of peoples everywhere is to believe that others are like themselves.

In actuality, there are very few nation-states in the world. They are a rare enough phenomenon that they have been the subject of serious study in anthropology (Fallers 1974). A few nation-states conform to the model—some European countries, Japan perhaps, a few of the new Pacific island states, and states formed from former British colonies—but this is about the extent of it. The majority of the people of the world do not identify primarily with their nationhood, and certainly not with the central governments that rule the nations in which they happen to live. The notion that one would sacrifice one's life for one's president or prime minister is a patent absurdity in virtually every nation on earth.

2. *The East-West power struggle is the most important event in world politics. All other political relationships must be ranked in terms of it.* Before World War II, the prevalent belief was that the world was organized on a multipolar basis. Now the United States has accepted a basically bipolar model, for which the United States and the Soviet Union are the only nations that "count." Taking this as the most basic "fact" about world order, United States policy makers then structure the entire world order within this framework.

For most nations on earth the East-West struggle is very nearly irrelevant for the conduct of everyday life, except as an enormously bothersome obstacle which they must confront at every turn. The possibility of nuclear destruction is a paramount concern for thinking people everywhere, but it is the height of bitter irony that the bulk of the people who will suffer or be destroyed in a nuclear holocaust have absolutely no interest in the ideological struggle that will be the basis for that holocaust.

Few nations would accept the American belief that all nations must eventually assign themselves to one camp or another, and some, like India, have had to work very hard to stake out an independent position.

3. *Economics and power are the bases of relations between nations.* Power politics as a philosophy has been with the United States only a short time. It was articulated in an extremely effective way by Hans Morganthau, perhaps the principal teacher of the current crop of United States politicians currently exercising executive power in the United States foreign policy community.

Military and economic power are realities in today's world. It is the belief that they are the only basis for relations between states that is problematic. For anthropologists of all shades it is particularly galling to see that in the United States' conduct of foreign policy almost no attention is paid to factors attributable to cultural differences between nations. It is assumed that wealth and military might are universal levellers and that little else matters. Occasionally it is recognized that pride, greed, and altruism may be factors in the course of human events, but such matters are often dismissed as unpredictable factors.

Nowhere is the structure of this belief so clearly seen as in the composition of United States embassy staffs. There are always economic attachés and political attachés, but in no embassy in the world is there a single officer whose primary duty is to interpret cultural differences which could cause misunderstandings between nations. This lack is reflected in mistake after mistake in the conduct of United States diplomatic personnel everywhere—events I hardly need detail for anthropologists.

Parenthetically, I do not wish to malign the United States State Department here. Many employees of the State Department are dedicated career personnel who have worked hard on their own time to acquire cultural skills to better perform their jobs. Unfortunately those that do learn exotic languages or cultural skills are rarely rewarded for their work, and career advancement is seldom tied to knowing these things. Indeed, too much knowledge of a region may result in a transfer to a completely different world area, on the theory that anyone who has bothered to learn so much must have become dangerously sympathetic with the people of the host country and may be impaired from carrying out United States interests. This condition is dubbed with the unfortunate name "clientitis" in foreign service circles. Thus it is not surprising that, when cultural matters become the principal issue in foreign relations, there often is no one around who can deal with the problem with much skill.

In fairness, the United States is not alone in having unskillful diplomats or in being unable to analyze cultural differences. I think the world could use many more anthropologists on diplomatic staffs everywhere to compensate for those who believe that money and guns are the only basis for international understanding and that when push comes to shove their own cultural ways are the only correct ones.

4. *Nations are ruled by a small group of elite individuals.* It is difficult to understand why the United States, with a strong internal ethic supporting democracy and broad-based grass-roots participation in public affairs, finds it so difficult to take these same broad-based processes seriously in other nations.

Yet again and again, the conduct of United States foreign policy is based on identification and support of narrow elite political structures: elite elected officials, elite dictators, elite religious officials. Broad-based popular political and social movements are ignored or taken seriously only insofar as they threaten the elite order.

Clearly, the only power which counts is believed to inhere in these narrow elite structures. An office is the chief sign of this power, perhaps reflecting the earlier stated belief that the world consists of nation-states. Thus the United States cannot easily see underlying cultural processes which contribute to social change or, seeing such processes, automatically feels them to be negative in nature.

There is an exception to this principle. If broad social movements prove to be important in terms of the United States' interpretation of the East-West struggle, then great significance is attached to them. Thus broad-based movements ideologically supportive of the Soviet Union or opposed to them are taken very seriously indeed. Often their importance is exaggerated to ridiculous proportions.

5. *The normal conduct of foreign policy thus consists of the elite leaders of nation-states meeting in seclusion to discuss matters of power and economics, presumably in the context of the East-West conflict.* This final point is not a separate belief, but rather the congruence of the preceding beliefs into an image—a scenario which, in fact, describes much of the conduct of foreign policy carried out by the United States in recent years.

My own, perhaps iconoclastic, belief is that this conduct rarely yields anything productive or lasting, because it is not based on reality. It is based rather on the mythic structure of the United States' idiosyncratic view of what the nations of the world are and how their peoples are motivated to act in their own interests.

THE IRANIAN HOSTAGE CRISIS: A CHALLENGE TO BELIEF

The Iranian hostage crisis (perhaps better titled the Iranian-American hostage crisis) lasted over a year, from November 1979 to January 1981. During this period a number of individuals from the academic community, myself included, had the opportunity to observe the United States policy process in action. We served as informal advisors to the State Department and to the White House during this time.

The hostage crisis was remarkable in that it successfully challenged the basic foreign policy beliefs which I have outlined above; it literally threw the American foreign policy community into a panic. Typically, State Department and White House officials exhibited behavior recognizable as typical of "culture shock." One State Department official was most articulate: "They just don't play by the rules, these Iranians. We can't figure out who is in charge. Nothing they tell us seems to have any basis in fact. They promise to do something, and then they do something completely different. How do you work with people as irrational as this?" Many individuals used language far more vivid than this in speaking about Iranian political behavior during this period.

Taking the points in the belief system cited above one by one, it is possible to see how the Iranian situation caused severe cognitive dissonance for American policy makers.

Iran and the Nation-State Model

Iran in the Middle East comes closest to emulating a nation-state model, but it is not a nation state in the Western sense of the word. It is more properly an empire where a monarch (the late shah) was able, after many centuries, to subjugate a vast number of disparate groups who had only the loosest allegiance to his, or any central authority's, rule.

Until the twentieth century Iran had permeable boundaries and no clear sense of sovereignty of territory except as defined by conquest. There was great identification with Persian culture throughout the area of Iran's sphere of influence, but little identification with Iran's nationhood. The sense of Iran as a nation-state is in a real sense an invention of the Pahlevi era.

After the revolution, the Khomeini regime was faced with the same old difficulties of keeping the nation together. Tribal groups throughout the country moved swiftly to re-establish the semi-autonomous rule they enjoyed in vast areas in past decades, a rule usurped by the strong-handed tactics of the Pahlevis. Religious divisions were strong and exerted great turmoil. Clashes between religious and secular forces made consolidation of power in the country very difficult.

United States negotiators assumed that because officials of the newly formed revolutionary government had the normal titles of heads of government, they actually were nation-state leaders in some normative sense. During this turbulent period, however, it was impossible for any individual to fill this role—to have the authority to speak with the voice of the nation as a whole. More importantly, anyone who presumed to do so and made an error was likely to be toppled from power rather quickly.

Thus there was never a single voice or voices which could speak authoritatively for the Iranian nation during the entire period of the hostage crisis. Indeed, even the settlement of the crisis was never attributed to one person or group of persons. In Iran no one wanted to be associated with the event.

The Irrelevancy of the East-West Power Struggle.

The hostage crisis was one event which provided no normal models for confrontation in post-World War II United States sensibilities. The crisis had nothing whatsoever to do with United States-Soviet confrontation, despite numerous feeble attempts to demonstrate that the Soviet Union might have had a hand in the proceedings. The result for the foreign policy community was that it was forced to deal with Iran as Iran and not as a projection of the global chess game. Sadly, the policy community was almost totally unprepared for this eventuality. The number of Iranian experts in government posts was (and continues to be) woefully small.

With no automatic responses available, the foreign policy community found itself in a frantic search for ideas. The White House in particular pursued a number of amateurish attempts at contacting "fixers" to achieve the release of the hostages. An ill-planned military rescue ended in fiasco. It was only when a solution was found which perforce touched Iranian cultural sensibilities that the release was effected.

Power and Money as Irrelevancies.

The hostage crisis was a true confrontation of cultural values, played brilliantly for internal consumption in Iran by Ayatollah Khomeini and his supporters.

The United States had no economic or military force capable of releasing the hostages. This was clear from the beginning. The Iranians were able to withstand a long economic boycott, sluff off threats, and turn the abortive rescue mission into positive support for the Islamic Republic.

The United States failed to realize that by addressing its concerns primarily to questions of power and money, it was playing directly into the hands of the clerical leaders bent on establishing an Islamic Republic with themselves in control. The clerics set up an internal moral dialogue in Iran, with the United States at one pole of morality and Iran at the other. The United States was characterized as "The Great Satan," concerned with the material world and with corrupting influence. By contrast, the revolutionary leaders were portrayed as spiritual men, concerned with morality and righteousness. The moral questionableness of taking the hostages was subsumed under the greater moral directive (actually a tenet in Shi'a Islamic doctrine) of "resisting the Wrong and promoting the Right" (cf. Beeman 1983b; Keddie 1981). Thus the crisis from an Iranian standpoint was not a differential power struggle but rather a moral struggle. The more the United States blustered and postured during this period, the more it reinforced the picture painted of it by the clerics.

In the end the Iranians suffered considerable financial losses in allowing the settlement. Some oppositionist politicians attempted to use this as a means of discrediting the officials of the regime. Instead, that the nation lost financially was taken by many as demonstration that Iran was not after material gain in the hostage takeover but was truly concerned with the moral and spiritual questions involved.[2]

The Irrelevance of Elite Actors

In keeping with its projection of nation-statehood on the new Iranian revolutionary government, the United States also attempted to project an elite power structure onto the new regime. Thus it was assumed from the beginning that somewhere there must be somebody with the authority to push a button and get the hostages released.

Iran's leadership, as stated above, was highly diffuse at this time. The leaders were conscious of the fragility of their situation and their need to curry public favor at all times. Thus though often posturing as though they had power, individuals such as Sadeq Qotbzadeh or even Abol-Hassan Bani-Sadr had almost no ability to control day-to-day governmental affairs. Indeed, Qotbzadeh was quite skillful in increasing his own influence in Iran by manipulating the American public and government officials.

Still the White House continued an unceasing search for a "plumber" who would carry out the United States' bidding on this matter. It sent advisor Hamilton Jordan to Paris in a wig and false moustache in search of an Argentinean businessman connected with a French lawyer who could reach the Iranian officials. Even the president's own brother, Billy Carter, hardly a diplomat, was dispatched to Libya to tap some secret pipeline to Khomeini. These attempts were pitiful and ludicrous and demonstrated how sadly U.S. officials were in the grip of their own myths about how governments operate. Not able to see the reality of the Iranian situation, they persisted in running after chimeras of their own making.

The clearest instance of firm belief in elite government power during the crisis was shown in the behavior of United States officials themselves. Despite the fact that the State Department and other government agencies had after a year accumulated considerable knowledge concerning Iran, its motives, and its probable reactions to United States overtures, hostage crisis negotiating was centered exclusively in the White House and delegated to individuals who had little or no experience in dealing with the Middle East or with Iran.

Zbigniew Brzezinski, the president's national security advisor, filtered all reports coming in from the State Department and other agencies and only let President Carter see those things which accorded with his ideas of how the situation was proceeding. Secretary of State Cyrus Vance was effectively cut out of the negotiations. He was not told of the abortive rescue mission (which he opposed) until it was underway, prompting his resignation.[3]

Unexpected Diplomacy

The normal, expected patterns of diplomacy anticipated by United States officials were not to be found in the hostage crisis. Iranian officials could not speak for their nation as a whole during this period, they were not swayed by considerations of economics and force, and they were not elite leaders in any sense understood by the United States. Moreover, because this problem could not be construed in the context of East-West confrontation, there were no easy, pat responses available for United States leaders to utilize in dealing with the situation.

The worst problem of all for United States leaders was that they could not make contact with Iranian officials at all. Rhetoric against the United States was so virulent and potent that any officials associated with the United States in any way were tainted by the contact. Their own enemies could then use this against them to destroy them. Thus "secret" messages sent by President Carter and others were revealed publicly almost as soon as they were received. Often they would be read to the masses during Friday prayers. For the United States, diplomacy as an elite operation is carried out in secret. For the Iranians at this time, secrecy was the kiss of death in dealing with Americans.

The eventual release of the hostages came when Brzezinski relinquished control of the operation and it was taken over by the new secretary of state, Edmund Muskie, and his team of advisors. The eventual solution was culturally correct both for Iran and the United States. It involved a mediator—Algeria; no face-to-face contact between American and Iranian officials; and a combination of ideological and economic agreements. More to the point, it involved bargaining, an area which both nations understand in certain specific contexts.

The United States unfortunately did not re-evaluate its belief system concerning foreign affairs following the hostage crisis. For most members of the foreign policy community, Iran was an aberrant state which refused to play by the rules. Thus the basic belief in what the rules are remains unchanged.

SHI'ITES IN LEBANON: ANOTHER CHALLENGE TO BELIEF

During 1983 and 1984 the United States found itself once again challenged by a conflict over which it seemed to have little control. United States troops were sent to Lebanon, along with French and British forces, to provide for peacekeeping in an ongoing civil war between various religious and ethnic factions in that nation. On April 18, 1983 a suicide bomber drove a truck containing massive amounts of explosives into a United States Marine barracks which already had a large amount of explosives warehoused in it. The resulting explosion killed 65 United States Marines and injured many more. As a result of this and many similar incidents, the United States eventually withdrew its military presence entirely from Lebanon.

United States officials were bitter in their denunciation of the terrorist activities, calling them "animal acts," among other things. Not only were they unable to deal with terrorism under these circumstances, they were also unable to comprehend the reasons for it. Lack of understanding in this case as well can be traced to a discrepancy between the actual situation in Lebanon in 1983–84 and the belief system prevalent in the United States foreign policy community as outlined above.

Lebanon as a Nation-State.

Of all nations in the Middle East, Lebanon is least qualified as a nation-state. It is an amalgam of small ethnic and religious communities which

identify primarily with their community long before they identify themselves as "Lebanese." The state was literally cobbled together by the
French after World War I out of bits and pieces of Ottoman territory.
The French tried to create a state which would be dominated by the
Maronite Christian community, and, indeed, the Maronites were the
largest ethnic group until shortly before World War II. After that time,
demographics in Lebanon shifted. By 1983 they were the third largest
group in the country. Shi'ite Muslims constitute today the largest single
group in the nation, but they are also the most economically disad-
vantaged and least powerful politically. They have languished for years
without any hope of realizing improvements in their economic or political situation, since an informal agreement established in 1935 assures Maronite Christian domination of the government.

The United States has taken the position that Lebanon has a dem-
ocratically elected government, and therefore grievances of individual
communities in that nation should be handled through ordinary state
governmental processes. This is fine for true nation-states, but in Lebanon communities the Shi'ites do not have the opportunity to participate fully in government. By supporting the Christian-dominated
central govermnent, the United States declared itself, in the eyes of the
Shi'ite community, to be enemies of the Shi'ites.

With the Iranian revolution as a model, the Shi'ites then moved
to redress their grievances by driving out the Christians and their foreign supporters—the United States, France, and Great Britain—who
seemed to be maintaining them in an illegitimate position of power.
Terrorism was the only means which the community saw as possible
under conditions where they could obtain no power through democratic processes.

The Superpowers in Lebanon.

The United States supports the Maronite government primarily because
it views that government as inherently more "stable" than any alternative. The reasons for this belief are based solidly on calculations
drawn from a world view based on superpower political considerations.

The United States views Israel as the chief bulwark against Soviet
penetration into the Middle East. Thus anything which threatens Israel
is automatically a threat to the security of the entire region. The Christian government in Lebanon is seen by Israel as far more likely to respect
its integrety as a state than any Muslim government which might replace it. Therefore the United States views support of the Maronites
as an essential point of foreign politics.

The United States continues to support the Maronite Christian community for another, related reason: the belief that increased Muslim power in the Lebanese government would result in increased Syrian influence and, by extension, increased Soviet influence since the Soviet Union is an ally of Syria. For this reason, a great deal of speculation was voiced that Iran, Syria, or the Soviet Union itself might be supporting the terrorist attacks against the United States. The notion of "state-supported terrorism" was advanced as a theory to explain the attacks, implying that the Shi'ites would never have engaged in such actions unless they were prompted to do so by outside forces.

The Shi'ite community, frustrated and angry, had every motivation to strike out at people seen as its opressors. Even if support was supplied from outside Lebanon for terrorist acts, those acts would never have been undertaken were the Shi'ites not at the breaking point. The attacks directed against the United States were not aimed primarily at lessening Western power in the region to the advantage of the Soviet Union, they were aimed at lessening Western support for the Christian dominated government.

Economics, Power, and the Shi'ites.

The Shi'ite community was of course interested in increasing its own power and economic status in Lebanon, but it was even more concerned with the general issue of legitimacy. The Christian government and its Western supporters were seen as illegitimate overlords in an essentially Muslim nation. The Shi'ite community was convinced that the only legitimate future for Lebanon was the establishment of an Islamic government. Moreover, extremist members of the community were willing to risk severe hardship and even death to achieve that goal. No amount of force applied by the United States, the Christian central government, or any other agency would dissuade them.

Elite Actors.

The United States was confused by the terrorist action because it could not find any specific agency or individual(s) who could be assigned responsibility for the terrorist events. The general sobriquet "Islamic Jihad" (translated incorrectly as "Islamic Holy War" in the Western press) claimed responsibility, but it was never clear whether this was one organization or a loose coalition of oppositionist forces. Lacking ability to identify an elite leadership structure for the extremists, the United States found itself powerless to address the threat, except to bluster. Washington was far more comfortable with the identifiable leaders of the Lebanese central government even though they were essentially powerless by this time.

Business as Usual.

The United States was unable to deal with the terrorist threat in Lebanon in an effective way precisely because the situation could not be handled using the U.S. models for dealing with foreign policy issues. It was not a nation-state issue, was not relatable to the East-West power struggle, could not be treated using economic pressure or brute military force, and was not addressable through elite actors. Under these circumstances, President Reagan was forced to withdraw with some embarrassment, scratching his head with wonder at the "incomprehensible chaos" in that nation.

THE UNITED STATES AND THE GULF WAR

The United States undertook an unusual action beginning on July 22, 1987. On that date it began to protect oil tankers belonging to the state of Kuwait by placing them under the United States flag and providing a military escort for their passage through the Persian Gulf. The reason given for doing this was to protect "free shipping" in the Gulf, specifically from Iranian attack as a result of the then eight-year-old war between Iran and Iraq. By "reflagging" the Kuwaiti tankers the United States signalled its entry into formal conflict in the region. This was an extremely dangerous—some would say foolhardy—action. By September of that year Iran resorted to mining the sea-lanes, causing one major skirmish between the U.S. and Iranian naval forces, when a United States helicopter attacked an Iranian vessel, the *Iran Ajr*, purportedly laying mines near Bahrain. The United States attack killed ten Iranian sailors and injured a number of others. Iran asserted it was wronged in this incident because it had not launched an attack against a United States vessel and claimed the right of revenge. In the weeks that followed Iran did not attack any United States ship but increased its attacks on ships flying under other flags.

The irony of these incidents is that the United States did not begin the reflagging operation for the reasons originally stated: to ensure free shipping or to curtail the Iran-Iraq conflict. The United States action actually caused an increase in attacks against international ships and succeeded in expanding the hostilities of the war. The operation was actually begun because the Soviet Union offered to lease three oil tankers to Kuwait and to protect those tankers militarily. The Soviet action caused the United States to respond with a counteroffer. Once again the belief system outlined as the framework for this discussion had worked to create actions which achieved exactly the opposite effect from that desired.

Nations and States in the Gulf

There are many states in the Persian Gulf region, but very few nations. The sheikhdom of Kuwait is one of the most problematic of these. It is claimed by Iraq and has been regularly threatened with annexation for most of the twentieth century. Since the beginning of the Iran-Iraq conflict, Kuwait has been the only reasonable point for the transshipment of large-scale war materiel for Iraq. It has thus become Baghdad's chief *entrepôt* for the war. Kuwait acquiesces in this in part because it feels it has no choice. Although the decisive battles of the Iran-Iraq war are taking place on the land border between the two countries, Iraq has tried to cut Iran's economic lifeline by bombing Iranian tankers to prevent Tehran from exporting oil from its fields in the Gulf region. Iran for its part has tried to cut Iraqi supply lines by attacking supply ships bound for Iraq. Iran is also interested in making life hard for the Kuwaitis, in hopes of getting them to halt the transshipping operations. The problem of violence in the Gulf is thus a multistate problem hinging on a very complex set of interdependencies, not the least being Kuwait's position of weakness *vis-à-vis* its neighbors.

The Superpowers in the Gulf

Note that the United States took no military action to halt violence in the Gulf until the Soviet Union became involved in the overall situation. This is in keeping with America's long-standing, predictable stance whereby little of significance is carried out in foreign policy unless it can be tied to a Soviet threat. In this case the Kuwaitis were playing the United States off against Moscow. In 1984 Kuwait had requested military aid from the United States, which was refused. It promptly established low-level diplomatic relations with the Soviet Union. The Soviet offer to lease three tankers with military protection touched off a panic in Washington—the Persian Gulf was in danger of becoming a "Soviet lake"—and thus the proposal to reflag the Kuwaiti tankers.

Economic and Military Power

Whether prompted by a perceived Soviet threat or not, the United States still finds itself embroiled in conflict with Iran at this point. The military posture the United States has adopted is coupled with a move to isolate Iran by establishing an embargo or sanctions against it if it does not accept a cease-fire in the war. The United States does not understand Iran's basic motivation in continuing the war. Iran may be interested in regional hegemony or demonstrating its strength against Iraq, but the basis for the continuance of the war is Iran's righteous indignation at having been the wronged party in the war, while continually being branded as the agressor in the conflict. Iran has only one message for the world at present: it is not the aggressor in the Iran-Iraq war. Iraq attacked first.

The attack on the *Iran Ajr*, which the United States apparently caught mining international waters fifty miles northeast of Bahrain, has the same quality as the war itself in Iranian eyes. The Iranians have already pointed out that they did not attack the United States. They were the subject of American aggression.

The United States' defense is the same as the Iraqi defense in the war: although the United States attacked first, Iran's mining operation was ample provocation. Iraq's defense in the war is that Iran was working to undermine its government and therefore had to be attacked to stop the subversion.

The attack on the *Iran Ajr* took place the day before Iranian President Ali Khamenei was due to address the United Nations on the United Nations peace resolution and on the anniversary of the war itself. President Khamenei, already facing loss of power at home due to implications of involvement with the United States-Iran arms scandal, had no choice but to deliver the most vituperative speech possible under the circumstances. This is sad, for many had anticipated a far more conciliatory address. Iranians have come to entertain a deep belief in conspiracy, especially conspiracy by the United States against them, and this whole set of coincidences looks too pat to be true. Very few Iranians will believe American claims that mines were actually being laid. The whole series of events looks too much to Iranian eyes like a put-up job. The end result for Iran is that the United States attack will never be seen as justified. It was viewed as another instance of Iran being attacked and then blamed for being the aggressor. The attack further fed the war fervor in that country and strengthened the most extreme elements in Iran's government.

"Plumbers"

The background to the United States military action was a three-year operation to improve relations with Iran by identifying "moderate elements" in the Iranian government who would be instrumental in helping to improve relations. The end result of this effort was a series of abortive negotiations resulting in arms sales to Iran in return for Iranian intervention in aiding the release of United States and other international hostages in Lebanon. This was yet another instance of the United States trying to identify a small, elite body of actors who would help accomplish American aims. The Iranians were much more clever than this and ended up purchasing a large quantity of arms, but not doing much of anything the United States wanted. When the scandal broke in the United States, the government was deeply embarrassed in the region and had then to take a strong policy against Iran, thus relinquishing a long-standing policy of neutrality in the Iran-Iraq war in order to maintain its credibility with other Arab states.

The Pattern Continues

Thus in United States involvement in the Gulf region, the pattern in foreign policy belief noted in other contexts continues to operate. Washington seems unable to take account of regional forces that transcend normal nation-state dynamics. Policy makers are excessively concerned with the Soviet Union, to the point that they will take unreasonable, even foolhardy actions when Moscow is involved that they would not otherwise consider. They fail to allow issues of national pride or injustice as legitimate motivating forces, and they continue to search for plumbers to accomplish their goals rather than to work through political processes which require understanding of the actual local circumstances.

Hope for Cultural Solutions to Crisis

The United States has had terrible difficulties in dealing with other nations which are not nation-states in the true sense of the word, such as Lebanon, Pakistan, and the Sudan. It continues to jam regional conflicts into the irrelevant model of the East-West confrontation, as in Central America. It negotiates on the basis of power when cultural understanding is the more immediate need. It looks for power elites and tends to take those in office seriously even when they have no real power, as in El Salvador.

Most serious of all, it continues to ignore the broad social and cultural processes which motivate the vast majority of humans in the conduct of their day-to-day affairs. Because it believes these processes irrelevant in foreign relations, it gives them no place in its own calculations. The end result is continual repeated miscalculation about the course of world events and the United States' proper role in them. The United States ends up on the wrong side of the fence almost every time. This is not the result of bad luck; it is the result of an inaccurate system of beliefs.

In a world growing rapidly interdependent, those who can reform their mythology to accord with the actual course of observed events will have a better chance of survival. The present rigid mythology which governs United States foreign relations does not bode well for the future survival of this nation.

SOME PRACTICAL SUGGESTIONS

Unfortunately, a great deal of the activity of academics in the area of foreign policy has consisted of self-righteous sniping, which some will also say is the central purpose of this chapter. I mean to do more than merely snipe, however. There are a number of practical suggestions we should be pursuing to bring a greater sense of reality to United States foreign policy as we transit into the twenty-first century.

Anthropologists and other academic specialists with broad cultural understanding of different world areas should:

(1) Work actively to insist on a higher standard of understanding on the part of governmental officials of the cultures and social systems of other nations.
(2) Integrate topics of relevant current interest, such as the Middle East conflict or Latin American revolutionary movements, into anthropological teaching.
(3) Write actively for journals of opinion and newspapers to provide cultural perspectives on breaking news. Most local and nationally recognized newspapers are delighted to receive timely, concise, well-written editorial pieces that provide unusual perspectives on news.
(4) Work to develop careers in public and foreign policy for anthropology graduates.

These are minor suggestions, but they are the kinds of things done by our colleagues in political science and economics which have had a powerful effect in shaping the philosophy of United States foreign and military policy today. By staying aloof in daily conduct and in the definition we maintain of our own profession, we anthropologists have only ourselves to blame if public officials remain insensitive to the insights we are able to provide by virtue of our understanding the ways humans work and think.

NOTES

1. These principles of belief were first expounded in 1983 (Beeman 1983c) and are included in two subsequent publications (Beeman 1986b; 1986c). This chapter is an expanded version of Beeman (1986c).

2. Cf. Beeman (1983a, 1983b) for additional discussion of Iranian leaders' moral characterization of the United States and its political uses in establishing the Islamic Republic.

3. Cf. Beeman (1981) on negotiation problems during the hostage crisis.

5

WITCHCRAFT
AND THE COLD WAR
Paul R. Turner

Witchcraft, the hostile use of extraordinary power, is usually thought of as being practiced in the twentieth century only in tribal or peasant societies. If it is conceded that witchcraft is practiced in modern societies, it would be limited to small groups of deviant people. Twentieth century witchcraft, then, is considered to be a localized phenomenon that does not exist on the national or international level. I will attempt to show in this chapter that witchcraft is not just a localized phenomenon in our century but has been practiced on the national level and is now being practiced on the international level.

WITCHCRAFT ON THE LOCAL LEVEL

My data for witchcraft practiced on the local level come from the village of Santiago, one of nineteen Highland Chontal villages located in the southeastern part of the state of Oaxaca, Mexico.[1] Santiago is a small Indian village of about 500 people linked to other villages by mountain trails.

The people of Santiago are slash-and-burn farmers of land on the sides of mountains. Their only farming tools are digging sticks for planting their crops of corn, beans, and squash and hand hoes for weeding their crops.

Santiagoans are bilingual, having native control of their own language and varying degrees of mastery of Spanish. Only a few people are able to read Spanish with comprehension or speak it fluently. Spanish has been the language used in the recent past for contacts with outsiders. Because of their limited knowledge of Spanish, Santiagoans have only vaguely understood some of the ideas that priests and schoolteachers have tried to convey to them. More than 400 years after the Conquest of Mexico, the people of Santiago hold beliefs that probably go back to pre-Conquest times.

One such belief is in the power of secret formulas that can be used for good purposes, healing and protection, or for bad purposes, illness and death. Curers use these formulas for good purposes; witches use them for bad purposes, but always in complete privacy, since other people may not be able to tell the difference between the two.

A witch in Santiago uses his power to frighten and coerce people. He does this, not by admitting he is a witch, but by making a threatening statement in private to a victim he is attempting to intimidate. The implication is that misfortune in the form of sickness or death will happen to the victim if he does not do what the witch wants done. Backing up the threat are the formulas that are followed for carrying out witchcraft rituals. Since the rituals are performed in secret, only the witch knows whether they have been performed or not. The public aspect of witchcraft, the only part ever witnessed by anyone other than the witch, is the threatening statement.

Threatening statements are also made by angry people who are not witches. These statements are not taken seriously unless the person making them has extraordinary power. Such a person is thought to have that kind of power if the victim, his immediate family, or his animals become sick or die shortly after the threatening statement is made. The witch does not have to continually make threatening statements to coerce people. Once they are convinced he has unusual power and will use it, they are reluctant to antagonize him in any way.

A witch has the greatest influence over people who consider themselves defenseless against his power. People less easily influenced believe they are invulnerable to the witch's power, or that they are vulnerable but can take direct action against him.

In one type of action the victim of witchcraft gathers together a sympathetic group of men armed with clubs, machetes, or guns. They go to the house of the witch and kill him at night. The victim of witchcraft tries to involve a group of men in killing a witch because one person, even armed, may not be equal to the task. Another reason for involving a group of men is because it indicates a consensus of belief that the person killed is a witch and not an ordinary person. This group consensus helps to convince the relatives of the slain person that the killing was justified, even though they might never have considered their relative to be a witch. If some of them are still unconvinced, the idea of revenging their relative's death against a group of people discourages them.

Sometimes the victim cannot persuade a group of people to kill the witch and takes action himself or hires a gunman. In these instances the killing could be considered a murder that needs to be revenged by the sons or other close relatives of the slain person. The victim has to take these relatives into account and how likely they are to avenge the death.

The person practicing witchcraft also has to take his own close relatives into account. If he has none, or ones unlikely to avenge his death, he must be careful about whom he tries to coerce. Even if he restricts his coercion to people who can be easily frightened, he has to make sure it is not overdone. Too many frightened people can unite in a group action and destroy him.

A witch in Santiago has to be careful to maintain the proper level of intimidation. If he is powerful and has support from his close relatives but is too much of a threat to a strong individual, or many weak ones, he is likely to be attacked through fear—fear of annihilation if nothing is done to put an end to his witchcraft. If he is considered to be relatively weak and not supported by close relatives, then he represents too little a threat. Any attempt on his part to coerce others may result in an attack on him, based not on fear, but on overconfidence.

The people of Santiago believe that anyone who sheds the blood of a human being aligns himself with the devil. This partnership begins with a murderer supplying the devil with food, the shed blood of the slain person. Killing a witch, though, is not the same as killing an ordinary human being. Witches are the enemies who cause the misfortunes of good people.

Witchcraft on the local level usually involves a powerful witch and relatively powerless victims. Less common is the situation where two people with extraordinary power are hostile toward each other and wish each other ill. I have data from Santiago that applies to such a situation.

Florentino, when I knew him, was an elderly man who had a reputation for being a troublemaker. He owned the only book of formulas that I ever saw in Santiago. He claimed that his formulas were all good ones to be used for healing and protection only. At my urging he demonstrated several of them to me one day in a secluded place on his ranch, after I agreed to pay him for his services. He also denied ever causing the illness that had affected Porfirio in the past.

Porfirio had the reputation of being the most knowledgable healer in Santiago and the villages beyond. He also demonstrated a healing ritual for me one day at his ranch, without pay, and within hearing distance of his neighbors. He said that since his rituals were good ones, he had no reason to be afraid of what other people might think. But one of his neighbors who heard what was taking place came over and covered up evidence of the ritual as soon as it was performed. Perhaps he thought that even though the ritual was a good one, someone might misunderstand. Porfirio told me that day that Florentino used his formulas for bad purposes, once to make him seriously sick.

Porfirio was older than Florentino and died first. Porfirio's son, I think, was convinced that Florentino had caused the death of his father. I suspect that he persuaded several other men to join him in killing Florentino. I was not living in the village at the time, and there were no witnesses to the slaying. What is certain is that Florentino was brutally clubbed to death by several men who have never been identified. Santiagoans accepted the slaying, not as a murder, but as the elimination of a witch for the good of the community.

At the time of his slaying, Florentino also had a son who promptly moved away from the village. The son never impressed me as someone capable of protecting his father, and I think he moved away because of the pressure put on him. He could either admit that his father was a witch and live in peace with the slayers or avenge his father's death by killing them. Florentino did have a son who was capable of avenging his father's death, but that son had been killed in a land skirmish with another village.

WITCHCRAFT ON THE NATIONAL LEVEL

Because this topic is not my focus here, I will discuss only briefly one example of witchcraft on the national level in the twentieth century: the witch hunt of Nazi Germany directed against the Jews. Just as witches in Santiago are blamed for the misfortunes of good people, so Jews were considered to be Germany's misfortune (Meltzer 1976:36). They were blamed for contributing to Germany's humiliating defeat in World War I and for exacerbating its almost unsolvable postwar problems. It was relatively easy for Hitler to divert the attention of the German people from their own failures to the highly visible Jewish presence among them. Jews seemed to have the best jobs and positions of influence at the expense of other Germans. Jews were portrayed as also being international manipulators of sovereign nations without allegiance owed to any one of them. Just as Santiagoans accept the slaying of a witch without protest, so Jews were vilified until German leaders had no objections to Hitler's "Final Solution of the Jewish Question" (Meltzer 1976: 107).

Jews who took Hitler's threats seriously fled Germany while they could still leave. Those who thought that Hitler would never carry through with his threats, or would not be allowed to do so, stayed and went through the Holocaust. The judgments against the Jews and witches were the same: they had no right to live. The one judgment was made by the most scientifically advanced nation of its time, the other by an illiterate community of Mexican Indians, both living in the twentieth century.

WITCHCRAFT ON THE INTERNATIONAL LEVEL

My example of witchcraft practiced on the international level involves the world's two nuclear superpowers, the Soviet Union and the United States. Their extraordinary power comes from owning secret formulas like the owners of secret formulas in Santiago. If the Santiagoan uses his formulas for good purposes, he is considered to be a curer, but he is always suspect. He has power, extraordinary power; and it could be used for bad purposes, making him a witch.

The formulas of the superpowers are used to build nuclear weapons that can be used for good purposes, deterrence and defense, or for bad purposes, first strikes and offense. Each country insists that its formulas are intended for good purposes only while questioning the sincerity of the other country's intentions. Every owner of a formula in Santiago also insists that it is intended to be used only for good purposes.

Powerless people in Santiago, though, do not agree with this assessment. They have been threatened and coerced by hostile people with extraordinary power who have used that power in the past to destroy others.

Nor would the other countries of the world agree that the formulas of the superpowers have been used, and are being used, only for what they consider to be a good purpose, defense. Obviously the Japanese living in the cities of Hiroshima and Nagasaki during World War II were victims of offensive nuclear weapons. Not so obvious have been the veiled public threats and secret attempts at coercion by American Presidents directed against those countries that have frustrated our foreign policy.[2] Probably no living American President, though, would admit publicly that he had ever tried to coerce other countries with the use of our nuclear weapons.[3] Nor does any witch in Santiago ever openly admit to coercing others with his rituals.

A witch works in secret ways in carrying out his rituals, similar to a scientist in a nuclear laboratory. Both of them succeed in casting frightening spells which affect their fellow human beings, but on a radically different scale. The witch coerces only one person at a time with his rituals while the scientist's weapons threaten an entire nation, perhaps the whole world.

Stalin was perceptive enough in his time to see nuclear weapons as something with which to frighten people with weak nerves (Kennan 1976:32) and he refused to be coerced by a weapon that was too destructive to be politically useful. Coercion, too, is the function of a witch's ritual, only on a different scale. Stalin was also aware of the potentially suicidal aspect of nuclear weapons (Kennan 1976:32). Any city-state or nation that rises to power and threatens other city-states or nations collapses when it arouses the fear of more enemies than it can handle (Powers 1984a:54). Threatening people in Santiago is also suicidal when the witch has aroused the fear of more enemies than he can handle. To threaten others with death through the use of potentially suicidal rituals or weapons would seem to indicate a death wish on the part of the threateners themselves, whether individuals or nations. But when nuclear superpowers entertain death wishes for whatever reasons, their suicidal impulses have implications not only for themselves, but for every living person—even the unborn, for a nuclear conflagration might extinguish the human race (Schell 1982:146).

Witchcraft on the international level not only involves the powerful coercing the relatively powerless, a common occurrence in witchcraft practiced on the local level, but also the powerful confronting the powerful, a less common occurrence in witchcraft.

The use of witchcraft between witches is somewhat unusual not only because it is a power struggle between more or less equals, but also because each is involved in vilifying the other while asserting his own innocence. A witch does not normally vilify his victims, they are powerless. Witches, though, do vilify their victims when they are engaged in a power struggle, for each is the other's victim. It is a mirror image situation in which each sees the same things, but in reverse. Each sees the other as a witch and himself as an innocent victim.

The mirror image situation also exists on the international level between the Soviet Union and the United States and has been documented (Osgood 1962:139). Some 76 percent of the good attributes that each nation claims for itself as well as the bad qualities assigned to the other nation are the same. Like witches intent on destroying each other, each superpower attributes to the other the most fiendish and inhuman tendencies (Kennan 1976:177). American claims that the Soviet Union is an evil and bizarre episode in human history,[4] the focus of evil in the world,[5] are met by Soviet claims that the Reagan administration has maniacal plans (Gwertzman 1984:1D) and is comparable to Hitler's Reich in trying to overthrow lawful governments by force (Lewis 1984).

CONCLUSION

I have attempted to show that witchcraft is practiced on the international level in our times. The objection could be made, though, that my attempt to explain the cold war in terms of witchcraft is simplistic and does not do justice to the complexity of the situation. After all, I might know something about witchcraft in a Mexican Indian village because I lived there and I am an anthropologist. But, international relations between the world's superpowers is a different matter and it would be unlikely that my expertise would extend that far. Would anyone knowledgable about world affairs agree with my assessment that witchcraft, or something like it, is being practiced on the international level?

There is someone knowledgable about world affairs and an authority on war, Thomas Powers, who provides an answer to this question. In fact, his article on the cold war, entitled, "What Is It About?" motivated me to write this chapter. Powers summarizes his lengthy article with these words:

> Only Russia has the power to threaten the United States. Only the United States has the power to threaten Russia. We fear each other. We wish each other ill. All the rest is detail (1984a:34).

Powers uses the same words to describe relationships between the Soviet Union and the United States that I have used to describe witchcraft in Santiago: power, threaten, fear, and wish someone ill.

The objection could also be made that there is an important difference between the formulas of witches and scientists that has not been mentioned: the formulas of witches are only effective if the intended victims believe in their efficacy; the scientific formulas are effective regardless of whether their intended victims believe in their efficacy or not. In other words, witchcraft rituals are psychological weapons at best while nuclear weapons are part of the actual-factual world.

This distinction loses its significance, though, if current nuclear weapons are never used. There are several reasons why these weapons might never be used. First, if these weapons are built to be deterrents only, as claimed by each country, then neither country will ever use them. Second, even if these weapons are built for offensive purposes, despite claims to the contrary, it is becoming more and more unlikely that either country would risk nuclear winter to use them (Powers 1984b:64).

If the only use of these weapons for each country lies in their being a deterrent to the other country not to use its weapons, then current nuclear weapons, like witchcraft rituals, are psychological weapons. Nuclear weapons as deterrents are psychological weapons because they are only effective if their intended victims believe in their efficacy. Adding to the psychological characteristics of nuclear weapons is the emphasis on the symbolic, rather than strictly military, concerns of the nuclear policies of the United States. Richard Burt, an assistant secretary of state, underlined this emphasis when he expressed no concern about deploying the Pershing II missile in Europe even though it had failed early flight tests:

> We don't care if the goddamn things work or not. ... After all, that doesn't matter unless there's a war. What we care about is getting them in (Fallows 1984:138).

However, recognizing nuclear weapons as psychological weapons rather than "real" weapons does not eliminate the danger that they represent to the existence of life on earth. As long as hostile nations have these weapons pointed at each other, the earth will be in a precarious situation.

"How do you think the cold war will end?" is a question I insert in conversations whenever it is appropriate. Two answers that are given most frequently are: "I hope it doesn't become hot," and "It will become hot." Of course, no one knows the answer to that question, but the outcome of the struggle between the two hostile power figures in Santiago might provide insight into what will be the final outcome of the cold war.

These two extraordinarily powerful men were not able to live out their lives in peaceful coexistence. Porfirio was convinced that Florentino had used his power against him in the past to make him sick. But neither Porfirio nor his son tried to kill Florentino because the psychic attack, although serious, was not followed by other attacks. Then, too, Florentino was too strong at the time to be killed, perhaps psychically or because he had a son who would have avenged his death. A kind of balance of terror existed between these two power figures for years.

Once his son was killed, though, Florentino was left in a weakened position. When he was thought to have used his powers for evil again, causing the death of Porfirio, Porfirio's son was suspected of taking group action against him and killing him.

Just as these two men with extraordinary power could not live out their lives peaceably, so it is unlikely that the Soviet Union and the United States will be able to coexist without using nuclear weapons on each other. The attack may come once the balance of terror has been upset. That balance can be readily upset by a number of factors, including shifting alliances of nations, technological breakthroughs, radical economic changes, or a gradual process of ever-increasing military spending until one country or the other is brought to the brink of bankruptcy (Lemann 1984).

The attacking country would be operating from a position of either fear or overconfidence. A feeling of overconfidence would come from seeing itself so much stronger than its adversary that a first attack could be mounted with relative impunity. Feelings of fear would come from seeing itself so much weaker than the opponent that the advantage of a first strike would be needed to survive at all.

It might be interesting to speculate which country will launch the first attack. Identifying a potential aggressor, though, is not important because in an exchange with current nuclear weapons there would be no winner. Assuming the world would still be inhabitable, neither country would ever be a world power again. If the human race is extinguished in that exchange, there would be no one left to note anything.

Admittedly, this is a pessimistic prophecy and I find it unsatisfactory to end on such a note of despair. Something can be done to change the predicted outcome of a nuclear exchange between the two countries if they stop practicing witchcraft on themselves and the rest of the world.

Both countries must rise above their tribal mentalities to a global perspective (Cousins 1981:40). As individual nations, the Soviet Union and the United States may have the right to build suicidal nuclear weapons, but not as members of a world community of nations. The current weapons that can destroy both nations threaten the world with nuclear winter (Sagan 1984) and human extinction (Schell 1982:115).

Realistically speaking, the prospects of these two superpowers rising above their own narrow interests are not promising, based on past experiences. There are the vested military-industrial interests in both countries that maintain their positions of power and influence by feeding on each other. Any significant reduction in nuclear weapons would be perceived as personally threatening to them. After almost forty years of cold war privileged status and self-serving political manipulations, the military-industrial complexes of one or both countries may already be in covert control of their governments. President Eisenhower warned against this possibility in his Farewell Address:

> In the councils of government we must guard against the acquisition of unwarranted influence, whether sought or unsought, by the military-industrial complex. The potential for the disastrous rise of misplaced power exists and will persist. We must never let the weight of this combination endanger our liberties or democratic processes. We should take nothing for granted. (January 17, 1961).

Then, too, having extraordinary power is a "heady" experience for any individual, be he a witch in Santiago or leader of a nuclear superpower. President Truman's reaction at the Potsdam Conference to hearing the results of the Fat Man plutonium bomb test were clearly visible to those attending the conference. He was a dramatically changed man, tremendously pepped up and filled with confidence to deal with the Soviets at the conference table (Wyden 1984:224).

President Nixon boasted to a group of visiting congressmen in November 1973, "I can go into my office and in twenty-five minutes seventy million people will be dead" (Zuckerman 1984:59n).

What gives extraordinary power to both a witch in Santiago and the leader of a nuclear superpower is their control of death. Death is life's most crucial uncertainty, uncontrollable, unpredictable for most human beings. A witch is believed to not only be able to predict a person's death, but to actively cause it. As such, a witch has negative charisma in the sense that he is disvalued but has unusual influence over others. Adding to that influence may be his own unpredictability in choosing a victim or the time to exercise his power.

A leader of a nuclear nation also has negative charisma but on a much greater scale. Not only can he cause the deaths of millions of people but may also be able to extinguish the human race. Any unpredictability on his part could add to his power. President Nixon seemed to be aware of this and believed in the "Madman Theory" of the Presidency (Schell 1982:205). According to this viewpoint, developed by the nuclear theorist, Herman Kahn, foes of the United States would be more willing to submit to the President's will if they thought he was crazy, unpredictable. President Nixon is reported to have used this strategy against the North Vietnamese to bring them to the peace table, but without success (Zuckerman 1984:191n).

Unlike a witch in Santiago, the leader of a nuclear superpower also has positive charisma in the eyes of his countrymen. By deterring his counterpart from unpredictably unleashing his nuclear arsenal, he saves the lives of his fellow-citizens, even perhaps preventing the extinction of the human race.

Today, to my knowledge, no one is practicing witchcraft in Santiago. For a variety of reasons the people of this village have rejected the use of hostile extraordinary power. If the nuclear nations were to do the same, giving up their nuclear weapon sovereignty to international control, then the less dramatic problems of the world could be more adequately addressed: pollution, poverty, illiteracy, and ill-health. It remains to be seen, though, if these nations are mature enough to rise above their own militant nationalism to recognize their responsibilities to the world community.

However, a small but important step toward easing international nuclear tensions has already been taken. President Reagan, perhaps to increase his re-election chances during the last Presidential campaign, refrained from making hostile statements about the Soviets, with the exception of his "joke" about bombing them out of existence. If this temporary cessation of threats could be made permanent, prospects for coexistence would be improved because one of the major components of witchcraft on the local, national, or international level is the expression of verbal hostility by those who either have extraordinary power or see themselves threatened by it.

NOTES

1. Santiago is the fictitious name of a real village where my family and I lived from 1959 to 1963. The data were collected then and during brief annual field trips thereafter. The extended stay occurred while I was a member of the Summer Institute of Linguistics. The subsequent field trips were financed by grants from the University of Nebraska, the University of Arizona, the Doris Duke Foundation, and the American Philosophical Society.

2. Such instances include Truman's public warning to the Chinese in November 1950; Eisenhower's secret nuclear threats against China in 1953; the Cuban Missile Crisis of 1962; Nixon's secret threats of war escalation to the North Vietnamese in 1969; and the Carter Doctrine of 1980 aimed at the Soviet Union's encroachment into the Persian Gulf (Diamond et al. 1984:5).

3. I do not intend to imply that American Presidents who have coerced other countries with our nuclear weapons are witches. It is relatively easy to identify witches when witchcraft is practiced on the local level. It is much more difficult to identify witches when witchcraft is practiced on the international level. Rather than identifying specific individuals as witches in such instances, I think it is closer to the truth to say that the entire citizenry of such nations is involved in the practice of witchcraft as taxpayers, voters, workers, scientists, politicians, military personnel, and the like.

4. Statement attributed to William Clark, former national security advisor to President Reagan (Powers 1984a:50).

5. Statement made by Ronald Reagan (Powers 1984a:47).

II

NUCLEAR WAR
AND THE COLD WAR

6

THE DRIFT TO WAR
Laura Nader

Although our history books are filled with examples of incidents that touch off a declaration of war, the concept of drift (rather than incident) is central to an understanding of the processes that lead to war in the modern age. I refer here to the cumulative unplanned actions of people that have had the unintended consequence of moving their societies in a direction toward war. In this chapter, I will elaborate on an argument that suggests that the way in which nation-states have become structured on the basis of modern militarized science prefigures a "slope" toward war. In this view, what, independently considered, may appear to be relatively unimportant tendencies developing in systems, will be seen as a set of continuous changes increasing the likelihood of war (Nader 1983).

A recognition of this drift or slope should encourage us to change or broaden our present strategies for avoiding war. If unconscious or unplanned tendencies in social behavior result in deep structures which prefigure a drift to war, solutions cannot be found through rational analysis of single incidents. We cannot see contemporary social systems as fixed systems that can be pushed to move away from or toward war with slight changes in current policies. Analogies to war as a game, whether ping-pong or chess, are equally unhelpful, except as data on how warriors think. In other words, theories relying only on one independent variable such as conflict or confrontation, "limited good" or gamesmanship, for example, will no longer be adequate (if

they ever were) for the job of understanding why modern wars happen
or knowing what to do to prevent them from happening.

I distinguish conventional from nuclear warfare because I believe
that the two are basically different sorts of drift processes, as different
from one another as defense is from suicide. No one can win a nuclear
war, but conventional war can be won in terms of territorial gain or
increased control of other goods.

The historian E. P. Thompson deals with the idea of drift by in-
troducing the concept of inertia in his analysis of the current crisis:

> [T]o structure an analysis in a consecutive rational manner may
> be, at the same time, to impose a consequential rationality upon
> the object of analysis. What if the object is irrational? What if
> events are being willed by no single causative historical logic . . .
> but are simply the product of a messy inertia? This inertia may
> have drifted down to us as a collocation of fragmented forces
> (political and military formations, ideological imperatives, weap-
> ons technologies): or, rather, as two antagonistic collocations of
> such fragments, interlocked by their oppositions (E. P. Thompson
> et al. 1980:3–4).

The most important aspects of drift to war are its unplanned nature
and the fact that it is the cumulation of a series of decisions and actions
(related and unrelated), that have led the most powerful world nation-
states in the direction of war. It is the structural and ideological contexts
of this drift that should be probed because they create and legitimize
the "messy inertia" that Thompson describes.

STRUCTURE AND IDEOLOGIES

We have a number of studies of the power structures of twentieth-
century nation-states. The power structure of these societies—the dis-
parities of power and social distance between those with or without
control of decisions and the means of production—is relational (Adams
1975). This structure has generated close social relations between the
leading military, political, and economic groups of the nations producing nuclear weapons. Such relations provide the context in which
the following controlling processes have emerged: "institutionalized
insanity," organizational survival, and short-term self-interest.

I use the term "institutionalized insanity" to refer to isolated
groups with institutional power whose members are immune from the
heavy social sanctions imposed on insane individuals without such
power. This social insulation prevents group members from distin-
guishing delusions derived from ideology from reality based on empirical fact. Institutionalized insanity has not been widely recognized

as a social problem, although exhibiting many of the same features as insanity among individuals. Those who suffer from it are members of power groups and as such are not counted among the socially insane. We hear individuals like physicist Herb York say about the Reagan administration: "What's going on right now is that the crazier analysts have risen to higher positions than is normally the case." U. S. Senator Alan Cranston refers to T. K. Jones, a high ranking member of the Reagan administration, as "far beyond the bounds of reasonable, rational, responsible thinking," when Jones suggested in relation to nuclear war that, "If there are enough shovels to go around, everybody's going to make it." Psychiatrist Jerome Frank says that leaders of nuclear powers behave like mental patients when their strategies to cope with danger end up creating more danger. President Reagan's messianic reference to Russians as "godless monsters" is additional evidence of the kind of thinking that leads to reckless plans to defend presumed United States vulnerabilities. I say, "presumed," because both inside and outside the administration, deficiencies in arguments by the proponents of nuclear buildup have been challenged or qualified by many astute, responsible observers and participants including Admiral Hyman Rickover (1982) and more recently Frank Von Hippel (1983).

The architects of the present United States nuclear policies are said to be intellectuals who, in the words of Robert Scheer (1982) can separate their rhetoric from the consequences of what they advocate. Another view was revealed to me by a man who had worked in the Pentagon for more than twenty-five years. When I asked him if the Pentagon was studying the problem of depressed white middle-aged men in positions of power and responsibility, he added, "and who are being advised by depressed men." It must be difficult to manage the inherent contradictions between what is considered "sane" within the organization and outside of it as well.

In 1983 Theodore Draper published an exchange with the then Secretary of Defense, Caspar W. Weinberger. According to Draper, Weinberger argues that there is no contradiction between deterrence of war and planning to employ nuclear weapons to deny victory to the Soviets if deterrence fails. In his response to Weinberger, Draper labels as "indoctrination" the school of thought that believes in the feasibility of a nuclear war without mass destruction and civilian devastation (1983:33). The idea that nuclear warheads would drop with exact precision only on each side's military installations without mass destruction suggests that nuclear war can be limited, controlled, and clean. Weinberger and others erase these contradictions by blurring the distinctions and by thinking that we can end war by denying victory to the Soviet Union rather than winning a nuclear war outright.

Some scholars studying organizational behavior have found the concepts of organizational survival and momentum to be useful analytical tools for explaining resistance to change and innovation in organizations. No matter what the explicit goals of an organization are, its most central, albeit implicit goal, is its own survival. An organization takes on a life of its own because its members' livelihoods and self-esteem are dependent on its existence.

Institutionalized insanity and organizational survival are important factors in the nuclear arms race. If institutionalized insanity operates among military and defense personnel, behavior in their circles that outsiders might think crazy (like the idea that somebody can win a nuclear war) goes undetected and undebated. This situation can persist for so long that the very survival of such organizations depends on the continuance of policies arising from this insanity (Fallows 1981). When this happens, the survival of the organization itself becomes incompatible with national or even personal survival. Ideologies and rationales are developed within these groups to defend their plan of action. These defenses are reinforced by actual or imagined outside criticism, and often become so strong that organizational members' insanity becomes even more firmly entrenched. This happened in the 1962 Cuban missile crisis (Janis 1973).

The short-term self-interest of the defense industry has also contributed toward the drift to war. This problem has been accelerated by the building of a permanent war economy as described by Melman (1965). As Admiral Rickover made abundantly clear in his last testimony before Congress, the United States defense industry is self-interested and profit motivated. Barnet (1972) reports that after World War II, Charles E. Wilson of General Electric, who recognized the profitability of the emerging defense industry, talked of "building a permanent war economy." During the Eisenhower years, the theory was developed in the United States among liberal politicians, economists, and businessmen that large military spending would stimulate the economy. This theory was put into practice during the Kennedy administration through an enormous increase in military spending and investment in military science. Thus defense industries profited from long-term government contracts, interest-free loans, payment by government for most plant and capital equipment, and government willingness to pay prices subjected to continuous upward renegotiation. These industries are among the biggest, most powerful, technologically advanced units of economic power in the country, and United States national security policy is directed by elite groups largely recruited from such business.

To understand the drift to war we need to examine both the nonrational and rational aspects of the arms race. People have argued that high-level military spending has weakened the United States position in the international marketplace and contributed toward rising inflation at home. The idea of a permanent war economy is hardly rational if one method of coping with the economy actually worsens it. The insanity lies not so much in the idea as in its institutionalization. There may be something about the way United States society has changed since the 1930s that has prompted this apparent drift toward a war economy. Some have said that Americans never found a civilian economic solution to the Great Depression. We simply postponed solutions by going to war.

Preparing for war has become endemic to the superpowers which suggests that there may be internal structural reasons behind this pattern not only in the United States but also in the Soviet Union. E. P. Thompson (1980) focuses his analysis on structures and explores the political implications of the types of defense communities found in these two nations. He argues that dividing the world—particularly Europe—into two mutually hostile blocs, keeping a nuclear balance between these blocs, and freezing Europe and the world into a political scenario of cold war, legitimates the military buildup of the two superpowers. He sees more similarity than difference between the United States and the Soviet Union. Both are characterized by what Thompson calls exterminism—a situation in which the competition for nuclear dominance inevitably means fighting a nuclear war. He argues: "What may have originated in reaction becomes direction. What is justified as rational self-interest by one power or the other becomes, in the collision of the two, irrational" (1980:7), and concludes that both sides need this cold war for their economic and status survival.

In all this, ideology operates as an important driving force and is both political and manifest. Sutton et al. (1962:2) define ideology as "any system of beliefs publicly expressed with the manifest purpose of influencing the sentiments and actions of others." Sentiments are aroused in support of nuclear buildup by the normative elements of the ideology (democracy, freedom, egalitarianism, individual liberty, free enterprise, individual property ownership, free marketplace, and so on for the United States; for the Soviet Union, communal property ownership, the state representing the interests of all citizens, equality between citizens, and so on). Nuclear buildup means a war economy and permanent preparedness which legitimizes huge spending for military programs at the expense of socioeconomic programs (see Melman 1965). Public support for such programs has been elicited by the use of binary opposites in ideologies supporting each superpower; for instance, freedom *vs.* nonfreedom, censorship *vs.* noncensorship. Democracy with all its principles is pitted against communism as the only desirable political system. Anthropology has demonstrated that binary opposites in human thought exist in all societies. (For a discussion of the tendency to symbolize in terms of binary opposites, see Foster and

Rubinstein 1986.) Those opposites, which form the basis of their ideologies structures, help to maintain the actual power structures of particular social systems. The American and Soviet power structures have
become wedded to the ideologies linked to an insider/outsider di-
chotomy that mobilizes the people of each state to work for defense,
pay taxes for it, and be prepared for war. Ideology not only influences
sentiments, but also action. Communism prompts the seizure of territory and its control in order to prevent the incursion of the free market
of capitalism. Capitalism thrives on creating world markets and attempts to control those parts of the world that provide raw materials
and labor for its enterprises.

Thompson argues in another work, *Beyond the Cold War* (1982),
that the function of the cold war is primarily ideological, serving to
promote internal bonding among two rival states and to maintain cohesion and discipline within each bloc. While the ideologies of each state
may be seen to be different in their content, they may be mirror opposites that lead to similar consequences. Thompson speaks of the
profit motive as a driving force behind the growth of a massive arms
industry in the West, of competition between the branches of the armed
services as a way of increasing the complexity of weaponry, and of the
role of the weapons labs and the accommodation of politicians as a
way of enhancing their power. In the Soviet Union, bureaucracy and
communism are the driving forces and, as in the West, the arms industry
has become a major factor in the economy. In both countries nationalism, patriotism, and fear of the other are also part of the ideological
basis for national existence.

Religion is also called upon for ideological justification. American
leaders talk about the godless nature of the Soviet Union and see the
Pope's visit to Poland as a symbol of good versus evil of that nation's
communist government. Words like "nuclear gospel" are used to describe the notion of a controlled nuclear attack, capable of striking
military targets "precisely and discriminately" (Draper 1983:33, quot-
ing Wohlstetter). Rhetoric becomes important in ideological warfare.
Supporters of the nuclear buildup use a style of rhetoric that F. G.
Bailey (1968) terms pseudocerebral; they appear to use logic and scientific evidence to support their position, while in fact, distorting or
excluding important information. This appeals to the will rather than
the intellect of their listeners.

DISCUSSION

What are the implications of the foregoing? Is there any possibility of
a counterdrift away from war? To begin with, the drift to global war

must be de-legitimized by counteracting the controlling processes of institutionalized insanity, organizational survival, and short-term self-interest that emerge from the United States and Soviet military industrial structures, which themselves are buttressed by political ideologies. Identifying these controlling processes and their structural and ideological contexts is an important first step toward destroying their potency.

The antinuclear movement is wise to plan its actions in stages beginning with the nuclear freeze and no-first-use declarations. At the same time, we need to develop positive economies and plan futures for nation-state societies that are not dependent on war for continued existence. To achieve these goals, those concerned with the arms race might well link up with the environmental movements and with healthy alternatives being worked on by the women's movements. Specific recommendations that follow patterns of logical reasoning for stopping this drift toward nuclear war have begun to appear, for instance, the slogan: "Nuclear war is not good for your health, and here is a series of paths that lead to the exit."

We also need plans for drawing people away from nuclear drift and toward positive goals. We need to visualize a peaceful world bent on creation not destruction, and on communication rather than distrust among nations (see Calder 1981). By so doing, we weaken the influence of those political ideologies that foster belligerence. The role of citizens will be crucial in this process; our voices will not be hindered by bureaucracies. In *Our Depleted Society* (1965), Seymour Melman suggested alternative ways of using the $222 billion then earmarked for "defense" if the emphasis on the arms race were reduced. There has been talk about the economic successes of Japan and West Germany, nonparticipants in the arms race. Why can't we imagine what the economies of the United States and the Soviet Union might be without it? Can we envisage solutions for the Great Depression that do not include warfare and use these solutions as a positive enticement away from nuclear war? Can we address as part of the picture the very serious problem of personal powerlessness among top-level officials in the military bureaucracies of countries like the United States or the Soviet Union?

I am arguing that we must recognize the limits on what our military and civilian leaders can do to change our present direction. The public, I believe, is less limited. We need to realize the roles that ordinary people can play in order to participate actively in decisions affecting their lives. This might lead us to think about developing economies appropriate to the conditions of peace. Contests between nations might focus on developing peacetime high technology rather than on building war technology. Such projects could be carried out by people-to-people movements unconstrained by bureaucracies and alert to the potentials offered by the pursuit of non-military goals. It may be that nation-states make war but people make peace (Willens 1984).

7

STEPS TOWARD
WORLD WAR III
Albert Bergesen

How is the cold war to be understood? Certainly it is a competition or conflict between the United States and the Soviet Union. But why? Certainly they have their differences, from ideology to geopolitical ambitions. Much analysis of the cold war and Soviet-American interaction is predicated upon such a conflictual situation, which it is of course. But, there is a perspective on these conflicts that places the actions of these states within a larger world context, the world-system perspective as it has developed in sociology and political science. Here the world is viewed as a singular system composed of a political realm, the international state system, and an economic sphere, the world economy. These two fundamentally interact, and that interaction lies at the root of international conflict. States rise and fall in economic might and this corresponds to a rise and fall in political/military position. Because we are speaking of a world system that has existed since the sixteenth century, the process of rising and falling has occurred before, and there is an identifiable rhythm of circulating hegemonies. In short, the cold war as an instance of such conflict between a declining hegemonic state and a rising competitor is not new, although there is obviously much that is unique to the present superpowers.

In this chapter, then, I want to place the present cold war into the larger context of the world system, and particularly into the cyclical rhythms of war and peace that have characterized the system since its inception. More specifically I will identify four steps that characterized the breakdown of global order prior to World War I and argue that these seem to be repeating. This is not to say that "history repeats itself," but it is to take a world-system view which suggests that there are deep underlying logics of a geopolitical nature that the present cold war may very well represent.

It seems we are always in, or approaching, some period of world crisis. There are, though, greater and lesser crises and the remaining years of the twentieth century seem destined for major political and economic upheavals. Signs of this became increasingly apparent during the late 1970s, with the 1974–1975 and 1980 slumps in the world economy and the deterioration of détente between the United States and the Soviet Union. Are these recessions short-term fluctuations in the business cycle or deeper and more long-lasting economic problems? And the collapse of détente: Is it temporary, or will Soviet-American relations continue to deteriorate, making the specter of World War III a reality? The answer to these questions depends in large part in the framework in which they are viewed and, with this in mind, I would like to analyze a number of recent trends in world politics from the perspective of previous research I have conducted on various long cycles of the world system (Bergesen 1980, 1981a, 1981b; Bergesen and Schoenberg 1980).

The modern world system has passed through two general cycles of international instability and conflict. The first lasted from the six-teenth through the early nineteenth centuries (1500–1815), and the second from the late nineteenth through mid-twentieth centuries (1870–1945). It is the contention of this chapter that we are entering yet another such cycle. These periods are characterized by incessant competition and conflict among the great powers and the absence of any sustained economic/military hegemony by a single power. During the troughs of these cycles, a single power exercised economic/military hegemony: mid-nineteenth-century Britain and the United States of 1945–1973.[1]

CIRCULATING HEGEMONIES AND INTERNATIONAL TURMOIL

One sign that we are beginning a third cycle is the structural similarity between the international state system at the end of the nineteenth and the beginning of the twentieth centuries. This cyclical process of trans-formation, whereby the core of the world system circulated productive and military hegemonies, involved interstate competition and warfare as part of the restructuring mechanism, whereby the system as a whole recognized and renewed its basic social relations. It is an aim of this chapter to articulate the stages of decomposition that appeared during the last cycle and suggest that we are passing through these same stages of decomposition today. The world system is in the midst of passing from one hegemony to the next, from that of the United States in the mid-twentieth century to that of whoever will follow.

When a single state exercises hegemony, productive/military power is more concentrated, a condition referred to as unicentricity, or unipolarity (Bergesen 1976; Chase-Dunn 1978; Bergesen and Schoenberg 1980). Conversely, when there is no single hegemony, power is more equally distributed across core states, creating a more multicentric, or multipolar, international order. With the rise and fall of hegemonies, then, the core moves form unicentricity to multicentricity to unicentricity and back to multicentricity in long, cyclical waves.

This cyclical rhythm appears to be a constituent feature of the world system and one of the mechanisms that keeps the capitalist world economy from being transformed into a more redistributive world economy. Productive advantage can shift from state to state—from Britain in the mid-nineteenth century to the United States in the mid-twentieth and possibly on to Japan in the early twenty-first century. The important point to understand is that while individual states and national economies may rise and fall, the world economy as a whole continues to expand. Further, the failure of individual economies—Britain and now the United States—is part of the rejuvenation mechanism whereby the overall world economy reorganizes itself for yet another round of technological innovation and renewed capital accumulation.

The transition from hegemony to hegemony is not a peaceful one. The multicentricity phase is unstable and conflict-prone. During the first cycle (1500–1815), there was incessant warfare among the great powers. During the second cycle (1870–1945) there was the "Second Thirty Years' War" of 1914–1945. If we are entering yet another cycle (beginning in 1973), then there will be a World War III or IV.

Support for the idea of a third cycle is found in comparing the stages through which the core passed during the transition from British to American hegemony to the present passage of hegemony from the United States to whatever will follow. From the mid-nineteenth through the mid-twentieth centuries, the core passed through four identifiable stages that represented the underlying dynamic of increasing pluralization and concomitant interstate rivalry, competition, and eventual war. The four stages are interconnected and part of the overall pluralization of power involved in the historical movement from one hegemony to the next. These four stages are: (1) the beginning decline of the hegemonic state and the rise of serious competitors; (2) the appearance of treaties and alliances in an attempt to stabilize the decomposing international order; (3) open friction and major international incidents as the pluralization of power increases and states begin to "bump" into each other; and (4) the outbreak of general warfare as the friction of international incidents is transformed into general conflict. As the hegemonic power declines, the major core states become more equal. Power is pluralized. This creates an increasingly unstable situation, as there is no dominant state to underwrite international agreements or enforce international order. Instability grows. States reach out to each other through treaty and alliance in an effort to halt the growing friction, but that fails. The instability increases. Competition and rivalry become more open, resulting in international incidents and eventually open conflict. The core moves from the order of hegemonic dominance to international anarchy. The cycle then begins again with the appearance of a new hegemonic state and another period of peace and economic expansion. Following the first cycle (1500–1815), this period was the mid-nineteenth century. Following the second cycle (1870–1945), it was the 1945–1973 boom years. We have now entered the third general cycle, which began in 1973.

To examine this argument more closely, we must look at the stages in more detail.

Stage 1: Declining Hegemonic States and Rising Competitors

Our point of departure is the mid-nineteenth and twentieth centuries, when the core was dominated by the economic and military hegemony of a single state—Britain and then the United States. During the nineteenth century there was the Crimean War of 1854–1856, in which the major powers were not so much opposing each other as resisting the expansion of a more marginal core, or semiperipheral, state—Russia. But other than that there was a general peace, the so-called 100 years' peace of 1815–1914.

By both the 1870s and 1970s, however, changes in the international system were becoming clear, as there was a move toward a more pluralistic distribution of power. Both hegemonies were fading and both faced serious economic and military challenges. This process of equalizing the power distribution was a mixture of unilateral decline by the hegemonic state combined with industrial expansion by other core powers. For Britain the rivalry came principally from the United States and Germany; for the United States it came economically from Japan and the European Economic Community and militarily from the Soviet Union. In steel production, for instance, German production equaled about a third of Britain's output in 1880; it was more than twice Britain's by 1913. Similarly, the United States produced about as much steel as Britain in 1880 but four times as much by 1913 (Bergesen and Schoenberg 1980). This situation would repeat itself again in the twentieth century. The United States would go from producing over half the world's steel in 1950 to only 20 percent in 1970, and in 1981 she had fallen to being the world's third largest producer, behind the Soviet Union and Japan. There are many signs of American decline: low productivity, sluggish growth rates, loss of important world and domestic markets to foreign producers, and so on (Thurow 1980). But perhaps the most dramatic sign of American decline is shown in the production of automobiles, an industry in which the United States pioneered the modern assembly line technique, the establishment of marketing and sales divisions, and the extensive use of advertising—all hallmarks of twentieth-century industrial expansion. By 1980, though, Japan produced more cars than the United States, making Japan the world's number one auto producer.

UPWARDLY MOBILE SEMIPERIPHERAL STATES   The dramatic growth of Germany and the United States during the late nineteenth century reflected the appearance of a number of new and revitalized core states. The international system received a shock between the years 1865 and 1871 with the dramatic appearance of a number of new and politically strengthened older states. Starting in 1865, following the American Civil War, the United States emerged with a strengthened central government, which was important for the rapid industrial expansion that followed (Chase-Dunn 1980). Then, in 1867, Italy was unified, the Dual Monarchy of Austria-Hungary created, the British North American Act established the Dominion of Canada, and the Meiji Restoration centralized political power and commenced Japan's ascension to core status. Finally, in 1871, Germany was unified under Bismarck. Two of these states went on to seriously challenge and surpass Britain (Germany and the United States), but the mere advent of so many others helped create a much more polycentric core. There were now more strong states contending within the international state system.

The core received a somewhat similar shock when a number of more peripheral states, through state-led industrialization and emphasis on manufactured exports, rose to strong semiperipheral status by the later 1970s, and would conceivably move into the core by the end of the twentieth century (for a somewhat more pessimistic view on this prospect, see Frank 1979). I am referring here to what are variously called the "new influentials" or the "newly industrializing countries" (NICs), such as Brazil, Mexico, Argentina, India, Hong Kong, South Korea, Taiwan, and Singapore.

A centralized and strengthened state apparatus was central to the upward mobility of Germany and the United States in the nineteenth century, and the growth in manufactured exports by today's NICs also seems state-led. In South Korea, for instance, the boom in growth and exports was part of a strong government commitment in the 1960s

involving fiscal, monetary, and exchange-rate policies. Taiwan's trans-
formation was similarly state-led. Explicit policy reforms in 1960 reduced protectionist tariffs, unified and adjusted the exchange rate, and
relaxed exchange controls. Finally, there is Brazil, perhaps the most
discussed case of state-led industrialization. Following the military
coup in 1964, there was a shift in the national economic policy from
the import-substitution strategy of the postwar period to one of export-
oriented growth, with particular emphasis on manufactured exports,
which resulted in the "boom" years of 1968–1973. These eight NICs
account for over three-quarters of all manufactures exported from the
developing world. The recent growth of their manufactured exports
has been phenomenal. Between 1960 and 1975, manufactured exports
as a percentage of total exports went from 14 to 82 percent for South
Korea, 3 to 27 percent for Brazil, 12 to 52 percent for Mexico, and 4
to 25 percent for Argentina (Bradford 1980:9).

The manufactured exports of these NICs are part of the pluralization of world production that is transforming the postwar
(1945–1973) American hegemony in production and trade into a much
more competitive and polycentric world. These semiperipheral NICs
are part of the challenge to American economic dominance along with
Japan and the European Economic Community, as less developed countries (LDCs) in general accounted for some 22 percent of total imports
of manufactures into the United States in 1977, compared with 23
percent from Europe and 21 percent from Japan. In certain areas, like
miscellaneous manufactures, which include clothing and footwear,
LDCs alone account for 49 percent of American imports compared with
only 19 percent from Europe and 18 percent from Japan (Bradford
1980:7).

In general, the appearance of upwardly mobile semiperipheral
states seems to occur during a generalized upswing in the world economy. The upswings of 1848–1873 and 1947–1973 correspond to the
appearance of politically strengthened and centralized states embark-
ing on rapid growth and movement toward core status. It appears that
periods of world economic expansion involve growth in the world
division of labor which mobilizes or somehow cuts loose certain peripheral states and prompts their upward mobility. It is as if in the
swirl of an expanding world economy there is enough world demand,
and an open enough trading system, that a certain degree of upward
mobility for some states is possible. The growing number of firms during an upswing has an analog at the world level with an expansion in
the number of countries actively participating in world production and
the export of manufactures. The rise and expansion of these new states
is also tied to the following downswing in the world economy. The
expanded production of newly mobilized economies contributes to
problems of overproduction and the excessive competition that booms

invariably generate. The downturn that inevitably follows consolidates gains made by some of the new states.

In the case of the United States, the mid-nineteenth century world upswing was the context in which political centralization occurred (the Civil War), and the later nineteenth century was the context for the great wave of mergers that created the modern multiunit corporation (Bergesen 1981a, 1981c). The middle of the twentieth century (1947–1973) witnessed another sustained upswing and boom, with a number of new states being centralized and experiencing a dramatic burst of industrial expansion and a shift to exporting manufactures (the NICs of Brazil, South Korea, and so on). As before, their expanded production and exports are a contributing factor to the present world glut and slump, which began with the 1974–1975 recession and will probably worsen before the end of the century.

Downturns are also mechanisms whereby old hegemonic powers are weeded out, for they appear unable to perform the necessary restructuring of production to be competitive during the following upswing. It appears as if their hegemonic position protects them from the full effect of the pressure toward consolidation and merger. Hegemonies in production and military power arise through a crystallization of class coalitions that give a particular country its advantageous position at the time of its rise to power. Later, when international conditions change, the hegemonic state faces conditions in which its now firmly institutionalized social-economic-political coalition is no longer the most advantageous combination, and hence it is unable to adapt successfully to the new economic environment. Newer rising core powers, however, do make the necessary adjustment under the duress of the downturn and reorganize their infrastructures, making them powerful competitors to the faltering hegemonic power. This can be seen by looking at the rise and fall of British and American hegemony.

THE RISE AND FALL OF BRITAIN AND THE UNITED STATES   It has been argued that Britain successfully adjusted to the general economic downturn of the seventeenth century, while the Ottoman Empire, Spain, and the Northern Italian cities declined and failed to regain their previous leadership during the following eighteenth-century upswing (Frank 1978). Within England there was also a consolidation of capital, with the gradual elimination of artisans who provided draperies for the older Baltic trade and the growth of merchant capitalists who served the new European and American markets.

> It is this productive transformation in England, generated and enforced (or, at least, stimulated) by the seventeenth-century depression that gave England the competitive advantage over her European rivals in the subsequent eighteenth-century expansive development (Frank 1978:98).

British hegemony went on to reach its zenith in the middle of the nineteenth century, during the great 1848–1873 world boom and began to decline thereafter. During the Great Depression of 1873–1896, there began a wave of mergers that was most dramatic in the United States and Germany, creating the corporate structures of Standard Oil, General Foods, and the like, and similar industrial cartels in Germany (Chandler 1980). British industry, though, did not engage in this merger movement as successfully as did the United States and Germany. Their mergers were more cosmetic in nature, involving a linking or federation of family firms to control price competition and to purchase raw materials collectively. They did not, however, engage in the more fundamental reorganization of production that occurred in the United States and Germany, where the autonomy of individual firms was subordinated to the hierarchical command structure of the new corporation. With this failure to create corporations or cartels, Britain did not make as profound a shift from family-based entrepreneurial capitalism to the trusts, cartels, and corporations of what would come to be called monopoly capitalism. This failure to reorganize production was central to the decline of British industry and the emergence of the United States as the next hegemonic power.

This brings us to the present downturn and the question of American adjustment. If American enterprises follow the example of Britain, they too will fail to adjust successfully to the downturn and to participate fully in the wave of mergers that will provide the foundation for the generalized economic upswing of the early twenty-first century. The most significant merging will involve state and firm, in which the state will function as something of a firm itself, like the idea of "Japan, Inc." This state/firm will be the foundation for the next upswing, just as the traditional corporation was the foundation for the great 1948–1973 boom.

The model of the successful role of the state in production seems to be Japan, in which the state apparatus (particularly the Ministry of International Trade and Industry—MITI) represents something of a functional equivalent to the managerial hierarchy that allowed the modern corporation to coordinate the production of a number of individual firms. Here it is the state bureaucracy that manipulates market forces to maintain the overall vitality of the Japanese economy, as if it were a single firm, "Japan, Inc." During the long downturn between 1973 and sometime in the early twenty-first century, the state will take over, coordinate, regulate, and increasingly structure national production in a way similar to the corporate coordination of production that first appeared during the long downswing at the end of the last century. The Japanese idea of "sunrise" industries, of new areas for research and development, for lending capital, and for extending depreciation allowances involves a connection between state and firm that would be resisted in the United States, much as the British earlier resisted the merging of family firms to create the modern corporation. The point here is not that the state has never participated in economic life. From the mercantile Hudson Bay Company onward, the state has participated in one form or another. The point is that the state/firm (Japan, Inc.) will be the dominant form of enterprise in the world economy, the same way the earlier corporations were the dominant form after the crisis at the end of the nineteenth century. Throughout the ups and downs of world capitalist expansion, the firm has grown in size. From the family firm or partnerships of the early industrial era in Britain to the modern corporation and the multinational state/firm, capital continues to be more concentrated and more centralized. As the modern corporation was larger than the family firms out of which it was composed, so will the state/firm represent a yet larger enterprise than the multinational corporations out of which it will be composed.

The United States, though, will not successfully cross over from the private corporation to the state/firm. *American hegemony in world production will be lost during the coming economic downturn.* It is already slipping away. The convulsive restructuring of production that occurs during downturns represents the means whereby capitalism corrects for the overproduction and excessive competition of its previous boom. But this restructuring will not occur in the United States. As the hegemonic power, the United States will, as Britain did earlier, avoid the crunch of the merger and consolidation impulse and thereby be in a weaker position in the upswing of the early twenty-first century, as the state/firm will not be the basis of American production. Instead, the United States will bail out unproductive enterprises, like Chrysler, and resist the state management of production. The United States will still be utilizing the old-fashioned private multinational enterprise, while the next hegemonic power will be based on the multinational state/firm.

Stage 2: Treaties and Alliances

The first stage begins with the decline of the hegemonic state, and the next general stage centers on the appearance of treaties and alliances as core states try to stabilize the increasingly pluralistic distribution of power. Treaties represent efforts by individual states to establish the order and stability that were previously guaranteed by the hegemonic power. In this regard the world-system perspective provides a very counterintuitive understanding of treaties and alliances: while seemingly a move toward international peace—as in, say arms limitation treaties and the generalized United States/Soviet Union understanding known as détente—they actually reflect desperate efforts by states to provide international order on a state-to-state basis. In effect, if there is generalized peace and tranquility among the powers, there is no need for treaties or alliances. It is only when that situation begins to disintegrate that states "reach out" and try personally to stabilize an increasingly volatile international situation.

The growing international instability that accompanied the decline of British hegemony generated a number of treaties and alliances, beginning in 1879 when the newly unified Germany established a military alliance with Austria-Hungary, to which Italy was admitted in 1882. This created a power imbalance that was checked in a classic balance-of-power arrangement with the appearance of the Franco-Russian Alliance in 1894. Now Europe was divided into two camps, and all that remained was to incorporate Britain. This occurred with the *entente cordiale* with France in 1904 and the alliance with Russia in the Anglo-Russian Convention of 1907. With that, the final shape of the Triple Entente and Triple Alliance was formed.

The general point here is that the web of alliances that appeared to snare the great powers at the end of the nineteenth century was a direct by-product of the pluralization of power in the core. Imagine a number of persons standing in a rowboat. As the boat begins to rock back and forth, the individuals reach out to each other in an attempt to provide some kind of stability. Imagine further that the appearance of new and strengthened states in the 1865–1871 period acted like a number of people entering the rowboat at once and thus contributing to the instability.

If the analog with the late nineteenth century makes any sense, we should be witnessing some sort of comparative alliance building to accompany the decline of American hegemony. What I have in mind here are not the immediate postwar treaties of NATO, SEATO, SENTO, or the Warsaw Pact, but the more recent arms limitation and test ban treaties between the United States and the Soviet Union which reflect the appearance of nuclear parity and hence a growing equalization of power within the international situation. The instability and uncertainty that come with the equalization of nuclear power push the great powers toward arms limitations and test ban treaties. This was not necessary during the late 1940s and 1950s, when the American lead in nuclear weapons was so lopsided. As the lead dissipated in the late 1960s and early 1970s, there arose "détente," or an interest in some sort of cooperative working arrangement between the United States and the Soviet Union. The fact that negotiations for SALT II have temporarily broken down, along with the new "tough" stance taken by the Reagan administration *vis-à-vis* the Soviet Union, strongly suggest that international order continues to deteriorate.

Old alliances are also coming undone. The Soviet Union and China, for instance, have seen their alliance go from ideological bickering in the 1960s to border skirmishes and fighting proxy wars in the 1970s, as in the Vietnamese invasion of Cambodia in 1979. The Western alliance also shows strains. The complete dominance of the alliance by the United States is passing.

Along with once solid blocks unraveling, new alliances are forming that would have seemed impossible twenty years ago. Perhaps the most "unholy alliance" is that between the United States and China. The statement by Deng Xiaoping to the Americans—"If we want to be able to place curbs on the polar bear [USSR], the only realistic thing for us is to unite" (Deng Xiaoping 1979:34)—would have seemed impossible twenty-five years ago. This realignment of China can be clearly seen in the peace and friendship treaty with Japan in 1978 and the establishment of diplomatic relations with the United States in 1979, forming the possibility of a new Triple Alliance.

The possible creation of a new Triple Alliance has not gone unnoticed. Moscow Radio, for example, charges that a "Washington-Peking-Tokyo Axis" is being directed against the Soviet Union (Pillsbury 1979), and this is certainly reminiscent of the anxiety and paranoia that surrounded the Alliance system prior to 1914.

Stage 3: Open Friction and International Incidents

The next stage in decomposition is friction, as the treaty efforts fail to stabilize the continued movement of the core toward open conflict. We often see alliances as a cause of incidents and wars, but this is not so. It is the movement toward plurality that generates friction and conflict, and treaties are only a signpost along the way. They are only attempts to reach out and halt the drift toward war.

During the second cycle there were a number of international incidents that preceded World War I. These centered on rivalries and disputes over spheres of influence in the periphery, as when the French and Germans squared off in the first (1906) and second (1911) Moroccan crises. There were also minor wars over territory, such as the first Balkan war (1912) when Serbia, Bulgaria, Greece, and Montenegro invaded the Ottoman Empire, and a second Balkan war (1913), when the victors fought over the Ottoman spoils. The resolution of this incident brought the major powers very close to war. The final "incident," the assassination of the Austrian Archduke Ferdinand by a Serbian student, was followed by general conflict.

What of the 1980s and 1990s? It is my contention that we are just entering this phase of friction and incident. The efforts at new alliances will continue, as they did in the last cycle right up to 1914, but the next set of activities should be open friction. The Cuban Missile Crisis is a good example of the sort of incident that would bring the great powers close to conflict. That, however, was over twenty years ago. The crises of the 1980s and 1990s will be very similar to the incidents of the last cycle, in that they will center on questions of great power influence and control over the periphery (Falk 1980). Most likely are efforts by the declining hegemonic state (the United States) to halt the growing influence of other rising powers (like the Soviet Union) in the Third World.

The areas that seem the most vulnerable are those where stable states are rare or where the process of nation-building is more recent, as in Africa and Southeast Asia. The earlier years of nonalignment (1950s and 1960s) are by and large gone, as new states find themselves pretty much within the sphere of influence of the major powers.

Another example of big power rivalry in the periphery can be seen in the American response to reports of aid from Cuba and the Soviet Union being funneled to rebels in El Salvador in 1981. The American concern seemed almost entirely centered on stopping purported Soviet/Cuban aid. The real issue seems to be just what the Soviets can and cannot do in the Third World, with "drawing the line" against Soviet power being the dominant motive for American aid to the Salvadoran military.

The American reaction to El Salvador and Nicaragua suggests we are entering a period when any number of African, Asian, Middle Eastern, or even Central American states may be the place for future Soviet-American confrontations and international incidents. Americans seem increasingly intent on confronting expansion (real or perceived) of Soviet influence, and that can only suggest a return to the sort of international tensions and crises that preceded World War I, when, say, the French and Germans were concerned over the expansion of each other's power in Morocco.

Stage 4: War

During the last cycle, international friction finally gave way to overt conflict, first in 1914 and then again in 1939. This can be seen as the final stage in decomposition of international order that began during the last quarter of the nineteenth century when British hegemony began to decline. To speak of the possibility or inevitability of World War III is certainly not new. My point here is to suggest that we are in fact headed in that very direction and that we have passed through a number of stages that preceded World War I. There are signs of preparation for just such a war and some analogies to 1914. One sign is the way American nuclear strategy has changed.

NUCLEAR STRATEGY   In the 1940s and 1950s the United States, as the leading nuclear power, adopted the "massive retaliation" strategy, which would meet Soviet conventional thrusts with nuclear retaliation. During the 1960s, with the expansion of Soviet nuclear forces, Secretary of Defense Robert S. McNamara unveiled the "mutual assured destruction" (MAD) policy, arguing that both the United States and the Soviet Union could deter war by threatening each other's cities. By the early 1970s this policy was changing. Then Secretary of Defense James R. Schlesinger took the first step away from MAD by saying the United States needs to be able to undertake "selective" nuclear strikes against the Soviet Union. By 1980 the priority was on hitting military targets rather than cities and industrial sites. Strategy now requires the United States to launch small-scale nuclear strikes against Soviet military targets, including missile bases and troop concentrations. President Carter signed Presidential Directive 59 in 1980; it states that the best way to deter a major conflict with Moscow is to have the ability to wage a prolonged but limited nuclear war. American officials claim the Soviets have long been committed to such policy. In short, American nuclear strategy has gradually moved toward the ability to wage nuclear war. It is becoming not only thinkable but plannable.

THE NAVAL RACE   During the 1950s and 1960s the Soviet Union caught up in both nuclear weapons and naval strength, such that the 1980s will probably bring an expanded arms race fueled by the paranoia and uncertainty of arms parity. The most obvious similarity to the nineteenth century is the naval race between the United States and the Soviet Union, which resembles the earlier one between Britain and Germany:

> There is every indication that the USA and the USSR are on the verge of a naval arms race if, indeed, it has not already begun. . . . For the first time in the post-war period there is now a serious rival. Soviet naval strength has now reached the point at which it is possible to argue that further (unmatched) expansion will threaten U.S. naval superiority. In other words, a necessary condition for a naval arms race, previously lacking, now exists (SIPRI 1976:26).

That assessment seems borne out in the expanded defense budget of the Reagan administration and statements by defense officials that the United States desires to "regain" its dominance of the high seas.

NEW WEAPONS PARANOIA   There is a more elusive similarity with the earlier German-British rivalry, and that is the paranoia about the challenger developing various sorts of advanced weapon systems. One sign of declining hegemony seems to be a vague, paranoid feeling that "they" are up to something and that "we" are falling behind. The British worried about the development of various German armaments, and today the United States seems easily scared by stories about, say, Soviet killer satellites or the development of a Soviet death ray (proton beam). As the confidence of past military superiority slips, all sorts of things become believable—true or not.

REARMAMENT OF OTHER CORE POWERS   Part of the pluralization of power involves a more equal distribution of military strength. The international military situation is increasingly pluralized by the spread of nuclear weapons to semiperipheral states. There has also been a significant change in Japanese attitudes toward defense. "For the first time in 30 years the Japanese are not being shy about defense" (Pillsbury 1979). At the most general level, the increased Japanese interest in defense reflects the pluralization of power and the challenge to American supremacy in the Pacific by the Soviet fleet. With the decline in American hegemony, individual states must increasingly assume the burden for defense, which leads to increasing defense expenditures and, in the case of Japan, the possibility of serious rearmament. The Americans continue to press the Japanese to increase their defense expenditures, which have risen some, and the Americans also press the Europeans to increase their NATO budgets and place nuclear weapons on their soil. The pluralization of power means the United States now needs allies and others to support its declining position. This explains, in part, the *rapprochement* with China and the pressure placed on Japan and the Europeans to increase defense expenditures.

POSSIBLE 1914 SCENARIOS   Finally we can consider the similarity between the alliance system of the last century and present international arrangements. World War I started with an incident and a system of alliances that activated the major powers. A comparable situation appeared recently when China invaded Vietnam in 1979. This had all the signs of 1914. First there was an alliance system linking the participants to more powerful core states. Vietnam was an ally or even a client state of the Soviet Union, while China was in the process of working out an understanding with the United States. Just prior to the Chinese invasion, Deng Xiaoping toured the United States, constantly speaking of the dangers of "Soviet hegemony" and how the United States and China should unite to oppose Soviet expansionism. In some sense the warm welcome he received in the United States can be seen as the result of partial American backing to take military actions against the Vietnamese. Implicit American support for and approval of "punishing" the Vietnamese is very similar to the Austrians receiving German approval to punish the Serbs for the assassination of the archduke. Then there are the Russians. In 1914 they were the protectors of Serbia and today they are the protectors of Vietnam. Then, as now, the Russians did not want to see their ally severely punished. Then Russian troop mobilization was a step toward war; in 1979 Soviet warships in Haiphong Harbor provided a show of Soviet concern, although this time it did not lead to war. But what if the Russians and Chinese had become involved and the Americans were brought in on the Chinese side? World War III? Maybe. The general point is that throughout the Third World, Soviet and American client states often face each other in possible conflict situations that might draw in their great power protectors. North and South Yemen, Vietnam, Cuba, Angola, Thailand, Syria, Israel: the list is endless. All are potential points of crisis, friction, international incidents, and perhaps war.

If there is to be a third world war it would seem the Soviet Union will play the role of Germany during the last cycle. The Soviet Union will present the principal military challenge for the next hegemony but will fail in protracted conflict because of the weakness of its productive base. Japan seems to be playing a role similar to that of the United States during the last cycle—a rapidly expanding economy with little investment in defense and possibly a late joiner in any conflict between the declining hegemonic power and the serious challenger. If that is so, then Japan stands the best chance of assuming the hegemonic mantle. It must be recognized that her industrial challenge is already quite successful—which was exactly the position of the United States vis-à-vis Britain a hundred years ago. Political/military hegemony seems to lag behind productive hegemony, and as such the relatively small size of Japan's military establishment should not be seen as a drawback to her eventual assumption of hegemony.

CONCLUSION

Predicting the future is difficult, if not impossible, and certainly vain. But not to try to understand the drift of events and learn from the past is irresponsible, although it is not clear that it makes any difference. Many saw World War II coming, and no one stopped it. But pessimism is no answer either, and so we go on, making our predictions and trying to understand the forces that animate international life and propel nations into conflict and war.

One such set of forces I have tried to identify involves the recurring rise and fall of hegemonic states and the inevitable competition and conflict that follows before a successor emerges. That process is somehow part of the overall collective dynamics of the world system. The outbreak of world war is not a question of accidents or a temporary breakdown in international order. It is endemic as long as we have an international state system and with it the built-in anarchy of international politics.

During the last long cycle, from the mid-nineteenth through the mid-twentieth centuries, the core of the world system went from one hegemony to another, from Britain to the United States. The passage of power was neither easy nor painless. On the basis of the progression of events during the last cycle there do appear to be a number of stages through which the core passes in the larger transition from hegemony to hegemony. Throughout there is the continued equalization of power distribution, a condition created by both the absolute decline of the previously dominant state and the rise of serious competitors. There are efforts at stabilization through treaties and alliances, arms limitations, and ideas of détente. These do not stop the deterioration, however, and soon competition and rivalry give way to friction and international incidents. Finally, all restraints are gone, and overt conflict appears; there is a war, or a number of wars. After all, it may very well be World War III and IV, or V and VI, before we again come to a period of peace, economic expansion, and a new hegemony. There is also the very real possibility that we may never reach the next upswing, and the prophesied hegemony of China or Brazil or Japan may never be realized.

NOTE

1. For arguments about a possible Dutch hegemony in the seventeenth century and a Spanish hegemony in the sixteenth century, see Wallerstein 1980 and Modelski 1978; the latter believes it was a Portuguese and not Spanish hegemony during the sixteenth century.

8

BIOLOGICAL AND SOCIAL CONSEQUENCES OF A NUCLEAR WAR

Elizabeth Schueler

George J. Armelagos

The 1986 Chernobyl nuclear power plant accident has attracted a great deal of attention. This interest is due not only to the health consequences of its emitting radiation, but also to the fact that it gives policy makers an opportunity to monitor a population's reaction to such a serious and indeed life-threatening nuclear accident.

> Chernobyl was a tragedy for the Soviet Union and Europe. But it was also a reminder for America. It brought into sharp focus the very real scope and consequences of radiation exposure. Chernobyl is more than an unfortunate nuclear event. It is a mirror into which we can look and see our own imperfect past (Miller 1986).

We might add that it provides a window for us to look into the future.

The response to Chernobyl raises questions about our ability to meet the more serious challenge of a nuclear exchange. It makes one question the assumptions of the Crisis Relocation Plan that was developed by the Reagan administration's Federal Emergency Management Agency (FEMA) in response to planning for the possibility of a nuclear attack. The plan (the CRP-2B model) is based on a 6559-megaton nuclear exchange, which represents 524,720 Hiroshima bombs. It proposes the evacuation of the population from danger zones in high-risk urban areas to shelters in low-risk areas and predicts that 80 percent of the American population will survive a nuclear attack. The three to five days of heightened tension will give 150 million Americans living in high-risk areas time to travel 50 to 300 miles to designated low-risk areas (Leaning and Keys:xvii). Even in the relatively minor incident in Chernobyl, there were serious problems to which the social system was not able to effectively respond. In this chapter, we will address the biological and cultural consequences of a nuclear attack which include the health problems that the target population will face, as well as the impact of such an attack on the social structure of the group.

The devastating effects of a global nuclear war are obvious and numerous. Some researchers suggest that the most critical impact of the nuclear exchange would be the immediate loss of life from the blast. For example, scientists who have been involved in FEMA studies (Laney et al. 1976; Quester 1979; Johnston et al. 1978) believe that those who survive a nuclear war will be free of the effects within a few years, that a large segment of the population will survive, and that the ecology will not be disrupted enough to constrain human survival. However, recent criticism (Abrams 1984; Harwell 1984; Turco et al. 1983) of the Crisis Relocation Plan offers a bleak scenario in which the health of the population is severely impaired and the ecology is seriously disrupted. Further analyses (Abrams and Von Kaenel 1981; Coggle and Lindop 1982; Middleton 1982; Geiger 1984; Turco et al. 1983, 1984; Ehrlich et al. 1983) have suggested that immediate mortality during a nuclear attack may be greater than was predicted by the CRP and the long-term consequences of a nuclear war are severe and life-threatening to those who do survive the blast itself. The health of the population would be threatened both directly from the blast and radioactive fallout and indirectly from the explosion's effect on the physical and biotic environment. These problems would in turn transform the economic and political systems, and would further affect the psychosocial well-being of the survivors. Ultimately, these survivors may not be able to adjust to the postattack world. The social consequences of the aftermath of a nuclear exchange have been neglected in previous studies and will have to be examined more fully.

Scientists who are studying the global effects of a nuclear war use the term "nuclear winter," a term coined by Richard Turco to describe freezing temperatures which would result from the sun's inability to penetrate rising clouds of dust and smoke after a nuclear exchange. Much of the research on this topic has been based on a 5000-megaton exchange between the superpowers. The TTAPS study (Turco et al. 1983) includes a scenario of simulation of the climatic effects of a nuclear exchange. Their baseline case produces 225 million metric tons of smoke and 65 million tons of stratospheric dust. Much of the smoke would result if only one quarter of the combustible material in major cities in the northern hemisphere were ignited by nuclear fires. It is estimated that this alone would produce 50 to 150 million tons of smoke, of which 30 million tons would be soot. The TTAPS study suggested that this smoke will cause a fall in temperatures from 30 to 40 degrees Celsius. The report is based on a one-dimensional model, which treats the earth as a homogeneous sphere. It does not consider the heat capacity of the oceans, nor does it consider the north-south or east-west variability of climates (Thompson and Schneider 1986:984).

A more recent study, which does account for geographical variables, suggests that the temperature drop will not be as severe and may be as little as 15 degrees Celsius, lasting for only a few days (Thompson and Schneider 1986). These scientists argue that the nuclear winter world will not be as life-threatening as others have thought, because the less severe drop in temperatures would not threaten the survival of human populations. In fact, Thompson and Schneider argue that while these environmental factors are serious, they no longer constitute a doomsday machine that would eventually insure dire consequences for the perpetrators of the nuclear attack as well as for the victims. However, this temperature change could have a large impact on the already devastating health and social problems that the survivors would confront. Thompson and Schneider argue that the implications of their study suggest that

> despite the continued potential for serious nuclear winter effects, there does not seem to be a real potential for human extinction; nor is there a plausible threshold for severe environmental effects. Thus, the two unique conclusions of the original nuclear winter idea with the most important implication for policy have been removed (1986).

While the biological extinction of human population is not an issue in the review of nuclear winter, according to Thompson and Schneider (they suggest that the term "nuclear fall" would be more appropriate), it begs the question of the level of survival and if this level of survival is acceptable to human populations.

The social organization in a postattack world is a bit more complex to predict than are the more tangible biological and physical effects because clearly there are only a few populations that have experienced the consequences of a nuclear bomb and no societies that have experienced the consequences of a nuclear war. However, anthropologists can combine their studies of cultures that have become extinct with their knowledge of how people have coped with various disasters. We believe that this information is essential if we are to predict the social consequences of a nuclear winter. The response of various cultures to natural disasters can be very informative. While many groups have dealt successfully with the challenges of those disasters, other societies have broken down and become essentially incapable of reproducing or maintaining themselves. Earthquakes, plagues, typhoons, mud slides, famines, and the Hiroshima-Nagasaki nuclear explosion provide useful information on the social response to severe disasters. While many of the previous studies have focused on the biological consequences of a nuclear exchange, they have failed to consider that these biological effects will have a major impact on the ability of social systems to function effectively.

BIOLOGICAL CONSEQUENCES OF A NUCLEAR WINTER

Abrams and Von Kaenel have identified four periods during and after a 5000-megaton nuclear attack where specific deleterious health patterns are likely to occur (1981:1226). The first stage of their scenario is the "barrage period," in which the population will be subjected to trauma from the initial explosion and injuries due to radiation. Those most affected will be adjacent to the blast areas. They have calculated that, moments after the attack, 86 million people (40 percent) of the total population will be dead and 34 million will be severely injured (27 percent of the survivors). Those who do not perish will survive in the "shelter period." The length of the shelter period will depend on the intensity of the attack, but could range from one to many weeks. Survivors will be restricted to fallout shelters during this period in which 50 million additional fatalities can be expected resulting in a total mortality of 133 million Americans.

In the "postshelter" period which follows, the radioactive fallout will eventually decrease and survivors will be permitted to leave their shelters for limited periods of time. The survivors will find a world in which there is a scarcity of food and shelter, a contaminated environment with an abundance of corpses, and an infrastructure in ruins. Abrams and Von Kaenel estimate that 60 million Americans will survive the first three stages of the attack (a figure significantly lower than the FEMA estimates). Those who do survive the "recovery period" will find only a rudimentary social structure and a nonexistent food procurement system and will face short-term and long-term consequences to their health which will further challenge their ability to survive. Unfortunately, these effects will not be restricted to the northern hemisphere, for populations in the southern hemisphere will also face serious consequences of the nuclear winter.

Immediate and Short-Term Effects

During the barrage and shelter periods, there will be numerous detrimental effects on the physical well-being of the people who survive
the actual nuclear blast, the emitting ionizing radiation, and the thermal
radiation. In the barrage period the blast alone, which will physically
alter the environment from its tremendous force, can be expected to
cause buildings to fall, avalanches, dam bursts and landslides (Harwell
1984), all of which could prove to be fatal. Ionizing radiation would
alter the immune response of individuals and, coupled with difficult,
extenuating living conditions in the shelters, the immune system's
deficiency would give rise to an increase in viral infections (Ehrlich
1984). Radioactive fallout due to emitting gamma rays would induce
different sorts of health problems such as vomiting and diarrhea (Barnaby and Rotblat 1982). The fallout would also contaminate the water
which would lead to a deterioration in sanitary conditions, an increase
in diarrhea and a serious threat of dehydration from the lack of water
(Abrams and Von Kaenel 1981).

The effects that the radiation will have on the victims will, of
course, depend on the rate and intensity of exposure. In Chernobyl, as
well as in Hiroshima and Bhopal, there were problems of evacuation.
It took roughly thirty-six hours to evacuate people from the Chernobyl
area because of unanticipated problems. For example, bus drivers who
were called on to evacuate the victims were less than enthusiastic about
their duties for fear of being exposed to the radiation. Not only were
there more people exposed to the radiation than in the immediate area,
but those exposed were afflicted for a significant amount of time.

Fires will also cause an immediate hazard in a nuclear exchange.
The primary problem will be burns. However, the incendiary bombs
that were set off in Hamburg during World War II caused further problems. They produced fire storms and caused people to crowd into
fallout shelters that were filled to their capacity. Many of those who
remained in the shelters died of carbon monoxide poisoning (Harwell
1985).

The tremendous clouds of nuclear dust that will result from these
fires will be in the atmosphere and will also pose a serious threat to
the population. As a result, the number of respiratory troubles can be
expected to be great. This dust will also result in the cooling of the
earth's surface, due to its blocking of the sun's rays. The cooling temperatures will likely cause frostbite and hypothermia to those not protected. Although Thompson and Schneider's recent study on the
cooling of the postattack climate indicates that the temperatures will
not be as cold as earlier predicted, a ten or fifteen degree Celsius drop

in temperature, as they predict, will still threaten the physical capacity of the already stressed survivors.

The short-term health effects on the surviving population will be further exacerbated by the destruction of an estimated 80 percent of the medical resources (Abrams 1984) and the loss of the majority of the trained medical personnel. The Chernobyl incident taxed Russian medical facilities and personnel to their limits. In Hiroshima, 270 of the 298 doctors who were mobilized to respond to those struck by the atom bombs were themselves victims of the attack, and 80–93 percent of the nurses and pharmacists were among the casualties (Harwell 1985). In the event of a nuclear attack, not only will there be fewer to care for the sick, but it can be expected that there will be little if any pharmaceutical industry (Abrams 1984).

The availability of food will also be problematic. Much of the agricultural industry will either be contaminated, destroyed by fire, or decimated by frost. Some believe that stored grain will be the only comestible available after the nuclear exchange. It has been estimated that 95 percent of the agricultural capacity, 60 percent of the processing capacity, and 20 percent of the production capacity of the United States will be destroyed (Hjort 1984). In the accident at Chernobyl, the damage to private agricultural industry was extensive; for example, vegetables on the domestic market declined by up to 90 percent in the weeks after the accident (Diehl 1986:1). The food that will be available in a nuclear winter will not be easily accessible, as the transportation system can be expected to be destroyed. Although malnutrition will not be an immediate short-term threat, lack of food among the survivors will cause an increase in tensions and panic during the shelter period.

Long-Term Effects

The long-term effects that a nuclear winter will have on the health of the population present a devastating picture. Perhaps the biggest concern in the postshelter and recovery periods will be the ability to obtain food. The stored grain that will not be contaminated has been estimated to be able to sustain the population for roughly six months (Hjort 1984). Assuming that the population can subsist on only grain for six months, vitamin C deficiencies would be prevalent (Hjort 1984), as would deficiencies in vitamin A, B_2, B_{12}, iron, and calcium (Dirks 1986:11).

The likelihood that there would be any significant agricultural potential is slim, for numerous reasons. First, the upper layers of the soils which are necessary for regrowth will be destroyed or at least impaired from smog, a decrease in temperatures, and fallout (Ehrlich 1984). Therefore, crop yields, if possible at all, will be decreased significantly and contaminated by the radiation. Even assuming that re-growth is possible, manpower will be limited, farm machinery can be expected to be destroyed or unusable due to unavailability of fuel, and fertilizers will be destroyed. The insect population will increase rapidly because of its greater resistance to radiation, an increase in corpses which will serve as its food source, and a decrease in birds which feed on insects (Abrams and Von Kaenel 1981). With the depletion of pesticides as well, insects could pose a large threat to crops, making the outlook for the agricultural industry even more unpromising. Temperatures will also be significantly lower, further aggravating the growing conditions and making malnutrition and famine perhaps inevitable.

There is also a high probability of an increase in infectious diseases during a nuclear winter because of impaired immunity systems among the population and unsanitary conditions. Therefore, dysentery, hepatitis, salmonellosis, and cholera will be potentially serious threats (Middleton 1982). Radiation will also cause genetic defects, cataracts, and, because it seriously harms cells responsible for the production of red and white blood cells and blood platelets, individuals will become more prone to fatal hemorrhaging and septicemic infections (Coggle and Lindop 1982). These unfavorable health conditions will be further compounded by the scarce medical resources.

There will be a slim potential for future healthy populations in a nuclear winter world. Radioactive exposure will impair genes, and beta-emitting fallout has the potential for causing temporary, if not permanent sterility (Coggle and Lindop 1982). The fetuses in utero at the time of the attack will most likely be retarded in growth (ibid. 1982). Further, those babies born after the attack will have a high probability of being malnourished. At Chernobyl there was a significant increase in abortions performed after the accident because of the fear of radiation damage to the fetuses. Those who do survive will have problems producing a healthy generation.

SOCIAL EFFECTS OF A NUCLEAR WINTER

What will happen to the social organization of the surviving population and to their psychological makeup is perhaps the most important factor which must be considered. In a nuclear winter world, it is these social factors which have been neglected and remain to be fully understood. The economic system, political system, social relations, and psychological state of the postattack population are likely to be drastically altered. The destruction of the economic system of the superpowers will not only affect their own countries, but will have a serious impact on Third World countries as well. Our economic system can be expected to be virtually destroyed. We can not expect there to be any economic institutions, businesses, or companies remaining as viable entities. We can envision a society that will be thrown back to a subsistence economy of some form, one that is solely concerned with obtaining food and shelter. These basic human needs will be the primary economic concerns of a nuclear winter population.

The inability of the First and Second Worlds to support themselves would create even more significant problems for Third World nations. They would face the reality of having to sustain themselves with no outside help in the form of food or other essentials. Further, the trade between previous partners would disappear and irrevocable economic hardships would increase for Third World nations. They too would be faced with the threat of famine.

Our political system would be in serious jeopardy. Any government support program including transportation, education, and health care would be impossible to maintain. Those that do persist would be ill equipped with personnel or resources, and we can expect that it will be a world of chaos. Simply dealing with the predicted 155 million corpses alone will be a formidable task indeed. The cities which are the center of a government support organization will most likely be the most severely impaired by the attack. There will, then, be no sense of a centralized system, and if there is anything that resembles such a system, it will not be effective since communication systems will be broken down.

The situation of the economic and political organizations will further challenge the ability of the survivors to maintain social relationships. The survivors will be asked to change their form of subsistence virtually overnight. They could not be expected, as some have suggested, to revert back to a technologically primitive world of a hunting and gathering society. In a hunting and gathering society there is a division of labor by sex, and all members of that society have welldefined, productive roles. Our culture has virtually overcome the sexual division of labor. To revert to this form of economic and political organization would be extremely difficult, perhaps impossible for our technological culture.

Further, hunting and gathering societies are usually characterized as being egalitarian, that is, everyone has equal access to resources, and there is no formal leader. In a nuclear winter world, some would be more affected than others according to where they were when the bombs hit. It is unlikely that those who were less affected would share what little they have. In fact, those among the small group of Americans who call themselves survivalists train themselves to fight others in order to maintain the subsistence items they have accumulated. They do not see sharing with the less fortunate as a virtuous act.

Finally, would the nuclear winter survivors be able to hunt and gather food? Again, it seems highly unlikely. Societies adapt certain behaviors to their environment and create subsisting techniques in order to fit into their particular culture and surroundings. Our society is one that is completely dependent on industrial technology; in the event of the loss of most, if not all, of its technological capacity the surviving population clearly would not have the knowledge to subsist. We will look, then, at disaster situations where rapid environmental change has occurred to get a better understanding of how a nuclear winter population might react psychologically.

By analyzing the population's response to, for example, the bubonic plague and to various earthquake disasters, we can predict some of the feelings that those survivors of a nuclear winter may have. The plague is an important example for it is comparable to a random situation in that one cannot predict if one is going to be physically endangered, and if so, to what extent. There is a fear, then, of the unknown because contamination is omnipresent yet unable to be detected.

The psychological response to an earthquake is quite different from the response to a plague. Similar to a nuclear attack, a severe earthquake such as that in Tokyo in the early 1920s can have an irrevocable effect on the environment, will occur in minutes with little if any warning, and will cause major disruptions in the area of impact. In Japan people lost their houses, their communities, and in many cases their families. The feelings of devastation, helplessness, and sorrow that the survivors of this disaster felt would be very much like what members of a nuclear winter community would feel.

The cases of Hiroshima and Nagasaki provide further information on the potential psychological state of nuclear winter survivors. Harwell (1985) explains that the victims in these attacks felt initial panic and fear not only because of the destruction of their immediate environment and infrastructure, but also because of their inability to assess the level of radiation that had been emitted into their surroundings. Ishida (1973) explains "death guilt," which describes the feelings of sorrow and permanence of death combined with the fear of nuclear extermination (Harwell 1985:437) that was and is felt by the survivors. Harwell also explains the psychological feelings which persisted well after the bombings including fears of becoming affected by the radiation or producing children who were affected (1985:437). These psychological problems did not simply dissipate but instead persisted for years.

All of these feelings are ones that will most likely be experienced by the survivors of a nuclear attack. The nuclear winter situation, however, is very different from those which we have described above. It is different for two reasons. First, the magnitude of the worldwide impact of such an attack is unmatched in history, and perhaps can never be fully understood. Second, in a nuclear winter there will be no outside help as there has been for virtually every disaster in human history. And so there will be, a few days after the attack, no sign of hope but instead further anxiety, fear, despair, and feelings of helplessness.

While we can study past disasters in an attempt to predict the feelings that survivors in a postattack world would experience, we cannot realistically analyze how the social systems in this world would respond. We must turn, then, to a society which was forced to change its form of subsistence virtually overnight, as those living in a nuclear winter world will be expected to do. The Ik, who resided in the harsh, dry, mountainous climate of Uganda, were not able to maintain themselves under such stresses (Turnbull: 1972). The government of Uganda formed a game park where the Ik lived and subsisted. The government regarded hunting, the Ik's main form of subsistence, as illegal. The Ik were compelled to switch from hunting to some other form of subsistence such as agriculture. Living in a region where there is little rain, and knowing very little about agricultural techniques, the Ik were not able to provide an adequate diet for themselves. As resources became scarce, tensions in their community increased. They developed traits such as unfriendliness and mutual distrust toward community members. Communications and relationships between family and village members broke down as resources became more scarce, and competitiveness increased. When heavy rains came, the Ik could not work together to plant crops, and they lost virtually all hope. As their family relationships began to deteriorate, reproduction virtually ceased. Indeed, if there are Ik today, there are very few.

The nuclear winter world may conceivably look very much like that of the Ik. Survivors will be forced to change their form of subsistence virtually overnight. There will be a scarcity of resources and so an expected increase in competition for survival. This will produce increased tensions and hostility. It is perhaps unrealistic to believe that the surviving population will refrain from reproducing as the Ik did. However, it is the following generation which will be the most in doubt in terms of its ability to reproduce another generation (Bateson 1986).

Survivors will be forced to live without any kind of established support system. Teachers and psychiatrists, who provide our children and adults with formal support, cannot alone be expected to cope with such a disaster. Family and peer relationships may deteriorate. Some argue that, in such a world, religious groups would gain force, yet we find it hard to believe that such support will be possible. Certainly the government will not provide the confidence necessary to deal with such a disaster. The nuclear winter society, then, would be asked to live with a minimal support system. It would be a life of ubiquitous problems, frustrations, and despair. If we could in fact continue reproducing, we would be producing a society that would not in any way resemble our own.

In the event of a large-scale nuclear war, those who survive the blast will be faced with marginal conditions. The possibility that the population could remain healthy is highly unlikely. Those not affected directly from the blast will not escape its impact. They, too, would most probably face starvation due to heavy reliance on the food products and economic assistance from the superpowers—who will essentially be incapacitated and unable to assist themselves or others in the southern hemisphere. Even if humans are not wiped out by the environmental or biological effects of a nuclear attack, and if we are still able to continue reproducing in a nuclear winter world, we must recognize, as Catherine Bateson has stated, "that we are talking about something that we might not want to call human life" (1986:31).

9

STAR WARS
AND ARMS CONTROL
Robert M. Bowman

Perhaps the most insidious hoax ever perpetrated on the American people is the one attempting to sell "Star Wars" as an aid to arms control.

When the radical right swept to power with the first Reagan administration, they thought they could simply walk away from arms control and pursue their goal of military superiority without interference from Congress or the American people. They were wrong. By mid-1982, there had been enough leaks about defense strategies for a "winnable protracted nuclear war" ("Pentagon Plan etc." 1982:1) for the American people to see what was going on—and know they didn't like it. The Nuclear Freeze Movement gathered strength across the land, got a resolution through the House of Representatives, and was gaining strength in the Senate. The Catholic bishops were becoming openly critical of the nuclear arms race ("Bishops and the Bomb" 1982: 68–78). The allies were balking at deploying Euromissiles. The strategic "modernization" program (particularly MX) was under fire as going beyond the needs of deterrence toward a first-strike capability. The Executive Branch was clearly on the defensive. Something had to be done. It was.

First, the START (Strategic Arms Reduction Talks) and INF (Intermediate Nuclear Forces) talks were entered into—not with the objective of reaching an agreement, but as a sop to public opinion. Second, a determined campaign was intensified to convince the American public that the Soviets had cheated on all their arms control obligations, thereby discrediting the whole arms control process. Third, in a masterful political maneuver, the president made his "Star Wars" speech, deflecting attention from the Freeze and his offensive buildup.

Actually, the "Star Wars" program had been going on for years. When the author directed such research from 1976 to 1978, it had legitimate objectives:

> *(1) To prevent technological surprise by always understanding the technology well enough to be able to predict what the Soviets might be capable of, and by when.*
>
> *(2) To develop countermeasures so that, in the event the Soviets were silly enough to spend a trillion rubles on a "Star Wars" system, we would have the means available to render the system useless, using available technology and at reasonable cost.*
>
> *(3) To monitor the technology and the strategic situation so that we would be able to determine if it ever became in our security interest to consider the deployment of such a system of our own.*

For many years there had been a few on the "lunatic fringe" who warned of the imminent deployment of Soviet laser battle stations and urged us to go beyond our prudent research program into a crash development of our own "Star Wars" system. Fortunately, these few were kept in check by the majority of career military professionals, who understood the technical and strategic realities. They knew that the Soviets were even less capable than we of putting up a militarily meaningful "Star Wars" system, and that for us to attempt to do so would be counterproductive for our overall national security effort. (These realities have not changed, by the way. Only the relative positions of the players have changed.)

After the 1980 election, the new president-elect and most of his chief advisors had little military or strategic experience. The transition team was heavily populated with those on the radical right selling "Star Wars" (among other things) as a means to regain military superiority and thereby the ability to once again dictate Soviet behavior. Even before being inaugurated, the president was under tremendous pressure to pursue such unilateral technological fixes.

Out of the Transition Team activities evolved the so-called High Frontier project. The author was involved in informal discussions of the High Frontier group during the transition period. Later, the author reviewed an early draft of the High Frontier Proposal. It was technically flawed, strategically naive, and politically irresponsible. It was also unabashedly anti-Soviet and anti-arms control. Even after two years of polishing, the slick book put out by the Heritage Foundation on High Frontier betrayed its biases:

> *The High Frontier strategy of Assured Survival can be adopted and pursued without regard for further arms control agreements*

> with the Soviets. Indeed, one of the salient advantages of High Frontier is that it provides security to the West quite independently of any trust or distrust of the leaders of the Soviet Union. The usefulness of High Frontier's spaceborne strategic defenses are not affected by Soviet compliance with past arms control agreements. This important advantage should not be affected by any future arms control agreements. (Graham 1982: 104).

and again:

> A High Frontier decision by the U.S., if backed by effective implementation efforts, would severely impact the Soviet Union, perhaps decisively (Graham 1982: 84).

and:

> In the Soviet view, High Frontier would confirm its worst fear about U.S. military purposes in space. It would view the move as what the Soviets themselves have characterized as a possible "absolute weapon" capable of ensuring U.S. "invincibility" from missile attacks (Graham 1982: 163).

Even at this early time, there were indications of the coming plot to subvert arms-control community:

> The potential for public support of this concept is enormous. . . . Adoption of the High Frontier concept could even convert or confuse some of the traditional opponents of defense efforts and technological innovations. It is harder to oppose nonnuclear defensive systems than nuclear offensive systems. It is almost impossible to argue effectively for a perpetual balance of terror strategy if it can be negated by new policies. It is hard to make environmentalist cases against space systems. Even those naysayers whose basic concern is disarmament will be hard pressed to make a case against High Frontier, the ABM (Anti-Ballistic Missile) Treaty notwithstanding (Graham 1982: 82).

By the time the President made his "Star Wars" speech in March 1983, the various right-wing groups pushing space weapons had discovered their belligerent anti-Soviet approach didn't work too well with middle America. So they came up with a complex scheme for co-opting the arms control and peace issues through an elaborate "doublespeak"— an approach foreshadowed in the President's own speech:

> Wouldn't it be better to save lives, rather that avenge them?

and

> We seek neither military superiority nor political advantage.

To understand what is really going on, one has to listen in on space weapons proponents talking among themselves, or get hold of the secret Heritage Foundation plan entitled "BMD (Ballistic Missile Defense) & Arms Control." Here are some quotes from this latter document:

> [K]eep BMD program alive in 1984 and make it impossible to turn off by 1989. . . . [P]ermit US to move ahead forcefully & unilaterally [emphasis in original!] . . . represented as a bilateral effort—one with Soviet reciprocation and participation . . . make it politically risky for BMD opponents to invoke alleged "arms control arguments" against an early-IOC or any other BMD system . . . disarm BMD opponents by stealing their language and cause . . . their explicit or de facto advocacy of classical anti-population war crimes . . . with appropriate political and emotional packaging, this approach may be able to tap the freeze constituency (i.e. the "do something" approach to arms control).

We have recently seen this tactic flower into full bloom. The weapons proponents are now repeatedly invoking arms control as the necessary reason for continuing "Star Wars" (while, out of the other side of their mouths, these same people are trying to destroy public confidence in arms control by falsely accusing the Soviet Union of massive treaty violations).

The main purpose of this chapter is to show how the continuation of a Death Star program ("Star Wars," if you prefer) would destroy the entire arms-control process, leading to an unrestrained arms race in both offensive and defensive weapons, greatly reducing our security. But many might say, "Who cares?" There has been so much propaganda to the effect that arms control has never done any good because the Soviet Union ignores it and uses it to our detriment, that some actually believe it. We must, therefore, take a look at the real record of arms control and Soviet compliance.

THE TRUTH ABOUT SOVIET TREATY COMPLIANCE

Basically, we do not trust the Russians—and we do not have to. If we trusted them, we would not need arms control treaties with them. Our faith in arms control as one of the essential ingredients in preserving our national security does not rest on trusting the Russians. We have independent means of verification, means much better than most people suspect.

But in a larger sense, a good deal of the distrust we feel for the Soviet Union is manufactured. A policy of deterrence depends on fear. From the bomber gap to the missile gap to the megatonnage gap to the window of vulnerability, the American public has been besieged with distortions, exaggerations, imaginations, and outright lies. We are bombarded with vague references to Soviet violations and cheating on arms control agreements. Yet the facts tell a different story.

In response to allegations of Soviet violations from the anti-SALT II lobby, an interagency group was established by President Carter. It was composed of representatives from the Department of Defense, the Joint Chiefs of Staff, the State Department, the CIA, the Arms Control and Disarmament Agency (ACDA), and the National Security Council. The United States commissioner in charge of treaty compliance stated, "The Commission has never yet had to deal with a case of real or apparent clear and substantial non-compliance with an existing agreement" (Center for Defense Information 1984). Similar conclusions are contained in Congressional testimony by Alexander Haig and by former CIA director William Colby.

The truth is that until the most recent accusations, even the United States government acknowledged that the Soviet Union was still adhering to the provisions of both SALT I and SALT II even though SALT II has never been ratified by the United States and SALT I has expired.

So what has changed? Why are we suddenly being told that the Soviets have violated every agreement they have ever signed? Have they begun a new policy of violation? No. Have we discovered new evidence of old violations? No. For the most part, partisans are dredging up the same old accusations that were investigated and dismissed in 1979. In fact, most of the alleged "violations" presented to Congress by the current Administration are only allegations of behavior inconsistent with the "spirit" of the treaties. In only two instances is it alleged that the Soviet Union has violated the letter of a legal treaty obligation— and in both of those cases there is scientific evidence showing that no violation has occurred.

The fact is that the Soviet Union has had just as many questions about United States behavior in treaty compliance as we have had about them. And the evidence for American violations seems just as strong as that for Soviet transgressions. Several excellent analyses have been produced (Center for Defense Information 1984; Federation of American Scientists 1984; Office of Technology Assessment 1984) in which specific allegations are examined in detail. It is not our purpose to repeat them here. The bottom line seems to be that both the United States and the Soviet Union seek out every opportunity to exploit loopholes or vague language in treaties and care little for the spirit of an agreement. At the same time, both have an excellent record of abiding by the letter of treaty obligations as they interpret them. Both the United States and the Soviet Union have destroyed old weapons as new weapons have been deployed, in order to stay within SALT limits. At the same time, both have rushed headlong into deployment of weapons not covered by agreements. Arms-control agreements have not made us friends, but they have helped keep our competition within manageable limits, have helped reduce the cost of that competition, and have helped maintain a stable balance between our forces and thereby made war less likely. What more do we expect of arms control?

Paul Warnke, former director of ACDA (Arms Control and Disarmament Agency), has put it this way:

> *If you have a clear, unambiguous arms control agreement, the record of compliance on both sides is good. Now, I know there have been suggestions of cheating. We've had a Standing Consultative Commission that meets regularly in Geneva—has ever since SALT I, and they have found satisfactory answers to the charges on both sides. The record in this regard is good. The Soviets live up to the letter—now I emphasize the letter—of an arms control agreement. They have a selfish interest in seeing to it that agreements are reached. They have a selfish interest in seeing to it that those agreements remain in force 1985.*

Having dealt with the great cheating myth, we should now more carefully assess the question of compliance with the ABM Treaty. It is this treaty that would be violated by "Star Wars"; it is this treaty which has been most hated by the right-wing anti-arms control forces; and it is this treaty which the Soviets have most recently been accused of violating.

For fifteen years the Soviet Union has been in strict compliance with the terms of the ABM Treaty. As noted earlier, they could by now have deployed a massive system with in excess of 10 thousand ABM interceptors. Yet, they have never had more than the allowed 100. They have done a great deal of research which would prepare them for a breakout of the treaty. But, of course, such research is allowed by the treaty, and we have done the same (as is only prudent). What's more, the objective of the current "Star Wars" program is a system which would represent a massive abrogation of the treaty. And, as we shall see, current and planned United States activities may already be in violation of the treaty. The Soviets have, in addition, developed anti-aircraft systems which some analysts fear may have some utility against ballistic missiles. This represents, they say, an attempt to develop ABM capabilities in the guise of something else. On the other hand, this is precisely what Dr. Keyworth, the president's science advisor, has proposed that we do (and perhaps are already doing) in our ASAT (Anti-Satellite) program. For the most part, talk of the Soviet ABM violations has been a blatant attempt to soften up the American people for a unilateral United States abrogation of the treaty.

LEGAL IMPLICATIONS OF SPACE WEAPONIZATION

While no present treaty bans antisatellite systems, per se, they would seem to violate the spirit of the 1967 Outer Space Treaty. "Star Wars" ABM systems, on the other hand, would clearly violate at least the ABM Treaty, and in some forms the Outer Space Treaty and the Limited Test Ban Treaty as well.

It is important to point out that even the development of "Star Wars" systems or components for them is prohibited by the ABM Treaty. LANAC (Lawyers Alliance for Nuclear Arms Control) points out that there are unresolved factual and legal issues regarding the point at which research ends and development of ABM systems or components begins. Despite these uncertainties, they conclude that some projects within the Strategic Defense Initiative program "have either already crossed over in the prohibited area of development or will in the near future under current plans" (Sherr 1984).

They also conclude that there is no legal or factual basis for the argument that certain space-based projects are adjuncts rather than components of an ABM system and thus would not be banned even after they had clearly entered the development stage.

LANAC also refers to the loophole in the ABM Treaty discussed above, in that weapons developments which clearly would be prohibited if intended for ABM use can proceed unhindered if intended for use, at least initially, in an ASAT system. Their interpretation, however, is that capability, rather than intent, should be the applicable standard. Since some projects in both the United States and the Soviet Union have an ABM capability, even though currently serving in another role, LANAC would find such weapons in violation of the ABM Treaty even if not tested in an ABM mode. This interpretation, of course, is not universal.

In their discussion of the legal issues of "Star Wars," LANAC has the following to say about the Standing Consultative Commission:

> The Standing Consultative Commission established under the ABM Treaty provides a workable legal process for dealing with compliance and interpretive issues. Although serious questions regarding Soviet compliance have recently arisen, the practice of making public accusations of cheating without exhausting the administrative recourse to the Standing Consultative Commission is unnecessarily damaging to the legal process. The effort should be

on closing ambiguities and loopholes through agreed interpretations (Sherr 1984).

THE PRACTICAL EFFECT OF "STAR WARS" ON ARMS CONTROL

The argument of the space weapons proponents is that "Star Wars" defenses will decrease the effectiveness of ballistic missiles and thus make the Soviet Union more willing to give them up in arms control negotiations. They say that the Soviet Union might be willing to agree to deep cuts in offensive weapons if both sides were building defenses so as to depend on a balance of offensive and defensive forces. Finally, they say that ABM defenses are a necessary prerequisite to real disarmament, providing a hedge against one side cheating by keeping a few nuclear weapons.

These arguments seem plausible on the surface, even though they have been advanced insincerely by those who do not really want anything to do with arms control. But a little analysis shows these arguments to be totally false.

Look at it from the Soviet point of view. They have put nearly all their strategic nuclear weapons in land-based ICBMs. (This was more a case of using the technology available to them than making a conscious strategic decision against the type of balanced triad we have.) They have devoted a large portion of their resources to producing these weapons which give them, for the first time, nuclear parity with the United States. No longer can they be threatened and dictated to as they were up to the time of the Cuban missile crisis in 1962. They have also achieved, because of these nuclear weapons, an intangible sense of equality in the international arena.

What about "Star Wars" as a way to help both sides agree to total disarmament? There are many reasons why this rationale is also totally false. In the first place, there is no indication that either the United States or the Soviet Union would be the least bit interested in disarmament. At the moment, it is only military might which makes the Soviet Union a superpower. In a disarmed world, it could revert to the status of just another large developing nation. Nor is there any reason to think that the United States would be willing to give up the military power which has enabled it to intervene around the world on behalf of its "interests." Dozens of times we have sent military forces into developing nations (three times into Nicaragua, for example) to install governments which would protect the economic interests of our multinational corporations (in return for military protection for their regime). In a disarmed world, we might have to pay a fair price for what we got. The people in the Dominican Republic and Guatemala might even decide to use their land to grow food for themselves instead of coffee, sugar, and bananas for the Americanos. So the first problem in getting to disarmament is to get the nations to want it.

Assuming, however, that this obstacle would be overcome, would "Star Wars" help? Again, the answer is "No." In the first place, nobody has come up with any ideas for how to get from an offense-dominated deterrence to a defense-dominated disarmament without passing through a totally unstable situation in which a disarming first strike was not only possible, but likely. And "Star Wars" only exacerbates this problem, because it would be much more effective against retaliatory strikes than aggressive ones.

In the second place, "Star Wars" systems are not purely defensive systems. They are not even primarily defensive. Now, there *are* "defensive" weapons. One example is a shore battery. It sits on your coastline, pointed out to sea, and is able to shoot at vessels coming within your three-mile limit. Another example is an anti-aircraft battery. It sits next to one of your cities and is able to shoot at enemy aircraft flying overhead in your airspace. Such weapons are characterized by their location in your own territory and their inability to threaten anything that has not invaded that territory. "Star Wars" weapons do not fit that description. They orbit the earth in the global commons of space, passing just above the airspace of potential adversaries. They are capable of attacking anything in the no-man's land of space, and possibly even within the sovereign territory of other nations. They are much like the battleship *New Jersey* cruising the Mediterranean, able to attack any other vessel in international waters or even attack targets in coastal waters, port towns, and interior highlands (as happened in Lebanon). Would we call the battleship *New Jersey* a defensive weapon?

The *offensive* capabilities of "Star Wars" systems would be awesome. They could destroy all existing space systems of an opponent and any others he attempted to put into orbit. They would allow the nation possessing them to further fortify space, placing there space bombers capable of raining destruction upon the earth with little or no warning.

Perhaps another analogy might be helpful. Imagine two hostile tribes facing each other across an open field. Each tribe is encamped in a fortress made of sticks of wood and bales of straw. Each has a generous supply of fire arrows. Each is deterred from attacking the other because of its vulnerability to retaliation. Each sends unarmed tribesmen out into the field to keep an eye on the other side and provide "early warning" of attack. Both sides implicitly accept this as being consistent with their treaty to use the open field only for peaceful purposes. Both sides also use information gathered by their scouts to help target their fire arrows.

Now imagine that one side announces that it is going to send a number of tribesmen out into the open field with machine guns so that they can shoot down enemy fire arrows as they fly overhead.

For a while, there is an argument about whether such a thing is possible, since no one has yet built a machine gun and it is not clear whether, once built, it can be aimed well enough and fast enough to destroy a thousand arrows in a few seconds. Some in the tribal council point out the staggering cost of the project, which would include designing and building a steel mill and all the other industry necessary. Some of the warriors point out how very vulnerable they would be out there in the middle of the field with no place to hide.

Meanwhile, one of the originators of the idea proposes that having machine-gunners in the field will help get the other side to agree to destroy most of their fire arrows. He even hints that they might be willing to help the other side make its own machine guns. He points out that with machine guns to protect them, neither side will worry about the other hiding a few fire arrows, so real disarmament will become possible.

What gets lost in the argument is the fact that the "defensive" machine guns, regardless of their capability (or lack of it) to shoot down fire arrows, would be very effective on the unarmed scouts of the other tribe or on passers-by from neutral tribes that occasionally transit the field. What's more, if both tribes were eventually to have such "defenses," how long would it be before the machine gunners from one side turned their weapons on their counterparts?

In the above scenario, which would be more conducive to stability, peace, and eventual disarmament—initiating a machine gun race or concluding an effective treaty banning weapons in the open field?

Taking this analogy a step further, imagine that the tribes had years ago considered implementing various schemes for enclosing their fortress in gigantic brick "astrodomes" to protect them from fire arrows. They quickly discovered that the technology to build the walls was theoretically possible, but extremely expensive—and that providing the *roof* was clearly impossible. Still, each side seeing the other trying to make bricks, began to make larger numbers of even more powerful fire arrows, including those fired in bundles and others so heavy they could break through a single layer of brick. They also started designing cannon balls capable of knocking down walls in advance of a fire-arrow attack. Then both sides, realizing the futility of their defensive efforts, agreed to a package deal. It outlawed brick walls and all other defensive efforts with the exception of one brick hut apiece to protect the chief and a small number of his warriors, assuring survivability of each side's retaliatory forces. With defenses thus limited, both agreed to limit the number of fire arrows and cannons, since both had more than enough for any retaliatory attack.

In this situation, the attempt by one side to deploy "defensive" machine guns in the field raises two problems:

(1) The defensive capability of the system (even though questionable) would violate both the letter and the spirit of the intertribal treaty, which was the basis for all the subsequent offensive arms limitations. It would, therefore, undoubtedly re-ignite the fire-arrow-and-cannon arms race as well as the race in "defenses."

(2) The enormous offensive potential of the system, especially against other systems in the open field, would create new ways for war to break out, would threaten the unarmed scouts which both sides counted on for early warning and treaty verification, and would heighten fear on both sides.

Again, the question must be asked: Which would be more conducive to stability, peace, and eventual disarmament—initiating a machine-gun race or concluding an effective treaty banning weapons in the open field (and abiding by the existing treaties limiting defenses and offenses)?

The situation we face today is similar. Neither the Americans nor the Soviets were willing to limit offensive nuclear weapons until in the ABM Treaty they agreed to limit the defenses those weapons would have to overcome in carrying out their retaliatory role. If we insist on abrogating that treaty and trying to make Soviet missiles less effective, we can expect them to take whatever steps are necessary to maintain their offensive capabilities, including building more and better nuclear "fire arrows" and even-more powerful antisatellite "cannons" to blow holes in our defenses.

Perhaps one day technology will allow true defensive systems to provide additional security in a disarmed world. To serve that purpose they would have to be more like brick walls than machine guns. This purpose will not be served by "Death Stars" whose questionable defensive capabilities are accompanied by (and dwarfed by) unquestionable offensive potential.

To understand the relationship between offensive and defensive capabilities, it is necessary to understand the relationship between antisatellite (ASAT) weapons and space-based antiballistic missiles (ABM weapons). A rational approach to arms control is impossible without such understanding.

THE RELATIONSHIP BETWEEN ASATs AND ABMs

In one sense, ASATs and ABMs are very different. The mission of an ASAT is easily accomplished. Its targets are extremely vulnerable, sensitive, complex sitting ducks, somewhat like aircraft carriers (minus power, escort vessels, and aircraft)—drifting predictably through the ocean of space. The mission of an ABM, on the other hand, is enormously difficult and perhaps impossible.

Yet there are important similarities between ASAT systems and ABM systems. They use much of the same technology and potentially much of the same hardware. The functions to be performed by the subsystems are identical. The differences are in the requirements for reaction time, accuracy, and power. In every case, the ABM mission is the more difficult. The result is that any system designed for an ABM mission, even if it turned out to be a complete failure in that role, would most likely be an extremely effective ASAT. It will thus be impossible to have an effective ban on ASATs unless we maintain and rigidly uphold the provisions of the ABM Treaty.

Because of the above noted similarities, George Keyworth proposed developing a geosynchronous ASAT capability in order to prove the technology required for an ABM. Such a ruse would never fool the Soviets, and they would rightly charge the United States with a violation of the ABM Treaty. If ASAT testing continues much longer, it will be almost impossible to keep the ABM Treaty from falling apart.

Thus it can be seen that neither an ASAT treaty nor an ABM treaty is viable without the other. Either we ban the testing and deployment of both ASATs and ABMs or we allow ourselves to become embroiled in an arms race in space with no limits and no good end in sight. The likely result of such a race would be mutual bankruptcy, mutual destruction, or both.

The questions then arise: is it possible to reach agreement on a treaty which would be verifiable and effective in forestalling such an arms race in space? Can it really be accomplished, or is the genie already out of the bottle? Is an effective and verifiable treaty impossible, as the Administration has claimed, or should it be pursued vigorously, as the Congress has demanded? If it is possible, how should it be approached?

THE PROSPECT FOR ASAT NEGOTIATIONS

Negotiations with the Soviet Union aimed at preventing an arms race in space were cut off by the United States at the time of the Soviet invasion of Afghanistan. Until recently, enamored with the possibilities of high-tech weaponry in space and engaged in a quixotic quest for a return to strategic superiority, the Administration has refused to resume those negotiations.

Then in response to growing Congressional and political pressure, the Reagan administration in the summer of 1984 agreed to a Soviet proposal to discuss space weapons. After an abortive attempt to get talks started in September in Vienna, both sides finally agreed to the Geneva negotiations which started March 12, 1985. One of the objectives of these negotiations was to "prevent an arms race in space." Whether or not an agreement can be reached is another matter. If each side is more interested in blaming the other for failure than in achieving success, little will be accomplished. There are, however, those in both governments who, for different reasons, clearly are sincerely interested in reaching an agreement.

It is clear that after four years of intransigence the United States agreed to discuss space weapons due to the following factors:

(1) The Tsongas Amendment to the 1984 Defense Authorization Act required such negotiations as a precondition to testing of the new United States ASAT against a space target. The 1985 version of the amendment was weaker in many respects, but still contained a requirement that the Administration indicate its willingness to negotiate some sort of limitation on ASAT weapons.

(2) The Democratic party made space weapons one of its main issues in the 1984 election, and the Administration needed to do something to defuse this issue as well as the larger issue of its lack of success at arms control in general.

(3) More and more people in government came to recognize the fact that preventing an unrestrained arms race in space is vital to the national security of the United States. An Office of Technology Assessment (OTA) Workshop on Arms Control in Space (Office of Technology Assessment 1984) held January 30–31, 1984, revealed differences in philosophy toward arms control, but also resulted in a rather broad consensus that there were verifiable steps that could be taken to restrict space weapons in such a way that American security would be enhanced.

The main substantive difference between the United States and the Soviet Union seems to be over how comprehensive a ban is desirable. The Soviets, although agreeing to discuss "limitations" on ASATs, would clearly prefer a total ban on all space weapons. The United States, on the other hand, wants to separate the ASAT and BMD issues and is insisting on pursuing its "Star Wars" program. Our position on ASATs seems to be developing along lines which would prevent the development of more capable Soviet systems, while allowing the United States to complete development of its new Miniature Homing Vehicle to be launched by the F-15. This can be accomplished in either of two ways: (1) "grandfathering" existing systems (which means exempting them from any ban) or (2) limiting ASAT capabilities to lower orbits and prohibiting systems capable of reaching geosynchronous or other very high orbits.

Such an approach by the United States satisfies the Administrations's political objectives. It even allowed the Administration to proceed with the September 13, 1985, test of our new ASAT against a target in space. But this approach has absolutely no chance of resulting in an agreement (which is precisely what some members of the Administration would prefer).

While all of the critical American strategic satellites are in very high orbits, Soviet communications and early warning satellites are in highly elliptical "Molniya" orbits which come very close to the earth over the southern hemisphere. Either of the above approaches would result in most Soviet satellites being threatened by a highly sophisticated system which could strike without warning from anywhere on the earth, while all but a few United States low-altitude "spy" satellites (and the shuttle) would have permanent sanctuary. And as a practical matter, prohibiting new ASATs while allowing "Star Wars" development to continue is impossible, because even crude "Star Wars" prototypes would be powerful ASATs.

If at any point in the last several years the Administration had been sincere in wanting an agreement, it could have had one almost for the asking. All that would have been required would have been to join the Soviet moratorium on ASAT testing and to avoid taking positions that are patently inequitable and non-negotiable. A testing moratorium can be verified. Space weapons might possibly be hidden, but their testing cannot be. The rate of approach of space objects to each other in rendezvous maneuvers can be limited to prevent homing systems from being perfected in the guise of civilian applications. The size and power of lasers can be limited so that allowed laser communications systems do not approach destructive potential. The proximity of orbiting systems to those of other nations can be controlled to prevent the deployment of space mines.

Some residual antisatellite capability will remain, at least as long as there are nuclear missiles, but the development of new dedicated ASAT systems can be prevented. The risk to either side of the residual ASAT capability is small compared to the risks inherent in an all-out arms race in space which would put at risk critical early-warning and communications systems. In summary, verifiable treaty agreements can be reached which would greatly enhance the security of the United States and of the Soviet Union by reducing the danger of war. We should end our recalcitrance and pursue such agreements immediately.

10

THE DILEMMA OF DISARMING
Keith F. Otterbein

Proposals to disarm nations and individuals are intended to benefit all by reducing levels of violent conflict between and within nations. Since arms races are seen as a cause of war, just as the possession of guns is seen as a contribution to high homicide rates, these alleged causes of violent conflict would be reduced in importance or eliminated by disarming nations and the citizens of those nations. Such proposals have been almost universally resisted by those possessing arms. The reason for rejecting such proposals is inherent in the use to which such arms are put—they are used to protect one's nation or one's person. The efficiency of weapons, particularly firearms, is so great that if an opponent is armed and one is not, the opponent is the certain winner. Thus, the very survival of a nation or of an individual may depend upon their being adequately armed. While the possession of armies and weapons may prevent the annihilation of a nation and give gun owners the means to kill assailants, it also gives them the ability to carry out, for reasons of aggrandizement (and sometimes just to test the weapons), attacks upon other nations and individuals. Not only may they be tempted to use the arms in non-self-defense situations, but their mere possession may provoke others to attack because they either fear being attacked or desire to take the weapons for their own use. Hereupon lies the dilemma of disarming: Weapons are needed for survival, yet their possession is likely to involve their owners in the very armed conflicts which the weapons were intended to prevent. Ironically, it is the basic need for self-preservation—as a nation or as an individual—which is both the reason for arms possession and the cause of the killing which the weapons were intended to prevent.

I first became aware of the dilemma of disarming in my research on warfare. Although I have always seen war as a type of armed combat, only recently have I seriously expanded my research interests to include internal violence. Homicide and gun control are two topics I have focused upon. The dilemma of disarming is as relevant to analyzing gun usage within a nation as it is to studying warfare. In this essay I will first describe the dilemma of disarming as it applies to warfare and relate my empirical findings from my warfare research to the dilemma; second, I will describe the dilemma of disarming as it applies to firearms ownership and discuss gun usage, primarily within the United States; and, finally, I will draw parallels between warfare (and disarmament proposals) and gun usage (and gun control legislation), showing that the dilemma of disarming pertains to both. I will conclude by making recommendations both for nations and for individuals, which may make them more secure and yet reduce the escalating levels of violence between and within nations.

The dilemma of disarming, as it applies to the study of warfare, can be described as follows: Nations build strong military organizations to defend themselves from attack. But merely having an excellent military organization is not usually seen as sufficient by political and military leaders. They reason that their nation must be stronger than any likely enemy or combination of enemies. This felt need to be stronger than one's potential adversaries arises both from the desire to prevent an attack and, if an attack occurs, to defeat the enemy. Military readiness prevents an attack by a potential aggressor by creating in the minds of its political and military leaders the belief that if they were to attack, their military would be defeated. This mode of reasoning by defense planners is, of course, known as deterrence theory. Briefly, deterrence theory argues that military readiness, by deterring potential aggressors, decreases the likelihood that a nation will become involved in war. It is today the official position of the major world powers. However, if the leaders of each nation attempt to make their nation the strongest militarily, then each nation will continue to build and improve its military organization. The consequence of such continuous and expanding military preparation is an "arms race." Arms races, as often noted, frequently lead to war (Richardson 1960; Beer 1981: 231–39, 269–73).[1]

Military preparedness can itself be considered a cause of war; that is, if a nation is well prepared militarily, it is more likely to become involved in wars than nations that are not so well prepared. Two reasons seem to account for the relationship (Otterbein 1973: 942): first, the possession of an efficient military organization may tempt leaders of the nation or of the military organization to attack countries that they believe are militarily less well prepared.[2] A study of twentieth-century warfare which focuses upon "conventional deterrence" (i.e., non-nuclear deterrence) shows that those nations which have developed a military armament program based on the concept of the blitz-krieg ("lightning war"), rather than pursuing programs based on the concepts of attrition or limited aims, are more likely to attack their neighbors—and they are usually successful in their use of the blitzkrieg (Mearsheimer 1983: 203–6). Second, an efficient military organization that is in readiness for operations, but not actually engaged in war, may provoke an attack by a neighboring nation, since the neighbor fears it may be suddenly attacked and wishes to have surprise on its side.[3] Again, the study of twentieth-century warfare shows that a blitzkrieg strategy may be developed in order to launch a preemptive attack (Mearsheimer 1983: 35–43).

Since military preparedness and arms races can be a cause of war, a finding which no one seems to dispute, many thoughtful individuals have proposed disarmament. Disarmament proposals are intended to reduce the likelihood of war by preventing arms races. These proposals call upon all nations involved either to stop increasing the strength of their military organizations or to reduce the magnitude of the strength (Myrdal 1982; Schell 1984). Such proposals are seldom adopted.[4] This is true even when negotiators for both sides have reached a tentative agreement. Political leaders from both nations may reject the agreement (Fallows 1984: 138, 140). The reason for rejecting disarmament proposals lies, in most instances, in the fear that political and military leaders have that, if they disarm to the extent that their nation is less prepared militarily than their potential adversary, they may be attacked, and, if attacked, they will be defeated. Thus, the dilemma of disarming. Strong military organizations are needed for survival, yet military preparedness leads to arms races and wars. Ironically, the basic need for self-preservation is both the reason for building a strong military organization and the cause of war which it was intended to prevent.

In a cross-cultural study of warfare, using a sample of fifty societies ranging in size from hunting and gathering bands to large states (Otterbein 1985), I developed a scale of military sophistication which measures the fighting ability of political communities, a technical term for a maximal political unit. The scale score for a political community reflected eleven efficient military practices, including both weaponry and characteristics of the military organization. The hypothesis tested stated that the higher the scale score the more likely that the political community would defeat its enemies and survive in intersocietal struggles. It was found that political communities with high scale scores were likely to have territorial boundaries expanding, while political communities with low scale scores were likely to have constant or contracting territorial boundaries, a clear indication that being well-armed contributed to societal survival (1985: 92–108). Moreover, more than two-thirds of the political communities with high scale scores were found to attack neighboring societies continually or frequently; the less well armed the political community, the more likely it was to attack neighbors only infrequently. And, the data provided no evidence that possession of a strong military organization deterred enemies from attacking (1985: 87–92).[5] Only four societies out of the sample did not have military organizations and warfare. There are indications that the members of all four of these societies were driven from other areas and forced to seek refuge in isolated locations such as islands, Arctic wastelands, or mountaintops. Protected by their isolation, they have found it unnecessary to maintain military organizations (1985: 20–21).

The dilemma for political leaders: They must create a strong military organization if their political community is to survive or have a chance to survive, yet the possession of a strong military organization may involve the political community, both as attacker and as defender, in warfare. Faced with the realization that societal survival depends upon maintaining a strong military organization, political leaders are unlikely to seriously consider disarmament for their political communities. With these results in front of me, I drafted a dedication to my book which was intended to highlight the dilemma: "To all those who have died in defense of their political communities" (1985: vii). Students have frequently either been mystified by the dedication or felt it to be an expression of a pro-military attitude. The parent of one student, an academic economist who had not read the study, was disturbed that his son was required to read the book (in an advanced course in political anthropology); he conjectured that I had guns hanging on the walls of my home.[6]

The dilemma of disarming, as it applies to the study of firearms ownership, can be described as follows: Many individuals purchase and practice with firearms in order to have a means of defending themselves from attack. Body armor may even be worn. In addition, they may secure their homes with quality locks, alarm systems, and watch dogs. In many parts of the world houses are surrounded by walls, and bars are placed over windows. Sometimes glass or barbed wire is embedded in the tops of walls. The most affluent may hire bodyguards or maintain private security forces. Generally the wealthier or the more important politically the person is, the more likely the use of fortress architecture.[7] The reason for firearms ownership and other defensive measures is the felt need to be stronger than those who would harm or steal.

These measures are taken to dissuade potential criminals from attacking oneself or one's home or, if an attack occurs, to prevent its success by thwarting or killing the assailant.[8] Firearms ownership and other defensive measures prevent attack by creating in the minds of potential criminals the belief that they will be unsuccessful; lack of success can range from inability to enter the property to the apprehension or death of the attacker. The deterrence of crime is a major concern of security planners. Briefly, criminal deterrence argues that firearms ownership and other defensive measures, by deterring potential criminals, decreases the likelihood that the "law abiding" will be robbed, injured, or killed. Criminals, however, may go to great efforts—if what they want to steal is of immense value or the person they wish to kill is politically important—to achieve their ends by using weapons that can penetrate defenses (including body armor) or by devising means of defeating security systems. Indeed, it appears often that those seeking greater security and those seeking to defeat that security are involved in a domestic "arms race."

The possession of firearms gives individuals, whether they are homeowners or security personnel, the ability to kill. They may at times use their weapons in non self-defense situations, either in anger or in furthering their own self interest. Also, the possession of weapons may provoke an attack by criminals, either out of fear that the weapons may be used upon them or to take the weapons.

Since firearms ownership has been seen by many as a cause of violent crime and homicide in the United States, gun control legislation has often been proposed (Clark 1970: 101–14; Newton and Zimring 1969). Such legislation is intended to reduce the number of weapons in private hands, thereby lowering the homicide rate, a result which will occur because fewer firearms will be used in the commission of crimes[9] and guns will not be available to those involved in domestic quarrels. Such proposals, at least in the United States, have been vigorously fought by legitimate gun owners (Kennett and Anderson 1975: 165–256). The reason for rejecting such legislation lies in the fear that gun owners have that "if guns are outlawed only outlaws will have guns."[10] Thus, the dilemma of disarming. Firearms are needed for self-defense, yet their possession may involve their owners in armed confrontations. Ironically, the basic need for self-preservation is both the reason for gun ownership and the cause of the homicides which the weapons were intended to prevent.

Gun ownership in the United States is extensive; one national survey indicates that guns (long guns—rifles and shot guns; handguns—revolvers and pistols) are possessed by about half of the households in America, with nearly half of these households possessing a handgun (Davis et al. 1981: 233). The long guns are owned primarily for hunting and target shooting, with self-defense being a secondary purpose. Handguns are owned primarily for self-defense, although many owners use handguns for hunting and target shooting.[11] Some research shows that handguns are being bought by citizens not to commit crimes, but out of fear that crimes will be perpetrated upon them (Lizotte and Bordua 1980). Policemen and other security personnel carry handguns, likewise, for protection.[12] Practicing with handguns for self-defense, by both police and nonpolice, is on the increase; "combat shooting," in contrast to traditional target shooting, stresses practice with larger-caliber handguns rapidly fired at human-like silhouettes. New magazines devoted to combat shooting are appearing on newsstands. The possession of handguns and the skills to use them increase the likelihood that citizens and police will kill those threatening them.[13] Indeed, law enforcement agencies are concerned with this problem; the term "deadly force" is used to refer to police self-defense. Although it is not legally classified as murder, such deaths contribute to the homicide rate. The availability of handguns in homes and on the police provides criminals, who cannot legally purchase handguns, a source of weapons.[14] Whenever the police make an arrest there is the possibility that their handguns may be snatched from their holsters; and being shot without warning is a constant possibility.

The dilemma to citizens and police: they feel they must arm themselves, as well as devise other defensive measures, in order to avoid becoming victims, yet the possession of firearms is apt to involve them in self-defense homicides. And, believing that their personal survival may depend upon being armed, neither gun owners nor police are likely to consider seriously legal restrictions.

The dilemma of disarming emerges as a central issue both in the study of warfare and in the study of gun usage. Four striking parallels emerge: (1) The need for self-preservation compels nations to build military organizations and citizens to purchase guns (and police to carry handguns). Not to do so puts both nations and citizens in jeopardy of their lives. The only apparent alternative is for the nation to hide itself (an impossibility) or the citizen to move to a less threatening neighborhood (an impossibility if he does not have the financial means). (2) The possession of arms, intended for self-defense, is likely to involve the nation in war and the citizen and police in shootings. On the other hand, nations may build military organizations in order to go to war and criminals may steal guns (or obtain them from other criminals) in order to commit armed robbery. (3) The possession of arms may provoke an attack. The armed forces of a militarily strong nation may become the target of a "preemptive attack." Homes may be robbed and policemen may be assaulted for their weapons. (4) Disarmament proposals and gun control legislation, while aimed at reducing levels of violent conflict between and within nations, are strongly resisted by both nations and citizens who feel the need for self-defense. When the proposals are presented in a manner which would make them binding, as is the case with federal gun control legislation in the United States, well-financed organized resistance emerges. Disarmament and gun control are viewed by those who are to be disarmed as a threat to their safety. Moreover, it appears that the proponents of such proposals and legislation often exclude themselves from the group to be disarmed or prevented from arming. For example, at the international level, proposals to prevent the proliferation of nuclear weapons are sponsored in part by nations possessing nuclear power; at the national level, legislation to control handguns is backed by politicians who have private or government bodyguards.[15]

I believe there is a solution to the dilemma, both as it pertains to well-armed nations and to citizens within nations. The solution takes a slightly different form, depending upon whether the focus is upon nations or upon citizens, but the reasoning is the same. The solution is to be well prepared, but not so well prepared that it provokes potential adversaries.

For the individual the safest posture to take is to be well protected, but not to appear overly so. The open carrying of firearms and the use of security measures may suggest to criminals that the individual is carrying large sums of money or that his home contains objects of great value, such as silver, coins, or firearms. In order to prevent the criminal from imagining, correctly or incorrectly, that valuables are being protected, firearms should be carried concealed and the features of security systems should not be obvious.[16] The first line of defense is to avoid becoming a target of an attack, but if an attack comes, the individual needs appropriate defensive measures as outlined earlier. This would, when deemed necessary, include the carrying of firearms.[17]

For nations the safest posture to take is probably to be nearly as strong as the potential aggressor and to be perceived that way. Perception is all important. If one is weak, it is desirable to be perceived as strong; but if one is very strong, it may be desirable to be perceived as slightly less strong. The latter statement is contrary to deterrence theory. The purpose in appearing not too strong is to avoid provoking the potential adversary into an attack. The appearance of overwhelmingly superior strength invites preemptive attack. It would be better not to advertize such superiority. This military posture is likely, or so I hope, to create in the minds of the political and military leaders of the other nation the belief that they could win. However, they will probably not attack for two reasons: (1) The leaders do not fear an attack—they perceive their potential adversary as not strong enough militarily to attack and win; and (2) The leaders realize that victory, which they probably could achieve, would be gained only at great expense to their military forces. Indeed, this latter situation could leave them vulnerable to attack form other well-armed nations.[18]

The following diagram illustrates what I believe is the preferable level of military preparedness.

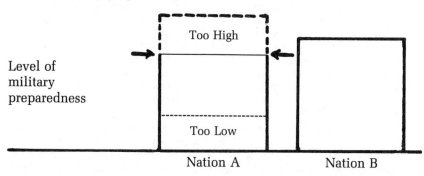

The preferred level of military preparedness for Nation A is marked by two arrows. It falls just below the level of military preparedness of Nation B.

If one or more nations were to adopt the above solution (I wish I had a fine-sounding term for it), several beneficial results would take place. First, the nation with the strongest military organization would no longer need to continue defense spending. If this occurred, there would be no arms race. That alone would contribute to a lessening of the possibility of war. Second, if the leaders of the strongest nation came to believe that their high level of military preparedness might provoke other nations into attacking them, they might subscribe to the solution. The effect of this would be that they would reduce the size and strength of their military organizations. Such an act would create deescalation, or an arms race in reverse. Third, arms reduction talks would no longer need to be a competition in which each negotiator tries to get the "best deal," that is, tries to get the other to give up more in the way of armaments than he himself gives up. Ideally, negotiators would compete to see who could give up the most in military preparedness.

NOTES

I am indebted to Barton Brown, Barbara Howe, Charlotte Swanson Otterbein, and A. T. Steegmann for helpful comments and criticism on this essay. A shorter version of this chapter appeared in the *Newsletter of the Association for Political and Legal Anthropology* 4(2):7–10 (October 1980).

1. Shaw (1985) states: "The future looks bleak, if only because the nuclear powers are embroiled in the advanced stages of yet another classical arms race. In keeping with the most widely used arms race model, the 'Richardson model,' there is every reason to anticipate the outbreak of the Third World War because we are now entering a critical final stage called 'fatigue.' . . . Crucial features of this stage are that (1) the nations involved in the arms race are approaching a position in which one is not clearly superior to the other, (2) the nations involved begin to exhaust their resources to maintain their military power balance, and (3) awareness of this exhaustion says, in effect, 'it may be better to attack now while there is still a chance of winning.' In other words, the USSR and the U.S. threatening parity in military power, with speculation that the USSR, if not the U.S. is in a state of exhaustion due to domestic economic troubles, and with the U.S. announcing plans for a massive military buildup by 1987, war might well break out soon" (pp. 159, 177).

2. Although it is obvious that President Harry S. Truman cannot be accused of starting World War II, he became an enthusiastic proponent of the atomic bomb when he learned of its first successful detonation. It gave him increased confidence in negotiating with the Soviets and an opportunity to take revenge on the Japanese (Wyden 1984: 223–6). When the first atomic bomb was dropped on Hiroshima, President Truman exclaimed, "This is the greatest thing in history" (Truman 1955: 421).

3. Even articles that argue—as well as demonstrate—that some United States policy makers hope to outspend the Soviets, thereby forcing them to continue massive spending that will eventually break them, are provocative. An example of such an article is one by N. Lemann in the October 1984 issue of *The Atlantic*

4. *The United Nations Disarmament Yearbook* for 1983 states that "no objective observer of the international stage can help but be struck by . . . the apparent contradiction between the quest of States for international security and well-being and their reluctance to promote those purposes by restricting their armaments" (Department for Disarmament Affairs 1984: 1). I do not see it as a "contradiction," but as a dilemma, a dilemma which I attempt to explain in this chapter.

5. Two other comparative studies of deterrence, one a cross-cultural study (Naroll 1966) and the other a cross-historical study (Naroll, Bullough, and Naroll 1974) obtained the same result.

6. At the time I had no guns hanging on the wall. Today I have three B.B guns on a gun rack that belonged to my father.

7. This is my term for such elaborate defensive measures. Domestic forts could be another term. Fortress architecture contrasts with a concept known as defensible space (Newman 1972).

8. Criminal law, with its penal sanctions (including incarceration and capital punishment), is another measure developed by all political communities for coping with those who steal and kill (Otterbein 1986).

9. A recent review of the literature by Wright, Rossi, and Daly (1983: 273–308) argues that evidence that gun control will reduce violent crime is not conclusive.

10. From a bumper sticker in the author's collection of progun, antigun memorabilia.

11. In the Niagara Frontier region (Erie and Niagara Counties of Western

New York) where I live, holders of pistol permits usually first purchase a handgun for hunting or target shooting. A subsequent purchase is likely to be a small, concealable pistol; in New York State handguns, if carried on one's person, must be carried concealed.

12. For the nineteenth century development of this practice in the United States see Kennett and Anderson (1975: 148–51). They describe how urban police were forced to carry weapons for self-defense.

13. For many years the *American Rifleman* has published a one-page feature titled "The Armed Citizen." Each month the feature reprints excerpts from approximately ten to twenty news reports that show how armed citizens have defended themselves with firearms. Often the assailant is killed. From 2 percent to 6 percent of American adults have actually fired a weapon in self-defense (Wright, Rossi, and Daly 1983: 145, 148).

14. It is estimated that as many as 275,000 handguns are stolen annually in the United States from legitimate handgun owners. Most thefts would, however, be from homes (Wright, Rossi, and Daly 1983: 177–88).

15. On January 9, 1986, Senator Edward Kennedy's private bodyguard was arrested at the Senate Office Building for carrying two submachine guns and a pistol. The bodyguard was charged with three counts of District of Columbia gun law violations. Senator Kennedy has been an advocate of gun control legislation (*American Rifleman*, March 1986, p. 40).

16. The trend in the installation of burglar alarm systems is toward concealing wires, contacts, bells or sirens, and control panels. Over ten years ago the display of these items was thought to have a deterrent effect. Today installers of alarm systems do not want potential burglars to know the extent and nature of the system; if the burglar has this information, it is easier for him to defeat the alarm system.

17. Christians should not find this position unacceptable. Even Jesus's disciples, when accompanying him, carried weapons: "[Jesus said] . . . and he that hath no sword, let him sell his garment, and buy one. . . . And they said, Lord, behold, here are two swords. And he said unto them, It is enough." (St. Luke 22: 36, 38, King James Version).

18. A similar proposal, which focuses solely upon the nuclear confrontation between the United States and the Soviet Union, has been advanced by Narveson (1985: 226–27): "My proposal, in effect, is that it [a state] make clear its defensive stance by limiting itself to a force that could not plausibly be employed to serve basically aggressive purposes. My proposal calls for A opposing B with a force that is clearly quantitatively inferior to that of B by any reasonable measure. . . .What is the rationale for the present proposal? Two different considerations converge to support it. In the first place, it is assumed that nothing is really lost in the way of defensive security by inferiority as compared with parity or even superiority. Thus the state following my policy will not expose itself to greater risk than is faced by anyone exposed to attack by nuclear missiles. And in the second, this stance offers a clear inducement to the opponent to reduce, and certainly not to increase, his arms establishment."

III

ANTHROPOLOGICAL RESEARCH AND THE COLD WAR

11

ANTHROPOLOGY AND WAR: THEORY, POLITICS, ETHICS
R. Brian Ferguson

In public meetings and in print, anthropologists are calling for greater disciplinary efforts to reduce the risk of war. The question is, how to do it? Lists of *potential* contributions have remained depressingly consistent for over twenty years (Bunzel and Parsons 1964; Commission on the Study of Peace 1983: 1:1; 1984:2:1; Nettleship 1975), yet it is difficult to see any practical results from these programatic statements. This chapter discusses some areas where anthropology can make a contribution now, and identifies other potential contributions which have not been emphasized in the past.

A major problem in anthropological efforts to date has been the gulf between those working on theories to explain nonstate warfare and those trying to apply an anthropological perspective to contemporary war. For the most part, the two are separate groups, so that insights offered by the applied group are often questionable in terms of contemporary theory. This raises the question: Why should we expect others to listen to an anthropological opinion if we ourselves do not seek understanding from anthropological theory?

The literature on nonstate or tribal war has grown substantially in recent years (Ferguson 1984a), although anthropological theory on war has been difficult to fathom because of the diversity and apparent contradiction of findings. Polemics aside, genuine contradictions are exceptional. Most of the solid generalizations found in the literature can be synthesized to form a general framework of explanation which does justice to the complexity of the phenomena of war. Elsewhere

(Ferguson 1986) I review that literature and develop a synthetic model. The plan of this chapter is to first summarize that model and then discuss its relevancy to contemporary war, both in its own direct implications and in what it indicates about various applied efforts.

The model is based mainly on data about nonstate societies. States are considered only as an endpoint to that evolutionary continuum. To attempt to analyze modern war with this model would require much work and many modifications and extensions of theory. The goal here is more modest: to show that the general features of the model *seem* relevant to contemporary conflicts and that this apparent relevancy suggests guidelines for future research.

The model is materialist in orientation, involving three premises. First, that the demographic characteristics of a society, its technology, and its pattern of extracting and processing resources from the natural environment ("infrastructure") shape the society's social, economic, and political organization ("structure"), and that both infrastructure and structure shape the ideological superstructure of the society. The relationship between these analytic levels is thought of as a nested hierarchy of progressively more limiting constraints. The more basic factors establish the general outlines or possibilities of a war system. Other factors operate within those limits, progressively narrowing possibilities towards a very limited range of actually possible patterns. Within this deterministic framework, there remains a significant role for individual variation and choice. Further, the model asserts that beliefs and attitudes, although largely derivative, are still an essential part of the functioning of war systems. This opens the possibility that ideas developed by anthropologists may have an impact "in the real world," provided they take into account the more basic constraints shaping contemporary war.

The second premise concerns the motivation of those who decide on war. It begins with the proposition that humans will attempt to maintain or enhance the existing level of the resources available to them, of the costs involved in obtaining these resources, and of the security of these and other basic living conditions. Since warfare typically endangers some or all of these, the decision to fight will occur when decision makers perceive material benefits which outweigh the expectable costs—wars will occur when decision makers believe it serves their material interests. This premise directs attention to the interests and actions of those who decide military policy and, in doing so, breaks out of a functionalist perspective in which social patterns are explained by their contribution to the maintenance of whole social systems. It does not suggest a "psychologistic approach," since the structure of leadership, interests, and options are all determined by social processes. And while this does contradict views that wars result from "aggressive instincts" or cultural values glorifying violence, it does not imply that war is always deliberate. War *may* occur by deliberate plan, or it may be an unplanned and unwanted last resort made inescapable by the consequences of previous self-interested decisions. Even in the latter situation, however, the impact on their material circumstances will remain a paramount concern for decision makers.

The third and final premise is that war can act as a mechanism of selection, eliminating societies which do not make adjustment for living with an existing pattern of warfare. The selection impact of war can be studied in relation to changes within as well as among societies. This premise is needed primarily for understanding processes of evolutionary convergence.

In the summary of the model which follows, I will stick with the format used in Ferguson (1986): first discussing the general significance and interrelation of all factors, mainly as found in relatively egalitarian societies, and then discussing the overall impact of historical and evolutionary developments on these patterns.

Beginning with infrastructural conditions, the model reaffirms that a change in the balance of a population to its available critical resources can create conflicts both within and between groups which can lead to war. However, depending on circumstances, these conflicts may be resolvable through non-violent means such as movement, trade, or modifications in production. Also, when resource scarcity does generate war, there will be variation in the specificity of conflicts thus created, depending on whether the conflict is one of general competition among several essentially similar groups, or one where two particular groups are locked into a direct conflict of interests. A range of possibilities exists, and the less specific the conflict, the more lattitude there is for the influence of structural factors in shaping it.

Besides generating some conflicts, infrastructural factors largely determine gross military potential. Technology, population characteristics, and the basic pattern of production all limit the tactics which can be used and, consequently, the strategies which can be considered and the type of war which can be waged.

Structural patterns are conveniently divided into three categories: kinship, economics, and politics. Kinship provides much of the structure of life in tribal societies. Its relevance to war is shown in a very strong cross-cultural correlation of postmarital residence patterns with major variations of war. Basically, patrilocality is associated with local (or "internal") war, matrilocality with long distance (or "external") war. The connection is that the two residence patterns involve different possibilities for mobilizing male combat teams. In this materialist model, the residence patterns are the derived variables, primarily determined by the nature of existing resource scarcities and related conflicts, combined with the exigencies of material production. Other major features of kinship systems likewise are reflected in the organization of military forces, and marriage and other kin ties are important in establishing and using alliances with other groups. The military significance of kin patterns declines with increasing societal centralization and complexity, however, and so kinship is of negligible importance for later discussions.

Economic systems, the societal and intersocietal organization of production, exchange, and consumption, operate within multiple infrastructural constraints. Nevertheless, economic relations have their own logics which have crucial effects in war. In contrast to kinship, these become more significant as evolutionary complexity increases.

Distribution and consumption patterns affect resource scarcity. Production and distribution patterns affect the possibility of intensification as a nonmilitary alternative response to diminishing resource availability. Labor needs can impel a pattern of raiding for captives. Variations in military conduct are expectable depending on whether the economic system allows for individual social mobility via military feats, for releasing large numbers of men from production tasks for part of a year, for creating a specialized warrior group, and for the production of a transportable surplus to support military campaigns.

Distribution networks, often accompanying kinship ties, define communities of interest which are reflected in groupings for war. External exchange is a key part of making alliances, with intergroup redistribution systems meriting special attention in this regard. Existing trade patterns often structure regional military alliances and can strongly affect readiness to fight over local issues. But war also affects trade patterns, leading to situations of unequal exchange or tribute. Sometimes trade can alleviate pressures associated with local resource scarcities and so reduce pressure for war. In other circumstances, control of trade networks is itself the principal objective in war.

Political organization in relatively egalitarian societies is based on patterns of kinship and economics, and the major features of both are reflected in politics. Different social categories of people have different inputs to the process of decision making. Leaders typically are adult males, and as a group or as individuals they may have their own special interests regarding war. However, adult males in leadership roles are responsive to their own subdivisions of closely related kin. For such an internally divided group to arrive at a decision to go to war often requires the use of considerable skills of conflict resolution and consensus management, and this fact creates a significant role for individual variations in leadership ability in the processes leading to war or peace.

Both structural and individual factors likewise affect the forging of actual politico-military alliances out of the potential alliances created by links of kinship and trade. As ephemeral as alliances may be, they give some structure to the constant flux of intergroup relations. They are necessary for survival and success in war, and all military options must be evaluated in terms of their likely impact on alliance patterns. These patterns, combined with existing differences in the military strength of groups, comprise an intersocietal system which has a crucial role in shaping processes of conflict.

As with economics, war has a reciprocal effect on politics. Authority patterns commonly are more defined within combat groups than in normal daily life, even though serious war threats often lead to a temporary augmentation of general leadership in routine activities. War is an important element in the evolution of more permanent social hierarchy and centralization both within and between autonomous groups, although the exact nature of its role remains controversial.

War is not a result of infrastructural and structural factors alone. Psychological patterns must also be considered. For one, the material rationality premise of this model obviously must operate within existing informational limits. Uncertainty, creating a "prisoner's dilemma" type of situation in a context of high military tension, can lead to pre-emptive attacks even though all parties may prefer peace.

Other emic patterns, apart from and sometimes contrary to a strict material calculus, also impinge on the practice of war. These take various forms. A general cognitive orientation may make war seem inevitable. Religious beliefs may sacralize fighting. Traditions may define situations where the use of force is expected. Value systems may confer prestige on warriors. Typical personality types may tend toward belligerence.

Any of these cultural patterns can make it more likely that people in a conflict situation will opt for war, in effect lowering the threshold for violence. But in the model argued here, they explain much less of the variance in military behavior than calculation of material interests, and are unlikely to lead to extensive fighting in the absence of such interests. Rather, they act as psychological reinforcement, bolstering the resolve of those who must fight. Given the potential costs to warriors, such reinforcement may be indispensible. Whether these "warlike" beliefs and attitudes are initially generated by design or by selection, when war is a likelihood, they will actively be fostered by childhood enculturation and adult peer pressure. And when war involves a different mix of costs and benefits for those who decide military policy and others, including those who must do the fighting, leaders expectably will manipulate these intangible incentives to further group support of their decisions.

The preceeding discussions sketched the significance of various factors involved in generating and shaping war complexes and patterns. To apply this model to actual cases also requires attention to two additional perspectives, historical and evolutionary.

In Ferguson (1986), the significance of history is argued in terms of the effects of Western contact, since most of the existing historical information on non-state warfare comes from contact situations. The consequences of contact typically include major changes in every aspect of warfare previously discussed. Failure to appreciate this has led to many misunderstandings about supposedly pristine war patterns. But history is always happening, everywhere. The contingencies of history generate actions and modifications of war systems which should always be investigated. Conversely, existing historical conditions will determine what impact any innovation will have. The uncritical lumping of data on warfare from different time periods can be an error fatal to analysis. (For an illustration of how an historical approach can be combined with a theoretical orientation similar to the one outlined here, see Ferguson [1984b]).

Sociocultural evolution involves increases in political centralization, structural inequality, productive intensification, and societal complexity, all of which have major consequences for war. These changes are felt at every point along the evolutionary continuum, but they are most obvious with the emergence of stratification and states.

It has long been recognized that the growth of centralized territorial administration leads to a decline in the significance of kinship structures in shaping military groups. Another general change is a relative decline in the significance of infrastructural sources of conflict. Things like an absolute reduction in critical natural resources certainly can still lead to war in states. But the increasing productivity and complexity of economic systems which is part of evolution tends to shield populations from natural scarcities, at the same time that it generates new structural demands and conflicts which can lead to war even without population pressure.

Another consequence of increasing economic complexity, accompanied as it is by increased structural inequality, is that one's material well-being is determined more by placement in the societal structure, rather than by overall balances of population to resources. The stakes involved in any conflict situation will be determined by structural position, as will the probable costs and benefits of actual war. A decision-making elite and the majority of a population may have parallel interests in a particular military policy, but their interests may also be divergent or flatly contradictory. A major source of divergent or contradictory interests is that members of an elite enjoy many benefits by virtue of their structural position, and so have a great interest in preserving that structure and their positions within it against any political threat. In many different ways, this can lead to "political wars," which do no more for the majority than waste their lives.

Such wars can occur because leaders in states can compel people to fight. The ultimately coercive nature of military recruitment in states is perhaps the most fundamental distinction separating state from more egalitarian patterns of war. Pure coercion, however, is a relatively inefficient and costly means of securing obedience to leaders' decisions. It is far better, for an elite, to rule by encouraging social structures which fragment resistance, and by fostering an ideology which portrays the objectives of the elite as representing the interests of all in society, a proposition which the elite may believe themselves.

Evolution affects military capabilities, and so the kinds of wars that are fought. States and near-states go to war with armies whose discipline, tactical sophistication, logistical support structures, and sometimes technology give them great advantages in combat against less evolved societies. Power imbalances of this sort mean that strategic goals are often achieved without the necessity of actual violence. With state armies, wars of conquest become a regular possibility. This expansionist potential gives new significance to war as a mechanism of selection. War can lead to the spread of state organization throughout a region of interaction, and to convergent trends in the internal organization of states opposed in war. One important trend, although its generality remains to be established, is toward the development of a distinctive military complex which comes to demand and receive larger shares of society's resources.

The model that has been outlined here was not developed to explain contemporary warfare. Nevertheless, it does have some direct relevance to understanding contemporary situations in that the model, and other considerations, contradict widely held beliefs that war is a "natural" part of the human condition. During an earlier arms race, Stewart (1964: 431) commented on the generality of such beliefs, and how they make war seem inevitable. Others recently have made similar observations (Falk and Kim 1980: 10–11; Tishkov 1983). My own informal investigation (casual conversations with nonanthropologists) confirms these observations and adds another disturbing element: that many, probably most, people base these beliefs on what they *think* are the findings of anthropology, that "primitive people fight for no reason." A great many people think that the message of anthropology is that humanity is doomed to war.

One version of the inevitability belief is that wars occur because humans are innately aggressive. As described elsewhere (Ferguson 1984a: 8–12), this proposition has been so thoroughly discredited that it is difficult to find serious researchers who still assert it. It is not an element in the model presented here. Besides its lack of scientific credibility, the proposition flies in the face of common sense. If war is the result of an aggressive instinct, why is it that societies with war need elaborate social reinforcement to make men fight? True, humans are known to inflict and even enjoy inflicting almost unimaginable violence on other humans. Yet humans are also known to adopt a pacifism so strict that it suppresses even mild expressions of anger. If this suggests any genetic program, it can only be a program *to learn* attitudes towards violence, without any particular predisposition.

Another version is that war is a natural form of expression for politically autonomous groups. This Hobbesian view is discussed and criticized elsewhere (Bennett Ross 1980; Ferguson 1984a: 19–21; 1986). Supporting the Hobbesian view is the corollary belief that war is universal, found in all societies. But there are societies without war (Fabbro 1980). In fact, the claim for universality can only be advanced by relying on several dubious procedures: letting one cultural subdivision with war represent a broader cultural grouping which includes some groups without war; letting war at any point in time count, and disregarding what may be much more typical periods of peace; and when these fail, falling back on the untestable assertion that a peaceful people might have had war before the Westerners arrived. Even if we focus on societies where warfare is an undisputed occurrence, periods of active warfare involving a given group usually are relatively brief. The vast majority of humans, living or dead, have spent most of their lives at peace. So one can agree with Hobbes that politically autonomous groups have the potential for war, but this tells us nothing about why real war occurs. Contrary to the Hobbesian image, peace is the normal human condition.

A third version is that war is the inevitable consequence of population growing until people are forced to fight over life-sustaining resources. (For a recent assertion of this premise as a base for a broad theoretical formulation, see Schmookler [1984: 20]). The model presented here contradicts this Malthusian view. Yes, population growth and pressure on critical resources can and often does lead to war. But there is no inevitability in this linkage even in "simple" societies, and with evolution, the significance in war of absolute scarcities fades in importance. The model suggests that the causes of war in modern complex societies will most commonly be found in economic and political relations. (For an anthropological refutation of a Malthusian explanation of one particular modern war, see Durham 1979).

The danger in the public perception that war is inevitable is that it may sap people's resistance to war. The model described here indicates that war is not destined, it is caused. Understanding the processes which lead to war creates the possibility that they can be redirected toward peace.

Serious investigators of contemporary conflicts do not need to be told this. Still, the model may be useful for peace research in that it provides something which is called for in several recent reviews of that literature (Eberwein 1981: 31; Falk and Kim 1980: 4; Gantzel 1981: 40; Singer 1981:3): a theoretical structure which encompasses and integrates the diversity of phenomena involved in war. The model also suggests resolutions of existing divisions within peace research. One division is whether war is "caused" or "chosen" (Beer 1981: 12–13). It is both. Another division is whether the genesis of war is to be sought in the authority structure of particular sovereign groups, or in the system of international relations (Falk and Kim 1980: 459, 531). Again, the model indicates that both are crucial.

But does this model really seem applicable to the circumstances of modern war? And if so, what does it suggest about applied anthropological research? These questions are addressed in the following section. Descriptions of current areas of more applied anthropological research are based on Foster and Rubinstein (1986), Givens and Nettleship (1976), and Nettleship et al. (1975); on research and conference topics described in many articles in the newsletters of The Commission on the Study of Peace and Anthropologists for Human Survival; and on my own participation in several conferences, sessions, and discussions on the issue.

Anthropological research and commentary regarding contemporary global militarism stands in an inverse relationship to the causal priorities of the model. There is a lot of work on superstructural factors, a little on structural patterns, and almost nothing regarding the infrastructure. Nevertheless, the importance of infrastructure in understanding modern war is obvious.

Hydrogen bombs and intercontinental missiles, and all their associated technologies, are part of our infrastructure. To that should be added all of the direct military ramifications of conventional weapons technology, national population characteristics, the distribution of critical resources, and geography, plus the role of infrastructural factors in shaping national and international economic systems. Further, the sudden insecurity of Western oil suplies markedly aggravated world military tensions after the mid-1970s (Tucker 1980: 246–7; Timberlake and Tinker 1984).

Infrastructural factors explain much of the qualitative difference between world military patterns of 1986 and, say, 1812. They also bear much of the responsibility for the broad outlines of contemporary world tensions. However, their responsibility for these tensions is also clearly limited, and infrastructural factors seem of limited importance in explaining most short-run variations in conflicts, which is what the model predicts. On this basis, anthropological neglect of infrastructural inputs to contemporary tensions is perhaps understandable. Besides, it is not readily apparent how anthropologists could offer a distinctive perspective on these inputs, with the very important exception of being able to describe the living conditions of Third World poor, which has been and will continue to be an important indirect factor in international tensions.

Anthropologists have done more work on structural aspects of contemporary war. Three lines of approach stand out. One is to focus on mechanisms of conflict resolution in tribal societies. This is an area where there actually has been a serious effort to apply lessons learned through the study of nonstate warfare to modern contexts (Koch 1974). The reasoning is that both "tribals" and "moderns" have to cope with similar problems of anarchistic intergroup relations, so lessons from the former might offer solutions for the latter.

Unfortunately, there are several problems with this approach. One is that this notion has been around at least twenty years (Bunzel and Parsons 1964: 430), and it has already received consideration by peace researchers who question the practical relevance of mechanisms from small-scale societies applied to present international relations (Falk and Kim 1980: 162). A second problem is that schemes for nonviolent conflict resolution, even those developed by peace researchers based on the study of contemporary industrial societies, face apparently insurmountable obstacles to implementation. (Compare proposals and projections in Beer [1979] with the course of events since the mid-1970s.) Even the Trilateral Commission, whose members certainly have clout, has failed to institutionalize its vision of an efficiently regulated world (see Sklar 1980). A third problem is that the focus on formal institutions of conflict resolution may distract attention from the most general reason why serious conflicts are resolved with minimal violence in nonstate societies—that the majority of people wish to avoid the costs of war. And this, I will argue later, is a lesson with practical contemporary relevance.

A second type of structural research is to engage in participant observation within a group somehow involved in war. The groups range from policy decision makers to members of armed forces to peasant villages supporting guerrillas. (One kind of group, war protesters, is discussed again below.) This type of work involves attention to both group organization and ideology, in varying mixtures. It can produce very useful information, but does entail certain complications.

By chosing to work with groups directly involved in processes of conflict, the anthropologist risks becoming a part of the conflict. The information produced may be used to further the interests of particular parties, so those who want to do this kind of work should consider, before starting, who is likely to use the data generated, and for what.

Participant observation in small groups also raises all the theoretical and methodological issues involved in the study of local communities or work groups within larger complex societies. To avoid the errors of early community studies, research should be built around the fact that these groups are part of larger systems, and that the latter determine many of the group's internal characteristics. If both of these concerns are attended to, one big contribution would be to explore characteristics of component subgroups of the military-industrial complex, since that complex as a whole does seem to bear much of the responsibility for military buildups (Rosen 1973a; Stubbing 1985).

Anthropologists could also study how parts of the military-industrial complex fit together, which indicates a third way anthropology can contribute to understanding contemporary world conflict—by helping explain the structures and dynamics of larger social systems. It is these, according to the model, which should be the major source of conflicts leading to war in complex societies. Their amenability to holistic study and their relation to internal and external warfare have been shown in transdisciplinary work on Central America, as reported in the journal, *Latin American Perspectives*, and publications of the North American Congress on Latin America (NACLA) (see also Durham 1979; Wolf 1973). Anthropological work on a higher level of organization, the nature of global interactions (e.g., Leeds 1975; Wolf 1982; Worsley 1984), even if not focused specifically on war, can help to rectify a relevant problem identified by Galtung (1980: 412): that the nature of imperialism has been obscured because analysis of its effects is fragmented into traditional academic specializations.

By far the most common anthropological approach to modern militarism is to examine its psychological bases. Specific interests vary widely. Anthropologists discuss the impact of nationalism, racism, and ethnocentrism; of values and orientations which encourage obedience or prestige seeking within the military; of psychopathologies which lead to violent responses to situations; and of ignorance which leads one nation to misperceive how an adversary state works, and to misunderstand the messages it sends. Perhaps the most common theme is that war is somehow the result of a negative image of the enemy.

Similar approaches have been used extensively in discussions of tribal war patterns, although they have not led to significant verifiable cross-cultural generalizations, and certainly not to any viable general explanation of war. In the model described above, these superstructural attributes are treated as largely derived correlates of existing conflicts. Nevertheless, a focus on psychological characteristics does fit well with a very extensive literature in peace research (Jervis 1980).

In regard to modern war Falk and Kim (1980: 230) argue that for this type of research to be productive, it should be "sharply focused on the role of 'war makers'," i.e., those who decide on policy. A well-known study on decisions to go to war indicates that more obvious factors of pride and prejudice have little importance (Abel 1941). The decisions are made through careful weighing of costs and benefits, although the ability to make such calculations can be diminished by stress-related effects of crises (Holsti 1980). More subtle cultural assumptions and attitudes, however, become apparent in any perusal of writings about international policy, and these reflect perceived options in crisis situations and in long-term strategizing.

What is not clear is the real significance of these often elaborate beliefs. Are they in themselves the generators of action, or is it more a case of ideological rationalization of actions intended to serve the interests of the powerful? The fact that preconceptions truly are believed in policy circles is inconclusive, since both cognitive dissonance and the processes of bureaucracy would result in belief of mandated policy. The model presented earlier points to ideological rationalization, as do the well-developed theories of imperialism (Kurth 1974: 12), the military-industrial complex (Rosen 1973b: 3), and most Marxist analyses.

This question suggests research topics for those who would study the beliefs of policy elites. Besides describing their beliefs, research should investigate why policy makers hold them, including the sources of ideas and mechanisms promoting ideological conformity. An even more important issue is to ascertain the consequences of ideology. Do the preconceptions actually make a major difference in how diplomatic and military personnel discharge their duties, or is that effectively constrained by bureaucratic, policy, and situational dictates?

Research into war-related beliefs of the national majority entails other issues. First, it must not be assumed, as some have, that majority beliefs push the nation toward war. In the current cold war, United States public opinion favoring increased defense spending took its big leap in 1979 and 1980, after the defense spending buildup had already begun. That increase in public support proved short lived, dropping to a minority position in 1982, and turning sharply negative in 1983. A negative balance of opinion regarding increases in defense spending has been the rule since the mid-60s. United States public opinion is also solidly against the nuclear arms race and against most possibilities of foreign intervention (Benson 1982; Ferguson and Rogers 1986: 25–32; Kriesberg and Klein 1980; Simon 1980; Yankelovich and Doble 1984). A recent poll of United States public opinion found that 53 percent thinks the United States would actually be safer if it stopped trying to halt the spread of communism to other countries (only 22 percent disagreed) (Yankelovich and Doble 1984: 44). Those who would direct United States military strategy recognize and lament the fact that the public tends to support military involvement only when they perceive an obvious threat to the United States (Kriesberg and Klein 1980: 104; Tucker 1980: 262–65 [see Stein 1980]). If there is a basic United States majority attitude toward military buildups, it is against them. Yet the current buildup goes on.

If prowar attitudes in the general public are to be studied, the model presented earlier suggests that a good place to begin is with the propaganda system. The material rationality premise is limited by the availability of information. In modern states, most people have no direct source of information about foreign affairs. Most information made available is controlled by established institutions. In all states, these expectably will reflect the interests and perceptions of the powerful.

The importance of propaganda is axiomatic when considering popular opinion in the Soviet Union, but it also applies in the United States. Here, various government agencies control and manipulate the information they make public (Fulbright 1970; Halloran 1986; *The Pentagon Papers*; the magazine *Covert Action*). Private corporations spend about two billion dollars each year to present their views on the world and to fund congenial research (Ferguson and Rogers 1986: 127–30). Entertainment media and advertisements serve up a steady diet of militaristic fare. Establishment news media reproduce the policy elite's view of military situations (NACLA 1983; Stone 1971). "Responsible" academics accept the positions of different segments of the policy elite as defining legitimate research and debate (Chomsky 1982: chs. 2, 4; Ravenal 1979: 83–86; Tucker 1984: 29). Much of the increased support for defense spending in the late 1970s can be attributed to the efforts of groups like the Committee on the Present Danger to convince the public that the United States had fallen dangerously behind the Soviets in military preparedness (Stubbing 1985: 851–52; Wolfe 1979: 25–27; Wolfe and Sanders 1979: 59–60; Kriesberg and Klein 1980: 105). Even though the case for Soviet superiority has been thoroughly debunked (Aspin 1978; Ferguson and Rogers 1986: 141–42; Holzman 1980; Posen and Van Evera 1983: 37–39), the myth has been kept very much alive.

An even more clear illustration of the significance of propaganda is found in the current Strategic Defense Initiative (SDI), a.k.a. "Star Wars." The public is often told that the goal of the SDI is to make nuclear weapons "impotent and obsolete," to create an impenetrable shield which would protect the United States from Soviet missiles. But the objective of the SDI is less to protect the United States population from incoming missiles, than it is to protect the United States' strategic ICBMs, and so to weaken Soviet first-strike capabilities (Bundy et al. 1984: 269; Clarke 1985: 166–69). At the same time, the United States is increasing its own first-strike and other nuclear capabilities via development and deployment of MX, Trident II, and Midgetman (Posen and Van Evera 1983: 24–28). Rather than making nuclear weapons obsolete, it seems that United States military planners are acting on recommendations to prepare to "fight and win" a nuclear war (e.g. Gray and Payne 1980); or at least, to regain a sufficient strategic advantage to allow it to return to the previous policy of credibly threatening to use tactical nuclear weapons against Soviet armies, a threat which previously had been the capstone of containment (Ellsberg 1981: v–vi; McNamara 1983; Record 1984: 13–22). It is very doubtful that public support would be forthcoming for a policy so stated—far better to speak of abolishing nuclear war and dazzle imaginations with talk of particle beams and laser stations. But if the SDI is "Star Wars," its planners have been "seduced by the dark side of the Force."

So propaganda does seem an important topic for understanding public attitudes. Anthropologists could study how propaganda works at every stage of the process, by attention to the people and organizations that make or present information on foreign affairs, by content analysis of the messages being transmitted, and by looking at how the information is received and perceived by the public.

Some would say that consideration of these matters is mixing politics and science. It is true that focusing on propaganda has political implications. But so does ignoring it. To ignore the possibility that the powerful use propaganda to generate support for policies which serve their interests is to risk portraying cause (a militaristic government policy) for effect (popular support for militarism). Further, since anthropologists are as exposed to propaganda as anyone else, to ignore these issues is to run the additional risk that propaganda assumptions will be incorporated into and so reproduced in their work. To study popular attitudes without attention to the propaganda system is to risk becoming part of that system. That is not just politics, it is also bad science.

In the recent upsurge of interest in war and peace, many anthropologists have expressed interest in going beyond research. They want to use the knowledge and skills already available in a direct way, "to get involved." This sense of urgency certainly seems appropriate in 1986. Activism is inherently political, more directly engaged in actual political processes than the research efforts already discussed. Consideration of the political implications of different types of action therefore seems appropriate. The following section considers two alternative paths toward relevancy, a policy route and a protest route.

THE POLICY ROUTE

A common theme at recent conferences on war is: How can anthropologists become more involved in formulating government policy?

Opportunities to influence policy should always be given serious consideration and evaluated on an individual case basis. Nevertheless,
there is reason to question this route as a general direction for those
wishing to promote peace.

Policy is the result of political struggle. Anthropologists brought
in as advisors or low-level functionaries will have no power, and often
little understanding of the policy-making process. As Sahlins (1967:
75) observed in regard to an earlier episode, when social scientists
thought they could reform war-related policy, "[T]he quixotic scholar
enters the agreement in the belief that knowledge breeds power; his
military counterpart in the assurance that power breeds knowledge."
Academic opinion is brought in according to its utility in furthering
established policy aims. A "good" academic is a technocrat, who does
practical, problem-solving work, not the "value oriented" scholar who
questions basic policy premises (Chomsky 1982: 89). (See Paige [1977]
on the impossibility of a truly value-neutral evaluation of policy assumptions.)

Even if an independent-minded anthropologist gets a foot in the
door, major obstacles remain if the goal is to change policy makers'
views on the world. Social psychologists have established the (not
surprising) fact that influencing basic assumptions behind policy is
very difficult and likely to happen only over long periods (Jervis 1980:
466–74). Meanwhile, the anthropologist would be exposed to the social
and institutional pressures of the policy machine. The more likely
result is that the system will change the anthropologist, rather than the
reverse (see Coser 1956: 27–29). "Realism" may come to mean working
within the established limits of policy. "Promoting peace" may be
equated with reinforcing the status quo.

Another political concern is the company one keeps. From a governmental view, the ethnographic and other information anthropologists produce may be considered "intelligence." The CIA has publicly
assumed the responsibility of seeking out scholars with unorthodox
and challenging interpretations of world issues (Engelberg 1986). Even
if a scholar purposely avoids the intelligence agencies, it may be impossible to refuse to cooperate with them if employed, say, on an
embassy staff. Given the history of these agencies, this raises many
political and moral issues. It also evokes the specter of disaster for the
profession of anthropology.

These are not hypothetical issues. Their reality is shown in the
history of Project Camelot (Horowitz 1967). "Camelot" was the code
name for a program of "insurgency prophylaxis" developed in 1964
by the Department of Defense (DOD). Social scientists, including anthropologists, were recruited to study the causes of insurgency around
the world. The participants saw themselves as reformers, but as a group

they lacked any clear conception of their role or goals, and their work in practice was shaped by their employer, the DOD. Project Camelot was terminated in 1965, killed by the scandal it caused in Chile and by political infighting in Washington. One of its legacies was to cast a pall of suspicion on anthropological fieldworkers around the world (Sahlins 1967: 73).

Another disturbing illustration of a military application of anthropological insights comes from the 1986 United States bombing of Tripoli. According to investigative reporter Seymour Hersh, the plan included bombing Qaddafi's family quarters because several senior CIA officers "claimed that in Bedouin culture Qaddafi would be diminished as a leader if he could not protect his home" (1987).

THE PROTEST ROUTE

An alternative to seeking acceptance by policy makers is to protest. This also is an attempt to shape policy but by pressure from the outside. Two complementary types of work are possible. One is to engage in participant observation or other study of peace organizations (Peattie 1986; Thompson and Smith 1981). Analytic skills could be applied to practical problems. What works? What should be avoided? What type of actions exert the most leverage? During the Vietnam War, many Americans who opposed the war were also opposed to the peace demonstrators (Simon 1980: 23–24). Why?

As argued in the earlier discussion of structurally oriented research, study of smaller groups should be combined with exploration of their place in the larger system. That applies here. A case illustrating the need is provided by the recent Nuclear Freeze Movement. It had spectacular success in promoting mass demonstrations in 1983 and then practically disappeared. The causes of this sudden rise and fall are not all clear, but one important factor is the capitalization of the freeze position by a segment of the elite, whose influence tended to depoliticize the issue, leaving it susceptible to co-optation by supporters of the strategic modernization policy called "Build Down" (Ferguson and Rogers 1986: 226–32).

The other kind of protest work involves developing a counter to the ideology that promotes war. First, we can show how and why the interests of the powerful may differ from the interests of the majority. The point is not that the two are necessarily opposed in any given case, but that they can easily be opposed. Because of this, any claims about the necessity of military action when no direct threat to the United States is apparent should be given close and skeptical scrutiny. Second, we can show how the goals of the powerful are promoted as being in the interests of all. Here the emphasis should be on the character and mechanisms of propaganda. Peace activists will never have the resources to keep abreast of every new wrinkle in ideology, but the general power of propaganda would be reduced if it were more readily recognized as such. Ideally, the counterideological message could reinforce and be spread by active peace organizations.

The protest route offers several advantages. First, the ideas of potentially divergent interests in war, of ideological manipulations by the elite, and of resistance by the societal majority as a way of avoiding war, are all direct extensions of the theoretical model.

Second, the basic idea in the approach is to bring democratic process to bear in determining military strategies. It represents the extension of a basic American value—democratic rule—to an area where it has previously been excluded (Medvedev and Medvedev 1981: 18–19; Posen and Van Evera 1983: 44–45; Thompson 1981: 38–39).

Third, there appears to be a social base responsive to this message. Public opinion polls show both a widespread distrust of political, military, and business leaders and a conviction that government is run by "a few big interests" (Crozier et al. 1975: 76–85; Ferguson and Rogers 1986: 18; Ladd 1976/77). Within the general population, people of lower socioeconomic status show systematically greater opposition to the use of United States troops abroad (Benson 1982: 594–95). These data suggest that many people would respond positively to the proposition:

> *If we hope to understand anything about the foreign policy of any state, it is a good idea to begin by investigating the domestic social structure: Who sets foreign policy? What interests do these people represent? What is the domestic source of their power? It is a reasonable surmise that the policy that evolves will reflect the special interests of those who design it.* (Chomsky 1982: 86)

In a sense, all this does is articulate what people already suspect. By giving the suspicion form and substance, it becomes a basis for action.

Fourth, we do not have to start from scratch in developing an audience for this message. We can begin with the very important audience we already have—our college students of military service age.

Fifth, public skepticism does act as an inhibitor of militaristic policies even now (Roberts 1986), which is why militarists put so much effort into propaganda. If public opinion were more informed, focused, and resistant to manipulation, its influence would be far greater. This in turn would slow military spending and encourage real efforts toward nuclear arms reductions. Public skepticism also has the direct effect of retarding unilateral United States military action. Military plans are based on possibilities and expectations, and the likelihood of popular support or opposition is very definitely included in their equations, often under the label of "Vietnam syndrome" (Tucker 1980: 269).

Sixth, this is one approach which can be applied to both East and West. A key concern for Soviet tacticians is the political reliability of Warsaw Pact armies. This is thought to be quite low, especially for offensive war (Herspring and Volgyes 1980). Currently, this is being compounded by clear signs that the antimilitarist, antinuclear sentiments of Western Europe are spreading in Eastern Europe (English 1984; Kamm 1986; Kaufman 1987). And while there seems little prospect of a similar development anytime soon within the Soviet Union itself (Medvedev and Medvedev 1981), top Soviet military officials have publicly worried that pacifist sentiments were sapping youth's willingness to fight (Strode and Strode 1983: 96–100). One recent study of the Soviet politico-military system suggests that perhaps the only way we can influence it is through a dialogue between peoples on the legitimacy of state militarism (Holloway 1981: 103).

In conclusion, anthropology does have a distinctive contribution to make towards promoting peace. The model outlined in the first half of this chapter seems applicable in its general form to contemporary war, and it suggests that much more research could be done. Besides the model, the mainstream of anthropology has been invoked in the references to other relevant areas of anthropological research, in the emphases on participant observation and a holistic perspective, and in the endorsement of a course of activism which involves articulating the interests and views of those who are normally excluded from policy circles.

In seeking to increase the influence of national majorities, the goal is to restrict the independent authority of those who at present make policy. The policies they have developed have lowered, step by step, the threshold of nuclear war to a point where they may be unable to avert it in a crisis (Cimbala 1986; Ford 1985; McNamara 1983). These policies have evolved in pursuit of the same type of strategic advantages always sought through military strength. Each incremental elaboration has had the backing of powerful interests and elaborate planning. But the end result is insane, the ultimate irrationality, a system which could end the world we know. No segment of the policy elite can control this whole system. Each merely acts within it. That is why it has become imperative that national majorities control their policy elites.

States usually do not work that way. Usually, rulers set policy, and the masses carry it out. But we live in a new situation—new because in the United States and Western Europe existing political structures allow the possibility of an increase in real democratic rule. And new because the danger we all face is greater than any in history. In the past, war has eliminated specific societies which did not adjust to their military environment. Today the possibility of selection remains, but it is against the whole species, and to avoid being eliminated we must learn how *not* to use military force. War has become far too important a matter to be left to our leaders.

12

ANTHROPOLOGISTS GOING INTO THE COLD: RESEARCH IN THE AGE OF MUTUALLY ASSURED DESTRUCTION

Steven L. Sampson
David A. Kideckel

The cold war and the tensions it spawns seem permanent features of the late twentieth century. As a document issued by the Methodist clergy suggests (Pace 1986), the policy of nuclear deterrence adopted by both superpowers has condemned East and West to endemic competition, conflict, and mutual suspicion. However, though the cold war's international dimensions are well known, the chief question that occupies us here is its influence on social scientific and, specifically, anthropological research (cf. Byrnes 1976a).

The social scientific ramifications of the cold war are many. In the West, particularly the United States, it shapes university budgets and grant priorities, affects basic social social scientific paradigms and preconceptions of other societies; and influences both the dissemination of research results and their public reception. Though these effects are general throughout the social sciences, anthropological research about Eastern European socialist societies is especially influenced. Since these so-called captive nations are a direct object of the cold war struggle, they have heightened sensitivity to the extremist politics of the period. Anthropological research, on the other hand, is predicated on face-to-face interaction and in-depth subjective understanding of other societies, practices which fly in the face of both Eastern and Western priorities in the cold war context.[1]

This chapter thus assesses some of the implications of cold war politics and culture for anthropological research. It particularly focuses on Western anthropologists in Eastern European research and the role of anthropological knowledge and practice for either bridging or reinforcing cold war-inspired cultural suspicions. Though this essay is based largely on our and others' experiences in Romania, we feel it has wider applicability in other Eastern European states as well.[2]

To be sure, fieldwork in Eastern Europe has much in common with anthropological research in general. Like others, anthropologists working in the cold war context are faced with problems of identifying research sites, gaining entry and building rapport in communities, steering clear of factional quarrels, gathering systematic data, and maintaining their health and emotional stability. However, as June Nash (1975) pointed out, there is more to fieldwork that the field worker. Conditions encountered in the field are shaped by its specific time-space location which, in Eastern Europe, is particularly colored by the cold war.

That the cold war provides the basic context of Eastern European research was constantly brought home to us during fieldwork and in subsequent discussions with interested parties in the West. Romanians of all walks had problems comprehending our presence in their country and often interpreted it in cold war terms. They often assumed we were agents of the United States government, various socialist governments, or descendants of expropriated kulaks returned to sue for patrimonial rights. Still others accepted our stated research goals but questioned their use for anything but political ends.

These suspicions were initially laid to rest during a decade of intermittent research as we established a degree of permanency in our social relations and became fairly well integrated into our host communities and became (we thought) familiar and unthreatening to regional officials. However, despite our integration in regional life, the mid-1980s was a turning point for us. Steven Sampson was denied entry into Romania and declared *persona non grata*, and David Kideckel had a number of restrictions placed on his research in a 1984 visit.

Meanwhile, home circumstances were analogous. For example, our discussions with academics and others were invariably interrupted with questions concerning how we were able to do research in Romania in the first place. Western colleagues especially questioned the veracity of our data and were skeptical of statistics garnered by us from local and regional censuses and other documents. Some people even suggested that lying was necessary to accomplish any sort of germane Eastern European research.

Thinking about these events and interpretations, we came to see that they were based on mutually distorted or mistaken assumptions about both Eastern European socialist society and the Western research enterprise. Given the mutual suspicion and caricatured images they reflected, it was logical to turn to the cold war as at least a partial explanation for these distortions. In particular, we were forced to reflect on how our own research experience was shaped by our and others' cold war assumptions and to examine what the role of American anthropologists in Eastern European socialist societies is and ought to be. Consideration of these questions, however, first demands analysis of both the nature of the cold war and how it shapes the Eastern European research environment as a whole.

CHILLING ASSUMPTIONS—COLD WAR CONCEPTIONS AND MISCONCEPTIONS

There are a number of common understandings about the cold war that must be addressed and enlarged in order to grasp its relationship to anthropological research in Eastern Europe. In popular terms, the cold war is the nonmilitary struggle between two competing world orders, the "Free World" and the "Communist bloc." As usually conceived, the struggle has both ideological and geopolitical implications. Ideologically, from the Free World's perspective, the conflict revolves around Western freedom *vs.* Eastern repression. In the Communist perspective it concerns the struggle between the exploitation of individualism versus the security of collectivism. The ideological struggle translates geopolitically into a struggle for international influence. The West talks of Soviet expansionism via surrogate regimes in places like Afghanistan, Ethiopia, and Nicaragua, while the East sees Western imperialism throughout the world attempting to protect its dying, exploitative world order.

For those who accept the Manichaean view of reality, the cold war is pervasive and all interaction between the competing powers is part of the struggle—with victories or defeats seen as the outcome of particular events. Any event (from chess tournaments to space disasters to nuclear meltdowns) is part of the overall struggle, and all exchanges are potential confrontations and tests of strength and/or weakness. Since all actions are thus part of the grand cold war scheme, the potential for conspiracy theories is extraordinary. Instead of simple distrust, the relations between the two competing blocs are elevated to a "culture of suspicion" whereby there are no coincidences. It is this culture of suspicion, then, that serves as the backdrop for anthropology in Eastern Europe and generates some particular pressures on the fieldwork enterprise.

POLITICO-CENTRISM AND THE VERDICT MENTALITY

The pervasiveness of the cold war has caused it to become fixed in Western and Eastern political consciousness. In the West, this is also fostered by an enculturation process replete with popularized images of Eastern Europe from the "Six O'Clock News," school history lessons (cf. FitzGerald 1979), air raid drills, and the whole range of international crises which punctuated the 1950s and 1960s. The permanent merging of cold war and consciousness engenders what we call "politico-centrism," an internalized belief in the superiority of one's own political system and an automatic suspicion of our "adversaries."

Though analogous to ethnocentrism, politico-centrism in some ways is even more pernicious due to the potential implications of the cold war struggle as well as the intellectual blinders it places on the researcher. Though all anthropologists have a degree of naivety about the people and places where they conduct research, it is our belief that notions of Eastern Europe are more ingrained in the American world-view than the hazy images we have of New Guinea, East Africa, or the Amazon. While anthropological research in the Third World is basically a matter of acquiring knowledge, Eastern European research requires a systematic purging of prior misconceptions before one can begin knowledge acquisition.

Without this purging politico-centrism colors the assumptions one brings into the field and shapes the questions asked of one's data. In particular it fosters a "verdict mentality" where one continually evaluates the overall worth of socialism as a social system—is it progressing or degenerating, good or bad, creating equality or inequality? The contrast here with tribal or Third World research is instructive. Though anthropologists who work in these regions are occasionally asked to explain them to others, they are not usually pressed for a comprehensive evaluation except during some crisis (often brought on, we might add, as a spin-off to cold war struggles; e.g., the civil wars in Nicaragua and Angola). Verdicts about Eastern European socialism, provocative as they are, do little more than confirm the preconceptions of the questioner and force the anthropologist to place the research into artificially contrived categories.

More to the point for actual fieldwork, the culture of suspicion makes human contact between the two camps difficult at best and fraught with numerous obstacles. Ideologically, it manifests in the fear of subversion or "ideological pollution," by which people with foreign ideas will negatively infect our or their society. Geopolitically there is the fear that espionage may weaken the political or military order. In the conduct of research, then, there is an *a priori* assumption that all individuals so engaged have dark motives until or unless they prove otherwise. Research and researchers are thus automatically constrained by host countries or their own concern lest they be so labeled.

TWO, THREE, MANY COLD WARS

Other conditions shaping anthropological research in and about Eastern Europe are the differential way the cold war affects individual states and its changing, cyclical nature over time. Typically, the cold war is often seen to affect all participant states fairly similarly. As the conflict revolves around the two superpowers, it is often assumed that their "allies" pretty much follow their lead. Thus, détente between the United States and the Soviet Union supposedly demands détente between the allied states as well. When the superpower conflict boils over, one also expects a chilling of relations between other participant states.

Despite this alleged homogeneity, variation in Eastern European national, political, economic, and cultural environments suggest that the cold war experience also varies. No doubt, United States-Soviet relations affect other countries; American and Soviet allies are often called on to follow their "big brothers" and demonstrate unity in boycotts, economic sanctions, and other diplomatic initiatives. However, there are other cold wars besides the United States-Soviet one. In fact, for the Eastern European states the cold war is as much a struggle for them to maneuver between the Soviets and the West to satisfy their own national interests, as it is their following the Soviet lead.

Given their differential integration in the overall conflict, the states of the competing blocs periodically readjust their diplomatic postures and political economies to the irregular shifts, obstacles, and possibilities of the basic cold war competition. Thus, each Eastern European state is involved in essentially three cold wars: the main one as Soviet client, its own separate "war" with the United States and its allies, and a cold war of sorts with the Soviet Union and its allies. Similarly, each of these cold wars runs in its own cycle of "détente-tension-crisis" that may, though not necessarily, parallel the main United States-Soviet cycle.

Romania especially illustrates these multiple cold wars. Over two decades in relations with the Soviets and its allies, Romania has pursued a policy of relative autonomy. It was the only "bloc" country to maintain relations with Israel after 1967, to denounce the invasions of Czechoslovakia in 1968 and Afghanistan in 1979, and to defy the Soviet-led boycott of the 1984 Los Angeles Olympics. Romania, in fact, has a pervasive suspicion of its allies. Work stoppages, industrial explosions, and the like are all attributed to Soviet intrigues, and there are constant confrontations over small and large issues. At the same time, there is fear of ideological or geopolitical subversion by the Soviet Union and by Hungary which, from their persistent conflict over Transylvania, Romania sees as a Soviet surrogate.

The cold war cycle between Romania and the West has its own logic separate from, though related to, the main United States-Soviet conflict. To facilitate its autonomy from the bloc, Romania was rewarded with a variety of perquisites by the United States and its allies. Richard Nixon visited it in 1969, and it was granted most-favored-nation trading status in 1975, extensively increasing its participation in Western capital markets from the mid-1970s. Romania has responded by allowing increased immigration from that time (though its human rights records is still one of the more dismal in Eastern Europe).

The expansion of anthropological research in Romania was thus coincidental to the developing tension in Romanian-Soviet relations and the warming of Romanian-Western ones. Romania in the 1970s was an attractive site for anthropological research because of its rapid industrial transformation, ecological and ethnic diversity, and archaic folk regions, among other reasons. However, its attractiveness was first possible due to the changing cold war context. In virtually every year of the 1970s at least two American anthropologists were among those utilizing part of the eighty "man months" quota provided to the International Research and Exchanges Board (IREX), and anthropologists were also grantees in Romania on various Fulbright exchanges. Simultaneously with the American research effort, there were also French, Swiss, and West German anthropologists active in the country.

RESEARCH IMPLICATIONS OF THE MULTIPLE COLD WAR

For social science in general and anthropology in particular the shifting nature of the cold war in Eastern Europe causes uneven research possibilities. American anthropological research on Eastern Europe began in the interwar period with Philip Mosely's Balkan research (cf. Byrnes, ed. 1976b) and continued in World War II with Columbia University's "Culture at a Distance" project (Benedict 1946, 1953; Halpern and Kideckel 1983). However, since the war, there has never been a time when each of the Eastern states has been simultaneously open for Western anthropological research. Instead, as illustrated by Romania, the multiple cold war cycle results in some states openly encouraging research while others actively prevent it.

A brief chronology clearly shows this. Tito's Yugoslavia, beginning with the break with COMECON and continuing through its ascendant role in the nonaligned movement, was the first Eastern state to allow a significant post-World War II anthropological presence, out of which an impressive array of diverse studies issued (Halpern 1958; Hammel 1968; Lockwood 1975; Simic 1972; Winner 1971). However, though East-West relations warmed in the early 1970s, Tito's worsening health, Yugoslavia's unique ethnic problems, and its problematic relation with the Soviets caused a restriction of anthropological access such that current research there is hedged around by a number of limitations.

As Yugoslav research diminished, Romania began allowing greater Western social scientific and anthropological research correlated with the campaign for most-favored-nation status, increased import of Western capital, and the Ceauşescu government's use of nationalism and anti-Sovietism as a device to further its own legitimacy. Romanian field research was in vogue through the 1970s and also resulted in a variety of diverse studies.[3]

As discussed above, Romanian research possibilities in the 1980s are restricted due to the economic crisis, deepening internal political problems, and its own ethnic restiveness and related problems with Hungary over Transylvania. Currently, then, in the midst of the Reagan-Gorbachev stand-off most American and Western anthropological fieldwork is concentrated in Poland and Hungary where diverse influences are at work. Poland continues to seek an opening to the West in the aftermath of martial law, while the general liberalization of Hungarian life also allows for an increased anthropological presence.

Aside from the resulting uncertainty about access to the field, cold war cycles have other implications for Eastern European anthropological research and the conceptualization of Eastern Europe. First, comparativism suffers as people study different areas at different times (cf. Halpern and Kideckel 1983:394). Second, cultural transformations are harder to gauge, since it is well nigh impossible to maintain steady access to particular nations over time. Third, the cold war cycle often paradoxically encourages naive or unrealistic views of Eastern European nations as Western anthropologists enter these countries on the upswing of the cycle, when conditions for research are optimal, instead of on the downswing when conditions are more difficult.[4] By themselves, each of the above implications is not fatal. Taken together, though, they constitute a serious deficiency in using Eastern European ethnographic description as a data base for developing theories of modern socialist life.

There are also implications for the conduct of fieldwork that derive from cold war conditions. First, as Western anthropologists in Eastern Europe come not just from other countries, but from the "other side," they are initially faced with depoliticizing their presence in each field setting. Second, the actual nature of field projects also makes anthropologists particularly vulnerable to cold war tensions. Unlike other social science studies, anthropological projects tend to be long-term, to be located outside capital cities, to deal with common people and current events, and to require fluency in local languages; all these make anthropologists more susceptible to the culture of suspicion.

Anthropologists are on the job twenty-four hours a day at the café, at home with host families, and in the fields with collective farmers and private peasants. They place a high value on all this information. Given the cold war notion that all knowledge is useful, the culture of suspicion can then play itself out with accusations regarding anthropological motives, activities, or intentions. In a culture of suspicion, anthropology and espionage are considered the same thing, since all knowledge about Eastern European countries (at particular times in their specific cold war cycles) is, in effect, a state secret.

THE COMMUNITY CONTEXT OF THE RESEARCH

With the general influence of the cold war on anthropological research outlined above, we turn now to a brief examination of its specific influence on our actual fieldwork. Romania's role in the multiple cold war manifested as we entered our respective villages. Since we were unlike British or French anthropologists returning to their former colonies as researchers or members of development projects, the Romanians were under no traditional obligation to accept us. However, our access to the field was made possible by the cold war dynamic of the mid-1970s. Once we received national permission for village residence, local officials were required to accept us, which they did with the usual mixture of caution, curiosity, and enthusiasm.

In the absence of established channels for placing American anthropologists into Romanian villages, there was a host of small problems to resolve. Before we officially settled into our communities there were inevitable delays, with resulting tensions and anxieties about losing valuable field time. These were increased by our ignorance of bureaucratic procedure and a range of simple cultural and linguistic misunderstandings. For example, one of us waited six weeks for permission to settle in one community only to find that he had been approved for the wrong village. The entire process had to be reinstituted.

As discussed above, like anthropologists working elsewhere, we experienced difficulties in clarifying our role in our communities. However, the cold war context particularly exaggerated the confusion about our presence. There were problems in building rapport specific to the circumstances of Americans doing research in socialist communities. In our local relationships we tried to treat all citizens equally in order to maintain good relations throughout the community. Our presence, however, often put villagers into ambiguous positions. Sometimes contact with us enhanced social prestige (e.g., our presence at a wedding); more often it was discomforting. Though most villagers talked openly with us about any variety of topics, the political implications of these conversations were never far from the surface.

Other citizens were obviously concerned about becoming too close to us lest they be politically compromised. As far as we know, nobody was sanctioned or threatened because of conversations with us, though many were asked to summarize their discussions with us, by security officials, after the fact. Thus, relations with some individuals always remained at the formal level. Given these deep-seated barriers growing from the culture of suspicion, we could only react by trying to define ourselves in our communities, specifying who we were, what we were trying to do, why we were trying to do it, and how we were going about it.

Suspicions about us and our activities often arose during public meetings. Meetings serve as forums for decision making, arenas of public controversy, and reflections of the social and political workings of the Romanian community. Permission for us to attend meetings was at the discretion of local officials, but due to legal restrictions some meetings were off-limits (e.g., meetings of Communist Party cells, normally open only to Party members). On some occasions our presence at a meeting caused anxiety for officials and/or participants. For example, a visiting county official was shocked to notice one of us taking notes during his speech, whereupon local officials were asked for a full explanation for our presence and we had to produce our authorizations.

At times we also felt the ambiguity, tension, and embarrassment of social interaction as keenly as members of the communities where we worked. For example, we were occasionally unduly suspicious about some informants and wrongly assumed them to be security officials. In other situations, and contrary to our expectations, some people were neither circumspect nor taciturn but expressed their feelings to us about state policies or their difficulties in the factory or on the collective farm, publicly, loudly, and often in response to an innocuous query on our part. Needless to say, our being used as public sounding boards provoked anxiety and uncertainty for our own position of social neutrality within the communities and made the field situation even more problematic.

There were also constant problems about how to interpret our field observations. On one hand, intense expressions about the frustrations of everyday Romanian life, as those described above, put a strain on our attempt to avoid politico-centrism and the verdict mentality about socialist society. Thus, we occasionally interpreted essentially short-term, personal problems like alcoholism or family conflict as illustrative of socialism per se, though at home we would never see them as proof of the decadence of capitalism.

On the other hand, as the fieldwork went well and we had the extensive cooperation of Romanian officials and collaboration with Romanian scholars, we also fell prey to the naiveté that a cold war thaw encourages. Though we were somewhat critical of certain regime policies, in our work we never really examined the basic premises on which the Romanian system was based and which, a few years later, would produce the extreme deprivation and repression the country now knows. We tended to avoid touchy political questions, such as legitimate Transylvanian Magyar grievances, and we also downplayed any disagreements we had with state policies and practices. On the whole, we rationalized an awful lot!

Our activities after formal on-site research ended also were influenced by the multiple cold war relationships in which we previously had been enmeshed. Thus, some of our post-fieldwork activities helped Romanian officials and scholars maintain trust in us but also embroiled us in the third cold war between Romania, the Soviet Union, and the rest of the bloc. A key event in this was the Romanian Research Group's polemic with a Hungarian-American anthropologist regarding the Transylvanian ethnic conflict (Romanian Research Group 1979; Sozan 1977, 1979). Here our response clearly overlapped with Romanian policy toward the province and its Magyar minority. This encouraged the Romanians to consider us as allied with their cold war position and dampened any negative repercussions about our other publications which were mildly critical of regime policy and practice.

Let us recapitulate aspects of our fieldwork in Romania and its aftermath in the 1970s. Basically, American anthropologists entered the country at a time of détente between the United States and Romania and tension/crisis between Romania and her allies. Anthropologists were seen by the Romanians as possible vehicles to help solidify relations with the West and as allies in their cold war with the Soviet Union and Hungary. This state of affairs was dependent on both internal stability in Romania itself and in its relations both with the United States and the Soviet Union.

We assumed that our relationship with Romania would persist, that once this trust had been established between us and our host nation and communities we could continue our work with only slight adjustments in consideration of developing international relations. We were wrong. We now know that this atmosphere of trust merely reflected a tactical alliance that developed under the specific cold war conditions of the 1970s and that once these conditions changed so too did the possibilities and nature of our research.

In summing up our 1970s fieldwork and postfield experiences, we could characterize them as relatively successful, if at times problematic. This success, as we have discussed, was partly due to the conjuncture between the three cold wars and the quality of United States-Soviet, United States-Romanian, and Soviet-Romanian relations at the time. This is not to say that other factors were inconsequential. Clearly, the atmosphere between American researchers and Romanian officials and scholars was relatively open and optimistic. We developed long-term rapport with villagers and scholars and officials, having returned to do fieldwork several times without any extreme repercussions on peoples' lives. In addition, we actively tried to allay the suspicion built up in the cold war atmosphere by providing as much information about ourselves and our research as possible. Our research and friendships flourished and we left the field with considerable optimism about both.

THE 1980s—CHANGING CLIMATES
AND FAIR-WEATHER FRIENDS

Several of the anthropologists who carried out Romanian fieldwork in the 1970s continued research into the 1980s. Now, though, they possessed greater knowledge of the society and language, more extensive connections, and a high degree of optimism about research possibilities. Yet, despite these more salutary conditions, research possibilities had changed drastically as an intensified culture of suspicion came to dominate relations between Western anthropologists and Romanian officials and some scholars. This renewed suspicion now causes long delays for foreign anthropologists in getting permission to consult archives or live in villages (if it arrives at all). Restrictions are also placed on their ability to conduct interviews or visit people without supervision, while greater numbers of locations and topics are off-limits.

Romanian officials and scholars meanwhile are more concerned that foreigners will abuse their privileged information and present hypercritical portraits of the country and that the foreign presence will be politically provocative and undermine national authority. Even officials and scholars who wish to go beyond the prevailing suspicion are constrained to do so (though they often apologize for the obstructions they erect). The extreme evolution of these patterns finally resulted in the recent expulsion of two anthropologists, one after incarceration and interrogation overnight in a provincial train station.

Scientific collaboration has also become difficult. Many Romanian colleagues are no longer available for consultation, and those who work with visiting scholars are regularly questioned by security forces and expected to provide lengthy written summaries of their conversations. Travel by Romanian scholars to foreign meetings, even those held in other socialist nations, has also been curtailed, as has the circulation of foreign publications. To give an idea of the restrictions on information flow, in the decade 1973–1983 the Romanian statistical annual shrank from 639 to 355 pages!

A number of factors relating directly to the evolving cold war explain this turnabout. Détente between Romania and the United States and the United States and the Soviet Union has evolved into tension, while tension between Romania and the Soviet Union has abated. Economically, Romania is more dependent on the Soviet Union and seems to have drawn closer to it in many policy positions (though the accident at Chernobyl may again change all that). Simultaneously, billion dollar debts to Western banks, severely restricted consumption, rationing, and increased labor demands have produced considerable social and political discontent in the country. In reaction, the regime is more repressive toward its own citizens and more xenophobic about foreign influences. United States-Romanian relations are increasingly strained due to these practices, United States criticism of human rights abuses, and Romanian bitterness about IMF repayment demands and related United States threats to withdraw most-favored-nation status.

The foreign researcher, now more nuisance than oddity, sits uneasily in the midst of this maelstrom. Anthropologists, with their strange requests, their desire to live among the people, and their informal methods, are perhaps the most bothersome of all. Thus, though Western anthropological research and publication about Romania remained fairly consistent, if slightly more critical, from the 1970s through the mid-1980s, the Romanian response to it was considerably intensified.

Two specific phenomena catalyzed this increasing Romanian disaffection. First, increased Romanian political and economic sensitivities heightened Romanian awareness of the critical nature of some of our publications and of the ways we presented our research results. Despite earlier articles of a similar tone which had appeared in Romanian journals and despite our soliciting Romanian criticisms of our work (e.g., Cobianu-Bacanu 1977; Costea 1976; Iordachel 1979), greater exception was now taken to these same articles. Moreover, great meaning was attributed by some Romanians to our presenting papers at conferences where Romanian cold war adversaries were prominent— in Budapest and Belgrade and before West European Romanian emigrés. Thus, we lost the label "friend" and became just another hostile force buffeting the Romanian state.

Second, our actual activities in Romania became subject to greater criticism and suspicion. As we learned the language and the ropes of Romanian society, met friends and colleagues outside controlled settings, and widened our social networks, our presence in Romania was less and less predictable. Similarly, our presence was viewed as a greater potential source of ideological pollution at the same time foreign contacts throughout the state were being severely restricted.

Once symbols of détente in the 1970s, anthropologists in Romania in the 1980s have become trapped "in the cold." For this situation to change significantly we must possibly await United States-Soviet rapprochement combined with some chink in the Romanian-Soviet dyadic relation (again, Chernobyl comes to mind). More critically, we hope for the arrest of Romania's serious social, political, and economic decay for our own research interests but especially for the well-being of all the peoples in the Romanian state and for the advance of Romanian scholarship.

CONCLUSIONS

Fieldwork in Eastern Europe is influenced by factors more complicated than just the East-West cold war. It is influenced by a variety of conflicts and their conjunctures over time which, depending on the way individual Eastern European nations are involved in them, either facilitate or neutralize anthropological research. These conditions transcend the particular problems of individual fieldworkers in Eastern Europe and demand the realization that the specific problems of the field have deep-seated structural causes based in international political economy.

Though understanding cold war effects on anthropological research is important, we also feel our discussion contributes to helping define the role anthropologists might play in the cold war. First, anthropology is uniquely suited to work toward diminishing cold war tensions precisely due to its nature that subjects it to such tensions in the first place. Since anthropological research produces in-depth understanding of Eastern European life, it is a natural counter to the rampant politico-centrism of West and East, locked in their multiple cold wars. The anthropologist's conduct and research activities in Eastern Europe and subsequent publication and dissemination of information about Eastern Europe must consciously try to bridge the gap in understanding and knowledge embodied in those same politico-centric views.

This is not to say that, in seeking to diminish cold war-based misconceptions, anthropologists should purposefully refrain from honestly examining socialist society "as it actually exists" (Bahro 1978) and developing informed critiques about it. We do not hold with the position that any criticism of socialist society only provides ammunition for the forces of reaction. Rather, in seeking a more just social order, we recognize the need to expose contradictions as the first step in their ultimate elimination. Thus, in-depth anthropological research also has the responsibility to enlighten about the concrete realities of East European life—its achievements, its problems, and most important, the relations between the two.

Our goal for anthropology—to bridge cold war-inspired gaps in understanding as well as to expose and criticize the contradictions of Eastern European life—is also self-serving. As this chapter clearly indicates, anthropological research especially suffers "in the cold," although it thrives wondrously under conditions of détente. Simply for this reason, anything we might do to identify sources of tension and injustice and reduce them should be a prime objective of our activities.

NOTES

1. For an extended discussion of the nature of "mainstream" views of Eastern European socialism by Western/American social scientists, see Cole 1985.

2. Most of the authors' research was part of a group project whose other members were: Sam Beck (marginal peasant communities, regional political economy); John W. Cole (village socioeconomic organization, domestic economy); Marilyn McArthur (ethnicity); and Steven Randall (domestic economy, mountain communities). For a more detailed discussion of this project, see Cole 1976 and Kideckel and Sampson 1984.

3. Other American anthropologists who carried out field research in Romania at the time include: Theresa Adams (prehistoric archaeology); Andreas Argyres (peasant economics); Joanne Bock (popular art); Regina Coussens (ritual and general expressive behavior); Diane Freedman (dance); Gail Kligman (ritual and symbolism); Joel Marrant (history and folk tradition); Erica McClure (sociolinguistics); Mitchell Ratner (education); Zdenek Salzmann (Czech-speaking minority); and Katherine Verdery (regional political economy).

4. Chris Hann (1987) quite accurately terms this skewed perspective "détente relativism."

CONCLUSION
Paul R. Turner

The focus in anthropology has traditionally been on tribes living in their own small, relatively isolated, and homogeneous worlds. Our main task has been to describe the specifics of a given culture without relating these to cultural universals. We have earned a reputation for studying the strange customs of powerless people and the media, at times, take delight in portraying us in the same way: powerless people with strange customs. Even our colleagues in other disciplines all too often find us to be curiosities and wonder what relevance we have for the world at the end of the twentieth century (Johnston 1985:15).

Usually our energies have been directed to descriptive rather than comparative work even though we pay lip service to the importance of the comparative method for our discipline. Our descriptive emphasis has little to offer in the way of a characterization of human nature because it stresses what is different about a group of people, without mentioning what that group shares with all other groups of people.

Perhaps we have assumed that the differences between cultures are more important than the similarities without approaching the issue with an open mind. Or, it may have been to our own self-serving interests to be "peddlers of the strange," "merchants of astonishment" (Geertz 1984:275), while overlooking what all people everywhere share as part of their common human nature.

Our emphasis on differences between cultures may have added to the tensions of the cold war by contributing to the image that some nuclear planners in the United States have toward Soviet leaders. Our officials talk as if these leaders may be prepared to do the unthinkable: sacrifice their entire population in a nuclear war. This extreme position, of regarding the Soviets as alien, hostile, derives from a sense of "otherness" (Coughlin 1985:7) that anthropologists have done little to change.

Perhaps the greatest differences are not between cultures, especially complex ones, but within them (Cousins 1981:41), even though most anthropologists believe otherwise. We probably do not have the data to deal with this issue because the kind of societies we usually study do not have the intracultural diversity of the Soviet Union and the United States. Actually, the leaders of each of these countries sound a great deal alike when talking about tactical nuclear weapons. It is within these countries that the differences are found in the hawk-dove struggles to influence nuclear weapons policy (Feld 1979:142).

We, the editors of this volume, suggest that cultural differences not be overemphasized when dealing with the cold war, be they intercultural differences between tribes and nations, or intracultural differences within modern societies.

The cold war has a tendency to strip away the veneer of civilization from the superpowers, leaving them to react on the level of tribes or "primitive" nations. Both countries put their own narrow interests ahead of the common good of the world. Each country asks far more than it is prepared to give and will accept no limitations on its right to make unilateral decisions (Cousins 1981:54), even if this involves blowing up the world. Neither country exhibits the characteristics of what is expected from "civilized" nations:

> [T]he political, philosophical and spiritual awareness of man as a member of a world species with world needs and with the capacity and desire to create world institutions to meet those needs (Cousins 1981:67).

Since the reaction between the Soviet Union and the United States is on the level of tribal warriors in the cold war (Cousins 1981:88), the insights anthropologists have gained from tribal conflicts should relate to conflicts on the international level. The first part of our book, "Tribal Mentality and the Cold War," has been organized around this theme.

The second reason why there are relatively few anthropologists contributing to a solution to the nuclear confrontation problem is because of our long-standing commitment to cultural relativism. This commitment is related to our focus on the tribes and our opposition to racism and ethnocentrism. Both racists and ethnocentrists used their own race or culture as the standard in assessing the differences in other races or cultures. Our reaction to both groups was to try and describe the differences in the other culture without making value judgments.

We were never completely successful in our attempts at value-free social science, but our nonjudgmental stance helped us to gain the acceptance we needed, from the people we studied, for our initial fieldwork.

Serious problems, however, arise when cultural relativism becomes more than a stance for initial fieldwork. Sooner or later, in one way or another, we have to deal with the issue of whether what these people do is approved by us or not. If we accept cultural relativism as our value position, then what they do is right and we as outsiders have no basis for criticizing what they, or any other groups, do. But each year the members of the American Anthropological Association pass resolutions that are critical of some group's practices, usually those of governments of the noncommunist world. In 1985 we voted on a Proposed Resolution Opposing Preparations for Nuclear War. One of the reasons given for such a resolution was the special responsibility anthropologists have for "ensuring the survival of humanity, which cuts across national boundaries" (*Anthropology Newsletter* 1985:34). This appeal to a universal value was not questioned by anthropologists supposedly committed to cultural relativism. Perhaps when the survival of humanity is at stake, anthropologists are no longer cultural relativists.

For the same reason, those of us who write about the cold war are not constrained by cultural relativism. The second part of our book, "Nuclear War and the Cold War," has a decided universalistic emphasis with one of our contributors, Laura Nader, applying the concept of institutionalized insanity to the power structures of nuclear nations.

The third part of our book, "Anthropological Research and the Cold War," describes some of the complicating factors that anthropologists experience in doing research on the cold war. In spite of these difficulties, our contributing authors are in agreement about the significant role that anthropology could have in preventing a nuclear conflagration.

We, the editors, are also convinced that anthropology could have an important part in ending the cold war. Anthropology is the only discipline with a world-wide data base to draw from in dealing with topics that are crucial to understanding the cold war: the causes of war, ethnocentrism, economic irrationality, human nature, and conflict resolution, to name a few.

The nuclear strategies of the two superpowers appear to be based on the notion of deterrence, believing that "war is an act of aggrandizement, and that nothing can prevent it but fear of the consequences" (Powers 1982:125). Actually we do not know the core causes of war because the topic has never been studied exhaustively from a cross-cultural perspective. What we know from the data we have suggests that war is more complicated than the nuclear strategies of the two superpowers would indicate. If a nuclear conflagration is to be avoided, then we need to identify the root causes of war.

Anthropologists have dealt with the problem of ethnocentrism to a greater extent than any other group of social scientists. We have had some success in educating our students to respect the cultures of tribal people. But we have had almost no success in tempering the crusading nationalism that characterizes the foreign policy of our country and that of the Soviet Union, both expressions of ethnocentrism. The combination of highly sophisticated scientific communities engaged in nuclear weaponry research in each country, with naive attempts on the parts of their governments to save the world from each other's political system, is a topic worthy of anthropological research.

Anthropologists have earned a reputation for pointing out instances of economic irrationality in tribal societies to other social scientists, particularly economists. The cold war offers yet another instance of economic irrationality, but on a massive scale. The two superpowers have plans to build nuclear weapons and defenses against such weapons that will bankrupt them. The war industry in both countries has been described as a form of economic cancer (Boulding 1982:xiv) that recent history suggests is progressive and incurable. Our capitalistic system, supposedly based on economic pragmatism, is perpetually preparing for war on a declining industrial base (Winpisinger 1982:108), a form of economic irrationality. Because of the arms race the Soviet Union's socialistic system, theoretically based on the primacy of the economy, is guaranteeing that it will continue to be a second-rate power, economically speaking, with little industrial significance in terms of products to sell in the world market—another form of economic irrationality.

People in tribal groups and people in nations act a great deal alike because they share a common human nature, influenced by similar biological, social, and cultural features (Spiro 1978:355). This common human nature that we share with the Russians can give us reason to be optimistic for they are not fiends, the focus of evil in the world, hostile, alien, the "other." They are parents and grandparents like we are, committed to their children and grandchildren having a future. They, like we, live lives controlled by universal values, the contents of which need to be filled in by anthropologists doing cross-cultural research.

Anthropologists might also be able to make a contribution to conflict resolution on the international level. We have lived in tribes that managed to handle conflicts, either between its members or with its neighbors, that resulted in the parties being reconciled. Anthropologists, more than anyone else, know about small communities and what binds them together with ties that go beyond the self-centered interests of individuals. If such a sense of community could be extended to the world as a whole, war as an option for societies might be eliminated.

We, the editors, encourage our fellow anthropologists to do more to end the cold war than pass resolutions at our annual meetings. The resolutions we vote on are probably ignored by those for whom they are intended and as such are ineffective. But these resolutions are important for what they imply about the universal values we hold, in spite of our relativistic posturing. If these implicitly held values were made explicit, we would have a clearer idea of who we are and what we have to offer in ending the cold war. In the process, we could exchange our own tribal mentality for one having global significance.

CONTRIBUTORS

GEORGE J. ARMELAGOS: Professor of Anthropology, University of Massachusetts, Amherst

WILLIAM O. BEEMAN: Associate Professor of Anthropology, Brown University

ALBERT BERGESEN: Professor of Sociology, University of Arizona

ROBERT M. BOWMAN: President, Institute for Space and Security Studies, Washington D.C.

DONNA BRASSET: Ph.D. Candidate in Anthropology, University of California, Berkeley

R. BRIAN FERGUSON: Assistant Professor of Anthropology, Rutgers University

WALTER GOLDSCHMIDT: Professor Emeritus of Anthropology, University of California, Los Angeles

DAVID A. KIDECKEL: Associate Professor of Anthropology, Central Connecticut State University

LAURA NADER: Professor of Anthropology, University of California, Berkeley

KEITH F. OTTERBEIN: Professor of Anthropology, State University of New York, Buffalo

DAVID PITT: Senior Research Fellow, Geneva International Peace Research Institute

STEVEN L. SAMPSON: Research Fellow, Institute of Ethnology and Anthropology, University of Copenhagen

ELIZABETH SCHUELER: Program Assistant, International Institute for Environment and Development, Washington, D.C.

PAUL R. TURNER: Professor of Anthropology, University of Arizona

BIBLIOGRAPHY

Abel, Theodore. 1941. The Element of Decision in the Pattern of War. *American Sociological Review* 6 (6):853–59.

Aberle, David F. 1966. Religio-Magical Phenomena and Power, Prediction, and Control. *Southwestern Journal of Anthropology* 22:221–30.

Abrahamson, Bengt. 1972. *Military Professionalization and Political Powers.* Beverly Hills: Sage.

Abrams, H. L. 1984. Medical Resources After a Nuclear War. *JAMA* 252:653–58.

Abrams, H. L., and W. E. Von Kaenel. 1981. Medical Problems of Survivors of Nuclear War. *New England Journal of Medicine* 305:1226–1332.

Adams, Richard N. 1975. *Energy and Structure: A Theory of Social Power.* Austin: University of Texas Press.

Alter, Jonathan, Pamela Abramson, and Vincent Coppola. 1984. Tickets to the Stars. *Newsweek.* 104:49. July 9.

Anthropologists for Human Survival. (various dates). Newsletter. c/o Eva Friedlander, 436 West 20th St., New York, N. Y.10011.

Anthropology Newsletter. 1985. Members Vote in October. 26: 1.

Aspin, Les. 1978. What are the Russians up to? *International Security* 3 (1): 30–54.

Bahro, Rudolf. 1978. *The Alternative in Eastern Europe.* New York: NLB.

Bailey, F .G. 1968. Parapolitical Systems. In *Local Level Politics.* Marc J. Swarts, ed., 281–94, Chicago: Aldine.

Baldwin, Gordon C. 1965. *The Warrior Apaches.* Tucson, Ariz.: Dale Stuart King.

Ball, Desmond. 1985. Nuclear War at Sea. Strategic and Defense Studies Centre. The Australian National University. This paper was prepared for a Conference held by the Institute on Global Conflict and Cooperation at the University of California, Los Angeles on April 26.

Baritz, Loren. 1985. *Backfire.* New York: Morrow.

Barnaby, F., and J. Rotblat. 1982. The Effects of Nuclear Weapons. *Ambio* 11:84–93.

Barnet, Richard J. 1972. *Roots of War*. Harmondsworth, Eng.: Penguin.

Barnett, Homer G. 1959. Status Symbols in Power Roles in New Guinea. *American Anthropologist* 61 (6):1013–19.

Batchelor, John. 1892. *The Ainu of Japan*. London: Religious Tract Society.

———1927. *Ainu Life and Lore*. Tokyo: Kyobunkwan.

Bateson, Catherine. 1986. Nuclear Winter: The Anthropology of Human Survival. Los Alamos National Laboratory Document LA–UR–86–370:31–37.

Becker, Ernest. 1971. *The Lost Science of Man*. New York: George Braziller.

Beeman, William O. 1981. How Not to Negotiate: Crossed Signals on the Hostages. *The Nation* 232 (20):42–44.

———. 1982. *Culture, Performance, and Communication in Iran*. Tokyo: ILCAA.

———. 1983a. Images of the Great Satan: Symbolic conceptions of the United States in the Iranian Revolution. In *Religion and Politics in Iran*. Nikki Keddie, ed. New Haven: Yale University Press.

———. 1983b. Patterns of Religion and Development in Iran from the Qajar Period to the Revolution of 1978–1979. In *Religion and Economic Development*. James Finn, ed. New Brunswick, N. J.: Transaction.

———. 1983c. Conflict and Belief in American Foreign Policy. Paper prepared for Pre-Congress Symposium on Peace and War. XI ICAES. Harrison Hot Springs and Vancouver, B.C. August 17–19.

———. 1986a. Iran's Religious Regime—What makes it Tick? Will It Ever Run Down? *Annals of the American Academy of Political and Social Science.* 483:73–83.

———. 1986b. Conflict and Belief in American Foreign Policy. In *War and Peace: Cultural Perspectives*. Robert Rubinstein and Mary LeCron, eds. New Brunswick, N.J.: Transaction.

———. 1986c. Anthropology and the Myths of American Foreign Policy. In *Anthropology and Public Policy: A Dialogue*. Walter Goldschmidt, ed. Special Publication No. 21, American Anthropological Association.

Beer, Francis A. 1979. World Order and World Futures. *Journal of Conflict Resolution* 23 (1): 174–92.

———. 1981. *Peace Against War*. San Francisco: W. H. Freeman.

Benedict, Ruth. 1946. *Romanian Culture and Behavior*. New York: Institute of Inter-Cultural Studies.

———. 1953. History as it Appears to Romanians. In *The Study of Culture at a Distance*. M. Mead and R. Metraux, eds. 405–15. Chicago: University of Chicago Press.

Bennett Ross, Jane. 1980. Ecology and the Problem of Tribe: A Critic of the Hobbesian Model of Preindustrial Warfare. In *Beyond the Myths of Culture: Essays in Cultural Materialism*. E. Ross, ed. 33–60. New York: Academic Press.

Benson, John. 1982. The Polls: U.S. Military Intervention. *Public Opinion Quarterly* 46: 592–98.

Berdichewsky, Bernardo. 1975. *The Araucanian Indian in Chile*. Copenhagen: International Work Group for Indigenous Affairs.

Bergesen, Albert. 1976. The Origins of the Expansion and Contraction of Center-Periphery Relations within the World-System. Paper presented at the American Academy of Arts and Sciences World-System Conference, Stanford University, April 3.

————.1980 Cycles of Formal Colonial Rule. In *Processes of the World-System.* T.K. Hopkins and I. Wallerstein, eds. 119–26. Beverly Hills: Sage.

————. 1981a. Long Economic Cycles and the Size of Industrial Enterprise. In *Dynamics of World Development.* R. Rubinson, ed. 179–89. Beverly Hills: Sage.

————. 1981b. A Research Design for Studying Long Cycles of the World-System. Unpublished manuscript, Department of Sociology, University of Arizona.

————. 1981c. The Effect of Cyclical Downturns in the World Economy upon the Organization of Industrial Enterprise: A Comparison of Britain in the 1880s and the United States in the 1980s. Paper presented at the Fifth Annual Political Economy of the World-System Conference, Madison, Wis. May 14–16.

Bergesen, Albert, and R. Schoenberg. 1980. Long Waves of Colonial Expansion and Contraction, 1415–1969. In *Studies of the Modern World-System.* A. Bergesen, ed. 231–77. New York: Academic Press.

Berlin, Isaiah. 1979. *Russian Thinkers.* Harmondsworth, Eng.: Penguin.

Bertrand, M. 1986. *Refaire L'ONU!* Genève: Éditions Zoe.

Best, Elsdon. 1924. *The Maori As He Was.* Wellington: Dominion Museum.

Binns, C. A. P. 1979. The Changing of Power. *Man* 14:585–607.

Bishops and the Bomb. 1982. *Time.* November 29.

Bogoras, W. 1904–9. *The Chuckchee.* Memoir of the American Museum of Natural History. vol. 11.

Boulding, Kenneth. 1982. Introduction. In *The Political Economy of Arms Reduction.* Lloyd J. Dumas, ed. Boulder, Colo.: Westview Press.

Boyd, A. 1962. *United Nations.* Harmondsworth, Eng.: Penguin.

Bradford, C.I. 1980. The Newly Industrializing Countries in Global Perspective. *New International Realities* 5:6–15.

Brink, J.H. Van Den. 1974. *The Haida Indians.* Leiden: Brill.

Buck, Peter Henry. 1949. *The Coming of the Maori.* Wellington: Maori Purposes Fund Board, distributed by Whitcombe and Tombs.

Bundy, McGeorge, George Kennan, Robert McNamara, and Gerald Smith. 1984. The President's Choice: Star Wars or Arms Control. *Foreign Affairs* 63 (2): 264–78.

Bunzel, Ruth. 1963. Report on Regional Conferences on Anthropology and World Affairs. Released by Wenner-Gren Foundation for Anthropological Research, Feb. 13.

Bunzel, Ruth, and Anne Parsons. 1964. Report on Regional Conferences. *Current Anthropology* 5 (5):430, 437–40. December.

Byrnes, Robert F. 1976a. *Soviet-American Academic Exchanges, 1958–75.* Bloomington, Ind.: Indiana University Press.

————, ed. 1976b. *Communal Families in the Balkans: The Zadruga.* Essays by Philip E. Mosely and Essays in His Honor. Notre Dame, Ind: University of Notre Dame Press.

Calder, Nigel. 1981. *Nuclear Nightmares.* New York: Vintage.

Carter, Ashton B., John D. Steinbruner, and Charles A. Zraket, eds. 1987. *Managing Nuclear Operations.* Washington, D.C.: Brookings Institute.

Center for Defense Information. 1984. Soviet Compliance with SALT I. Washington, D.C.

Chagnon, Napoleon A. 1977. *Yanomamo: The Fierce People.* 2nd ed. New York: Holt, Rinehart & Winston.

Chalfont, Alun. 1985. *Star Wars: Suicide or Survival?* London: Weidenfeld & Nicolson.

Chandler, A. D. 1980. The Growth of the Transnational Industrial Firm in the United States and the United Kingdom: A Comparative Analysis. *Economic History Review* 33:396–410.

Charles, Eunice A. 1977. *Precolonial Senegal: The Jolof Kingdom 1800 to 1890.* Boston: African Studies Center, Boston University.

Chase-Dunn, C. 1978. Core-Periphery Relations: The Effects of Core Competition. In *Social Change in the Capitalist World Economy.* B. H. Kaplan, ed. 159–76. Beverly Hills: Sage.

———. 1980. The Development of Core Capitalism in the Antebellum United States: Tariff Politics and Class Struggle in an Upwardly Mobile Semiperiphery. In *Studies of the Modern World-System.* A. Bergesen, ed. 189–230. New York: Academic Press.

Chomsky, Noam. 1982. *Towards a New Cold War: Essays on the Current Crisis and How We Got There.* New York: Pantheon.

Cimbala, Stephen 1986. Flexible Targeting, Escalation Control, and War in Europe. *Armed Forces and Society* 12 (3): 383–400.

Clark, Ramsey. 1970. *Crime in America: Observations on its Nature, Causes, Prevention, and Control.* New York: Simon & Schuster.

Clarke, Magnus. 1985. Nuclear Deterrence and the Strategy Defense Initiative. *Arms Control* 6 (2): 160–82.

Cobianu-Bacanu, Maria. 1977. A Romanian-American Dialogue. *Dialectical Anthropology* 2: 301–8.

Codere, H. 1950. *Fighting with Property.* New York: Augustin.

Coggle, J. E., and P. J. Lindop. 1982. Medical Consequences of Radiation Following a Global Nuclear War. *Ambio* 11:106–13.

Cole, John W. 1976. Fieldwork in Romania: An Introduction. *Dialectical Anthropology* 1: 239–50.

———. 1977. Anthropology Comes Part-Way Home: Community Studies in Europe. In *Annual Review of Anthropology.* vol. 7. B. Siegle, ed. 349–78. Palo Alto, Calif.: Annual Review.

———. 1985. Problems of Socialism in Eastern Europe. *Dialectical Anthropology* 9:233–56.

Commission on the Study of Peace. (various dates.) Newsletter. c/o Dr. Robert Rubinstein, Department of Anthropology, Northwestern University, Evanston, Ill. 60201.

Coser, Lewis 1956. *The Functions of Social Conflict.* New York: Free Press.

Costea, Stefan. 1976. Commentary. *Caiete de Studii, Referate, si Dezbateri.* vol 2. University of Bucharest Sociology Research Center. 36–38.

Coughlin, Ellen K. 1985. Sociologists, Psychologists Urge Study of Questions Concerning Nuclear War. *The Chronicle of Higher Education* 31: 7.

Cousins, Norman. 1981. *Human Options.* New York: Berkley.

Crozier, Michel, Samuel Huntington, and Joji Watanuki. 1975. *The Crisis of Demography: Report on the Governability of Democracies to the Trilateral Commission.* New York: New York University Press.

Davis, James, A., Tom. W. Smith, and C. Bruce Stephenson. 1981. *General Social Survey Cumulative File, 1972–1980.* Principal Investigator, James A. Davis. Ann Arbor, Mich.: Inter-University Consortium for Political and Social Research.

Dempsey, James. 1955. *Mission on the Nile.* London: Burnes & Oates.

Deng Xiaoping (Interview.) 1979. *Time.* February 5.

Department for Disarmament Affairs. 1984. *The United Nations Disarmament Yearbook.* vol. 8. New York: United Nations Publications.

Diamond, Stanley, et al. 1984. Anthropologists Speak Out on Nuclear Disarmament. *Anthropology Newsletter.* May.

Diehl, Jackson. 1986. Chernobyl's Other Losers. *Washington Post,* June 8.

Dirks, Robert. 1986. Nuclear Winter: The Anthropology of Human Survival. Los Alamos National Laboratory Document LA–UR–86–370:11–21.

Dixon, Norman. 1976. *On the Psychology of Military Incompetence.* New York: Basic Books.

Dobrizhoffer, Martin. 1822. *An Account of the Abipones, an Equestrian People of Paraguay.* 3v. London: J. Murray.

Doran, C. F., and W. Parsons. 1980. War and the Cycle of Relative Power. *American Political Science Review* 74: 947–65.

Draper, Theodore. 1983. On Nuclear War: An Exchange with the Secretary of Defense. *The New York Review of Books* 30 (13): 27–33.

Dunn, S., and E. Dunn. 1967. *The Peasants of Central Russia.* New York: Holt, Rinehart & Winston.

Durham, William 1979. *Scarcity and Survival in Central America: Ecological Origins of the Soccer War.* Stanford: Stanford University Press.

Durkheim, Emile, and Marcel Mauss. 1963. *Primitive Classification.* Rodney Needham, trans. Chicago: University of Chicago Press.

Eberwein, Wolf-Dieter. 1981. The Quantitative Study of International Conflict: Quantity and Quality? An Assessment of Empirical Research. *Journal of Peace Research* 18 (1):19–38.

Eggan, F. 1937. The Cheyenne and Arapaho Kinship System. In *Social Anthropology of North American Tribes.* F. Eggan, ed. 33–95. Chicago: University of Chicago Press.

Ehrlich, Anne. 1984. Nuclear Winter: A Forecast of the Climatic and Biological Effects of Nuclear War. *Bulletin of the Atomic Scientists* 40:25–147.

Ehrlich, Paul. 1984. When Light is Put Away: Ecological Effects of Nuclear War. In *The Counterfeit Ark.* J. Leaning and L. Keys, eds. 247–71. Cambridge, Mass.: Ballinger.

Ehrlich, Paul, et al. 1983. Long-Term Biological Consequences of Nuclear War. *Science* 222:1293–1300.

Eisenhower, Dwight D. 1961. Presidential Farewell Address.

Ellsberg, Daniel. 1981. Introduction: Call to Mutiny. In *Protest and Survive.* E.P. Thompson and D. Smith, eds. New York: Monthly Review Press.

Ember, Carol R., and Melvin Ember. 1984. Warfare and Aggression: Cross-Cultural Results. Paper presented at 83rd annual meeting of the American Anthropological Association. Denver, Colo. November 16.

Engelberg, Stephen. 1986. C.I.A. Aide Says Agency Will Let Scholars Acknowledge Backing. *New York Times* February 14.

English, Robert. 1984. Eastern Europe's Doves. *Foreign Policy* 56: 44–60.

Fabbro, David. 1980. Peaceful Societies. In *The War System: An Interdisciplinary Approach.* Richard Falk and Samuel Kim, eds. 180–203. Boulder, Colo.: Westview Press.

Falk, Richard. 1980. The Menace of the New Cycle of Interventionary Diplomacy. *Journal of Peace Research* 18: 201–05.

Falk, Richard, and Samuel Kim, eds. 1980. *The War System: An Interdisciplinary Approach.* Boulder, Colo.: Westview Press.

Fallers, Lloyd. 1974. *The Social Anthropology of the Nation State.* Chicago: Aldine.

Fallows, James. 1973. *Victims of Groupthink.* Boston: Houghton Mifflin.

———. 1981. National Defense. New York: Vintage.

————. 1984. What Good Is Arms Control? *The Atlantic* 254 (6): 136, 138–40. December.

Faron, L.C. 1961. Mapuche Social Structure. *Illinois Studies in Anthropology.* No. 1. Urbana, Ill.: Univ. of Illinois Press.

————.1968. *The Mapuche Indians of Chile.* New York: Holt, Rinehart & Winston.

Federation of American Scientists. 1984. Arms Control and the Compliance Mafia. Federation of American Scientists Public Interest Report. Washington, D.C.

Feld, Bernard. 1979. *A Voice Crying in the Wilderness.* Oxford: Pergamon.

Ferguson, R. Brian, ed. 1984a. *Warfare, Culture and Environment.* Orlando. Fla.: Academic Press.

————. 1984b. A Reexamination of the Causes of Northwest Coast Warfare. In *Warfare, Culture, and Environment.* R. B. Ferguson, ed. 267–328. Orlando, Fla.: Academic Press.

————. 1985. Class Transformations in Puerto Rico. PhD. diss. Department of Anthropology, Columbia University.

————. 1986. Explaining War. Paper prepared for the Conference on the Anthropology of War, sponsored by the Harry Frank Guggenheim Foundation, at the School of American Research, Sante Fe, N.M., March 24–28.

Ferguson, Thomas, and Joel Rogers. 1986. *Right Turn: The Decline of the Democrats and the Future of American Politics.* New York: Hill & Wang.

Fischer, Michael M. J. 1980. *Iran: From Religious Dispute to Revolution.* Cambridge, Mass.: Harvard University Press.

FitzGerald, Frances. 1979. *America Revised.* Boston: Little, Brown.

Ford, Daniel. 1985. *The Button: The Pentagon's Strategic Command and Control System.* New York: Simon & Schuster.

Foster, G. 1969. *Applied Anthropology.* Boston: Little, Brown.

Foster, Mary, and Robert Rubinstein, eds. 1986. *Peace and War: Cross-Cultural Perspectives.* New Brunswick, N.J.: Transaction.

Frank, A. G. 1978. *World Accumulation, 1492–1789.* New York: Monthly Review.

————.1979. Unequal Accumulation: Intermediate, Semiperipheral, and Sub-Imperialist Economies. *Review* 2: 281–350.

Freilich, Morris, ed. 1970. *Marginal Natives: Anthropologists at Work.* New York: Harper & Row.

Fulbright, J. William. 1970. *The Pentagon Propaganda Machine.* New York: Liveright.

Galtung, J. 1980. A Structural Theory of Imperialism. In *The War System: an Interdisciplinary Approach.* Richard Falk and Samuel Kim, eds. 402–55. Boulder, Colo.: Westview Press.

————. 1984. *There are Alternatives.* Nottingham, Eng.: Spokesman.

Gamble, David P. 1957. *The Wolof of Senegambia.* London: International African Institute.

Gantzel, Klaus J. 1981. Another Approach to a Theory on the Causes of International War. *Journal of Peace Research* 18(1):39–55.

Gard, Robert G., Jr. 1973. The Military and American Society. In *National Security and American Society.* Frank N. Trager and Philip S. Kronenberg, eds. 570–78. The National Security Education Program. Lawrence, Kan.: The University Press of Kansas.

Gatschet, Albert Samuel. 1890. The Klamath Indians of Southwestern Oregon. Washington D.C.: U.S. Geographical and Geological Survey of the Rocky Mountain Region, Dept. of the Interior.

Geertz, Clifford. 1964. *Agricultural Involution*. Los Angeles: University of California Press.

————. 1984. Distinguished Lecture: Anti Anti-Relativism. *American Anthropologist* 87: 263–78.

Geiger, H. J. 1984. *Dulce et Decorum Est:* Medical and Public Health Problems of Crisis Relocation. In *The Counterfeit Ark.* J. Leaning and L. Keys, eds. 159–82. Cambridge, Mass.: Ballinger.

Geilhufe, Nancy. 1979. Anthropology and Policy Analysis. *Current Anthropology* 20 (3):577–79.

Givens, R. Dale, and Martin Nettleship, eds. 1976. *Discussions on War and Human Aggression*. The Hague: Mouton.

Gluckman, M. 1960. *Custom and Conflict in Africa*. Oxford: Blackwell.

Goldschmidt, Walter. 1976. *The Culture and Behavior of the Sebei*. Berkeley and Los Angeles: University of California Press.

Goldschmidt, Walter, and R. Cohen. 1985. Peace and Peacemaking in Anthropological Perspective. Newsletter, Commission on the Study of Peace. *International Union of Anthropological and Ethnological Sciences* 3 (3):12, 13.

Gorer, G., and J. Rickman. 1962. *The People of Great Russia*. New York: Norton.

Graham, Daniel O. 1982. *High Frontier, A New National Strategy*. Washington, D.C.: Heritage Foundation.

Gray, Colin, and Keith Payne. 1980. Victory is Possible. *Foreign Policy* 39:15–27.

Grinnell, George Bird. 1889. *Pawnee Hero Stories and Folk-Tales*. New York: Forest & Stream.

————. 1915. *The Fighting Cheyennes*. New York: Scribner's.

————. 1923. *The Cheyenne Indians*. 2 vol. New Haven: Yale University Press.

————. 1962. *The Cheyenne Indians, Their History and Ways of Life*. New York: Cooper Square Publishers.

Gwertzman, Bernard. 1984. Gromyko Puts Deeds by U. S. First. *The* [Tucson] *Arizona Daily Star*. September 28.

Hackett, J. 1978. *The Third World War*. New York: Macmillan.

Halloran, Richard. 1986. Pentagon: Guardians of the Screen Image. *New York Times*. August 18.

Halpern, Joel M. 1958. *A Serbian Village*. New York: Columbia University Press.

Halpern, Joel M., and David A. Kideckel. 1983. Anthropology of Eastern Europe. In *Annual Review of Anthropology*. vol. 12. B. Seigel, ed. 377–402. Palo Alto, Calif.: Annual Reviews.

Hammel, Eugene A. 1968. *Alternative Social Structures and Ritual Relations in the Balkans*. Englewood Cliffs, N.J.: Prentice-Hall.

Hann, C.M. 1987. The Politics of Anthropology in Socialist Eastern Europe. In *Anthropology at Home*. Anthony Jackson, ed. 139–53. London: Tavistock.

Harner, Michael J. 1962. Jivaro Souls. *American Anthropologist* 64 (2): 258–72.

Harwell, Christine C. 1985. Experiences and Extrapolations from Hiroshima and Nagasaki. In *Environmental Consequences of a Nuclear War*. vol. 2. M.A. Harwell and T. C. Hutchinson, eds. New York: John Wiley.

Harwell, M. A. 1984. *Nuclear Winter*. New York: Springer-Verlag.

Henry, Jules. 1963. *Culture Against Man*. New York: Random House.

Hersh, Seymour. 1987. Target Qaddafi. *New York Times Magazine*. February 22.

Herskovits, Melville J. 1967. *Dahomey, An Ancient West African Kingdom*. 2 vol. Evanston: Northwestern University Press. (first published 1938.)

Herspring, Dale, and Ivan Volgyes. 1980. Political Reliability in the Eastern European Warsaw Pact Armies. *Armed Forces and Society* 6(2):270–96.

Hjort, Howard. 1984. The Good Earth: Agricultural Potential after a Nuclear War. In *The Counterfeit Ark*. J. Leaning and L. Keys, eds. 231–46. Cambridge, Mass.: Ballinger.

Hoebel, E.A. 1960. *The Cheyenne*. New York: Holt.

Hofer, Tamas. 1968. Anthropologists and Native Ethnographers at Work in Central European Villages: Comparative Notes on the Professional Personality of Two Disciplines. *Current Anthropology* 9: 311–15.

Holloway, David. 1981. War, Militarism, and the Soviet State. In *Protest and Survive*. E. P. Thompson and D. Smith, eds. 70–107. New York: Monthly Review Press.

Holsti, Ole. 1980. Crisis, Stress, and Decision Making. In *The War System: An Interdisciplinary Approach*. Richard Falk and Samuel Kim, eds. 509–27. Boulder, Colo.: Westview Press.

Holzman, Franklyn. 1980. Are the Soviets Really Outspending the U.S. on Defense? *International Security* 4(4):86–104.

Hopkins, T., and I. Wallerstein. 1977. Patterns of Development in the Modern World-System. *Review* 1: 111–45.

Horowitz, Irving Louis, ed. 1967. *The Rise and Fall of Project Camelot: Studies in the Relationship between Social Science and Practical Politics*. Cambridge, Mass.: MIT Press.

Hough, Walter. 1915. *The Hopi Indians*. Cedar Rapids, Iowa: Torch Press.

Hudson, A. E. 1938. *Kazak Social Structure*. New Haven: Yale University Press.

Hunter, Floyd. 1953. *Community Power Structure: A Study of Decision Makers*. Chapel Hill, N. C.: University of North Carolina Press.

———. 1959. *Top Leadership, U.S.A.* Chapel Hill, N. C.: University of North Carolina Press.

———. 1980 *Community Power Succession: Atlanta's Policy Makers Revisited*. Chapel Hill, N.C.: University of North Carolina Press.

Huntington, Samuel P. 1957. *The Soldier and the State*. Cambridge, Mass.: Harvard University Press.

Hyde, George E. 1951. *The Pawnee Indians*. Denver, Colo.: University of Denver Press.

Illich, Ivan. 1982. The Delinking of Peace and Development. *Alternatives* 7:4.

Iordachel, Ion. 1979. Conferinta 'Cercetarile in Domeniu Stiintelor Sociale din Romania. *Viitorul Social* 8 (2): 349–402.

Janis, I.L. 1973. *Victims of Groupthink*. Boston: Houghton Mifflin.

Ishida, T., ed. 1973. *More Against Atomic Bombs: Life History of Nagasaki Atomic Bomb Survivors*. Tokyo: Miraisha.

Janowitz, Morris. 1960. *The Professional Soldier*. New York: Free Press.

———. 1975 *Military Conflict: Essays in the Institutional Analysis of War and Peace*. Beverly Hills: Sage.

Jenks, Albert Ernest. 1905. *The Bontoc Igorot*. Ethnological Survey Publication. vol 1. Manila: Bureau of Public Printing.

Jervis, Robert. 1980. Hypotheses on Misperception. In *The War System: An Interdisciplinary Approach*. Richard Falk and Samuel Kim, eds. 465–90. Boulder, Colo.: Westview Press.

Johnston, D. R., et al.1978. Study of Crisis Administration of Hospital Patients and Study of Management of Medical Problems Resulting from Crisis Relocation. Research Triangle Park, N.C.: Research Triangle Institute.

Johnston, Francis E. 1985. Statement as Candidate for President-Elect. *Anthropology Newsletter* 26: 7.

Junod, H. A. 1927. *The Life of a South African Tribe.* 2 vol. London: Macmillan.

Kahler, M. 1979–1980. Rumors of War: The 1914 Analogy. *Foreign Affairs* (Winter): 374–96.

Kahnert, M., et al. 1983. *Children and War.* Geneva: Geneva International Peace Research Institute.

Kamm, Henry. 1986. For Rumania, A Vote Today on Military Cuts. *New York Times.* November 23.

Karsten, Rafael. 1935. The Head-Hunters of Western Amazonas. *Societas Scientiarum Fennica: Commentationes Humanaum Litterarum* 7(1). Helsinki: Centraltryckeriet.

Kaufman, Michael. 1987. Warsaw Journal: Hippie Foes of the Draft Handled with Kid Gloves. *New York Times.* January 2.

Keddie, Nikki. 1981. *Roots of Revolution.* New Haven: Yale University Press.

Kennan, George F. 1976. *The Nuclear Delusion.* New York: Pantheon.

———. 1986. "A New Philosphy of Defense." *New York Review of Books.*

Kennett, Lee, and James LaVerne Anderson. 1975. *The Gun in America: The Origins of a National Dilemma.* Westport, Conn.: Greenwood.

Kideckel, David A., and Steven L. Sampson. 1984. Fieldwork in Romania: Political, Practical, and Ethical Aspects. In *Economy, Society, and Culture in Contemporary Romania.* John W. Cole, ed. 85–102. Research Report No. 24. Amherst, Mass.: University of Massachusetts.

Kinnard, Gen. Douglas, 1977. *The War Managers.* Hanover, N.H.: University Press of New England.

Koch, Klaus-Friedrich. 1974. *The Anthropology of Warfare.* Addison-Wesley Modules in Anthropology, No. 52. Reading, Mass.: Addison-Wesley.

Kriesberg, Louis, and Ross Klein. 1980. Changes in Public Support for the U.S. Military Spending. *Journal of Conflict Resolution* 24(1):79–111.

Kurth, James. 1974. Testing Theories of Economic Imperialism. In *Testing Theories of Economic Imperialism.* S. Rosen and J. Kurth, eds. 3–33. Lexington, Mass.: Lexington Books.

Ladd, Everett Carll. 1976–1977. The Polls: the Question of Confidence. *Public Opinion Quarterly* 40(4):546–52.

Laney, M. N., et al. 1976. *Management of Medical Problems Resulting from Population Relocation.* Research Triangle Park, N.C.: Research Triangle Institute.

Leach, E. 1965. *Political Systems of Highland Burma.* Boston: Beacon.

———. 1976 *Culture and Communication.* Cambridge, Eng.: Cambridge University Press.

Leaning, J., and L. Keys. 1984. The Singularity of Nuclear War: Paradigms of Disaster Planning. In *The Counterfeit Ark.* J. Leaning and L. Keys, eds. 3–23. Cambridge, Mass.: Ballinger.

Leaning, J., and L. Keys, eds. 1984. *The Counterfeit Ark.* Cambridge, Mass.: Ballinger.

Leeds, Anthony. 1975. Capitalism, Colonialism, and War: An Evolutionary Perspective. In *War, Its Causes and Correlates.* M. Nettleship, R. D. Givens, and A. Nettleship, eds. 483–513. The Hague: Mouton.

Lemann, Nicholas. 1984. Peacetime War. *The Atlantic.* October.

Lewis, Flora. 1984. Moscow's Apoplexy. *The* [Tucson] *Arizona Daily Star.* May 27.

Lindgren, James. 1981. Organizational and Other Constraintson Controlling the Use of Deadly Force by Police. *Annals of the American Academy of Political and Social Science* 455:110–19.

Lizotte, A. J., and D. J. Bordua. 1980. Firearms Ownership for Sport and Protection. *American Sociological Review* 45: 229–44.

Llewellyn, K. N., and A. E. Hoebel. 1941. *The Cheyenne Way*. Norman, Okla.: University of Oklahoma Press.

Lockwood, William. 1975. *European Moslems: Ethnicity and Economy in Western Bosnia*. New York: Academic Press.

Lukes, S. 1973. *Power*. London: Macmillan.

Luttwak, Edward. 1984. *The Pentagon and the Art of War*. New York: Simon & Schuster.

McNamara, Robert. 1983. The Military Role of Nuclear Weapons: Perceptions and Misperceptions. *Foreign Affairs* 62(1):59–80.

McNeely, J., and D. Pitt, eds. 1985. *Culture and Conservation*. London: Croom Helm.

Marsh, Gerald. 1983. No Evidence of Cheating. *Bulletin of the Atomic Scientists*. Kenwood, Ill.: The Educational Foundation for Nuclear Science.

Mauss, Marcel. 1954. *The Gift*. London: Cohen & West.

Mearsheimer, John J. 1983. *Conventional Deterrence*. Ithaca: Cornell University Press.

Medvedev, Roy, and Zhores Medvedev. 1981. The USSR and the Arms Race. *New Left Review* 130:1–22.

Meggitt, Mervyn. 1977. *Blood Is Their Argument: Warfare among the Mae Enga of the New Guinea Highlands*. Palo Alto, Calif.: Mayfield.

Melman, Seymour. 1965. *Our Depleted Society*. New York: Delta.

Meltzer, Milton. 1976. *Never to Forget: The Jews of the Holocaust*. New York: Harper & Row.

Middleton, Hugh. 1982. Epidemiology: The Future Is Sickness and Death. *Ambio* 11:100–5.

Middleton, J., and D. Tait. 1958. *Tribes without Rulers*. London: Routledge & Kegan Paul.

Miller, R. L. 1986. Let's Not Forget Radiation in the United States. *New York Times*. June 23.

Mills, C. Wright. 1956. *The Power Elite*. New York: Oxford University Press.

———. 1959. *The Sociological Imagination*. New York: Oxford University Press.

Modelski, G. 1978. The Long Cycle of Global Politics and the Nation-State. *Comparative Studies in Society and History* 20:214–35.

Moore, S., and B. Myerhoff. 1977. *Secular Ritual*. Amsterdam: Van Gorcum.

Moskos, Charles C., Jr. 1973. The Emergent Military: Civil, Traditional, or Plural? In *National Security and American Society*. Frank N. Trager and Philip S. Kronenberg, eds. 547–9. The National Security Education Program. Lawrence, Kan.: The University Press of Kansas.

———. 1979. From Institution to Occupation: Trends in Military Organization. In *War, Morality, and the Military Profession*. Malkam M. Wakin, ed. 219–29. Boulder, Colo.: Westview Press.

Murdock, George P. 1934. *Our Primitive Contemporaries*. New York: Macmillan.

Murdock, George P., and Douglas R. White. 1969. Standard Cross-Cultural Sample. *Ethnology* 8: 329–69.

Murphy, Robert F. 1956. Matrilocality and Patrilineality in Mundurucu Society. *American Anthropologist* 58:414–34.

———. 1957. Intergroup Hostility and Social Cohesion. *American Anthropologist* 59: 1018–35.

———. 1960. *Headhunter's Heritage*. Berkeley: University of Calif. Press.

Musil, A. 1928. *The Manners and Customs of the Rwala Bedouins*. New York: published under the patronage of the Czech Academy of Sciences and Arts and of Charles R. Crane.

Myrdal, Alva. 1982. *The Game of Disarmament: How the United States and Russia Run the Arms Race*. (Revised and updated edition.) New York: Pantheon.

NACLA (North American Congress on Latin America). 1983. The Media Go to War. *NACLA Report on the Americas* 17(4), D. Hallin, issue editor.

Nader, Laura. 1983. Two Plus Two Equals Zero: War and Peace Reconsidered. *Radcliffe Quarterly*. March.

———. 1986. Nuclear Winter: The Anthropology of Human Survival. Los Alamos National Laboratory Document LA–UR–84–370:39–43.

Naroll, Raoul. 1966. Does Military Deterrence Deter? *Transaction* 3: 14–20.

Naroll, Raoul, Vern L. Bullough, and Frada Naroll. 1974. *Military Deterrence in History: A Pilot Cross-Historical Survey*. Albany, N. Y.: State University of New York Press.

Nash, June. 1975. Nationalism and Fieldwork. In *Annual Review of Anthropology*. vol. 5. B. Siegel, ed. 225–45. Palo Alto, Calif.: Annual Reviews.

Narveson, Jan. 1985. Getting on the Road to Peace: A Modest Proposal. In *Nuclear Deterrence: Ethics and Strategy*. Russell Hardin et.al., eds. 213–29. Chicago: University of Chicago Press.

National Rifle Association. 1986. "Glitch" in D.C. Gun Law Snares Kennedy Bodyguard. *American Rifleman* 134(3): 40.

Nettleship, Martin. 1975. Summary prepared by members of the Pre-Congress Conference, "War: Its Causes and Correlates." In *War, Its Causes and Correlates*. Martin Nettleship et al., eds. 775–85. The Hague: Mouton.

Nettleship, Martin et al., eds. 1975. *War, Its Causes and Consequences*. The Hague: Mouton.

Newman, Oscar. 1972. *Defensible Space: People and Design in the Violent City*. New York: Macmillan.

Newton, George D., and Franklin E. Zimring. 1969. Firearms and Violence in American Life: A Staff Report to the National Commission on the Causes and Prevention of Violence. Washington, D.C.: U.S. Government Printing Office.

O'Brien, C., and F. Topolski. 1968. *United Nations Sacred Drama*. London: Hutchinson.

Office of Technology Assessment. 1984. Compliance with the 1972 ABM Treaty. In *Arms Control in Space: Workshop Proceedings*. Appendix B. Washington, D.C.: U. S. Congress.

Ogburn, William Fielding. 1922. *Social Change*. New York: Viking Press.

Opler, Morris E. 1937. An Outline of Chiricahua Apache Social Organization. In *Social Anthropology of North American Tribes*. F. Eggan, ed. 173–239. Chicago: University of Chicago Press.

———. 1941. *An Apache Life-Way*. Chicago: University of Chicago Press.

Osgood, Charles E. 1962. *An Alternative to War or Surrender*. Urbana, Ill.: University of Illinois Press.

Otterbein, Keith F. 1973. The Anthropology of War. In *Handbook of Social and Cultural Anthropology*, John J. Honigmann, ed. 923–58. New York: Rand McNally.

———. 1985. *The Evolution of War*. New Haven: Human Relations Area Files Press. (Originally published 1970.)

———. 1986. *The Ultimate Coercive Sanction: A Cross-Cultural Study of Capital Punishment*. New Haven: Human Relations Area Files Press.

Pace, Eric. 1986. Ban on A-Arms Urged in Study by Methodists. *New York Times.* April 27.

Paige, Glenn. 1977. On Values and Sciences: The Korean Decision Reconsidered. *American Political Science Review* 71:1603–9.

Peattie, Lisa. 1986. The Defense of Daily Life. *Newsletter of the Commission on the Study of Peace* 4(1):3–12.

Pelto, Pertti J., and Gretel H. Pelto. 1973. Ethnography: The Fieldwork Enterprise. In *Handbook of Social and Cultural Anthropology.* John J. Honigmann, ed. 241–88. Chicago: Rand McNally.

Penniman, T. K., ed. 1938. *The Old-Time Maori, by Makereti, Sometime Chieftainess of the Arama Tribe, Known in New Zealand as Maggie Papakura.* London: Gollancz.

Pentagon Plan Specifies Methods of Winning Protracted Nuclear War. 1982. *International Herald Tribune.* August 16.

Pillsbury, M. 1979. A Japanese Card? Foreign Policy 33: 3–30.

Pitt, David C. 1976. *The Social Dynamics of Development.* Oxford: Pergamon.

———. 1983 *Using Historical Documents in Anthropology and Sociology.* New York: Holt, Rinehart & Winston.

Posen, Barry, and Stephen Van Evera. 1983. Defense Policy and the Reagan Administration: Departure from Containment. *International Security* 8(1):3-45.

Postman, M. V. 1899. *A History of Our Relations with the Andamanese.* Calcutta: Office of the Superintendent of Government Printing.

Powdermaker, Hortense. 1966. *Stranger and Friend.* New York: Norton.

Powers, Thomas. 1982. *Thinking about the Next War.* New York: Knopf.

———. 1984a. What Is It About? *The Atlantic* 253 (1): 35–55.

———. 1984b. Nuclear Winter and Nuclear Strategy. *The Atlantic.* 254(5): 53–60, 63–64.

Proxmire, William. 1970. *Report from Wasteland: America's Military-Industrial-Complex.* New York: Praeger.

Quester, G. 1979. Options for Accelerating Economic Recovery After a Nuclear Attack. Marina Del Ray, Calif.: Analytical Assessments.

Radcliffe-Brown, A. R. 1933.*The Andaman Islander.* Cambridge, Eng.: Cambridge University Press.

Rappaport, Roy A. 1967. Ritual Regulations of Environmental Relations among a New Guinea People. *Ethology* 7:17–30.

Raswan, C. R. 1935. *Black Tents of Arabia.* Boston: Little, Brown.

Ravenal, Earl. 1979. Foreign Policy Made Difficult: A Comment on Wolfe and Sanders. In *Capitalism and the State in U.S.-Latin American Relations.* R. Fagen, ed. 82–89. Stanford: Stanford University Press.

Record, Jeffrey. 1984. *Revising U.S. Military Strategy: Tailoring Means to Ends.* New York: Pergamon-Brassey's.

Richardson, Lewis F. 1960. *Arms and Insecurity.* London: Stevens & Sons.

Rickover, Admiral Hyman. 1982. *No Hold Barred.* Washington, D.C.: Center for the Study of Responsive Law.

Roberts, Steven. 1986. Congress Is Taking Exception to Reagan's Foreign Policy Agenda. *New York Times.* May 25.

Romanian Research Group. 1979. Transylvanian Ethnicity: A Reply to "Ethnocide in Romania." *Current Anthropology* 20: 135–40.

Roscoe, John. 1965. *The Baganda; An Account of Their Native Customs and Beliefs.* 2nd ed. London: F. Cass.

Rosen, Steven, ed. 1973a. *Testing the Theory of the Military-Industrial Complex.* Lexington: Lexington Books.

———. 1973b. Testing the Theory of the Military-Industrial Complex. In *Testing the Theory of the Military-Industrial Complex*. S. Rosen, ed. 1–25. Lexington: Lexington Books.

Rosen, Steven, and James Kurth, eds. 1974. *Testing Theories of Economic Imperialism*. Lexington: Lexington Books.

Ross, Howard Marc. 1983. Political Decision Making and Conflict: Additional Cross-Cultural Codes and Scales. *Ethnology* 22: 169–92.

Sagan, Carl. 1984. We Can Prevent Nuclear Winter. *Parade Magazine*. September 30.

Sahlins, Marshall. 1967. The Established Order: Do Not Fold, Spindle, or Mutilate. In *The Rise and Fall of Project Camelot: Studies in the Relationship between Social Science and Practical Politics*. I.L. Horowitz, ed. 71–9. Cambridge, Mass.: MIT Press.

St. Luke. The Gospel According to St. Luke. The Holy Bible. Authorized. 1973. Nashville: Gideons International.

Scheer, Robert. 1982. *With Enough Shovels*. New York: Random House.

Schell, Jonathan. 1982. *The Fate of the Earth*. New York: Knopf.

———. 1984. Reflections: The Abolition. I—Defining the Great Predicament. II—A Deliberate Policy. *The New Yorker*. January 2, 9.

Schmookler, Andrew Bard. 1984. *The Parable of the Tribes: The Problem of Power in Social Evolution*. Boston: Houghton Mifflin.

Schumacher, F. 1973. *Small Is Beautiful*. London: Blond & Briggs.

Scientific Research Council on Peace and Disarmament. 1985. *Atom Must Only Serve Peace*. Moscow: Nauka Publisher.

Seligman, C. G., and B. Z. Seligman. 1932. *Pagan Tribes of the Nilotic Sudan*. London: G. Routledge & Sons.

Shaw, R. Paul. 1985. Humanity's Propensity for Warfare: A Sociobiological Perspective. *Canadian Review of Sociology and Anthropology* 22: 158–83.

Sherr, Alan B. 1984. Legal Issues of the "Star Wars" Defense Program. Lawyers Alliance Issues Brief #3. Cambridge, Mass.: Lawyers Alliance for Nuclear Arms Control.

Simic, Andrei. 1972. *The Peasant Urbanites: A Study of Rural Urban Mobility in Serbia*. New York: Seminar Press.

Simmons, Leo 1942. *Sun Chief, The Autobiography of a Hopi Indian*. New Haven: Yale University Press.

Simon, Jeffrey. 1980. Social Position and American Foreign Policy Attitudes: 1952–1972. *Journal of Peace Research* 17(1):9–28.

Singer, J. David. 1981. Accounting for International War: The State of the Discipline. *Journal of Peace Research* 18(1):1–18.

SIPRI. 1976. *Armaments and Disarmament in the Nuclear Age*. Atlantic Highlands, N. J.: Humanities.

Sklar, Holly, ed. 1980. *Trilateralism: The Trilateral Commission and Elite Planning for World Management*. Boston: South End Press.

Skocpol, Theda. 1979. *States and Social Revolutions*. Cambridge, Eng.: Cambridge University Press.

Sozan, Michael. 1977. Ethnocide in Rumania. *Current Anthropology* 18: 781–82.

———. 1979. Reply to Romanian Research Group. *Current Anthropology* 20: 141–46.

Spencer, Sir Baldwin, and F. J. Gillen. 1927. *The Arunta: A Study of a Stone Age People*. London: Macmillan.

Spier, Leslie. 1930. *Klamath Ethnography*. Berkeley, Calif.: University of California Press.

Spiro, Melford E. 1978. Culture and Human Nature. In *The Making Of Psychological Anthropology*. George Spindler, ed. 330-60. Berkeley, Calif.: University of California Press.

Stearns, Mary Lee. 1981. *Haida Culture in Custody*. Seattle: University of Washington Press.

Stein, Arthur. 1980. *The Nation at War*. Baltimore: Johns Hopkins University Press.

Stephen, A. M. 1936. Hopi Journal. E. C. Parsons, ed. *Columbia University Contributions to Anthropology*, vol. 38, pt. 1.

Stewart, Omer. 1964. The Need to Popularize Basic Concepts. *Current Anthropology* 5:431, 442.

Stirling, M. W. 1938. Historical and Ethnographical Material on the Jivaro Indians. *Bulletin Bureau American Ethnography* 117: 1–148.

Stone, I. F. 1971. *The Hidden History of the Korean War*. New York: Monthly Review Press.

Strasser, Stephen, et al. 1984. Can We Fight a Modern War? *Newsweek*. 104:34–8, 43,44,48. July 9.

Strode, Dan, and Rebecca Strode. 1983. Diplomacy and Defense in Soviet National Security Policy. *International Security* 8(2):91–116.

Stubbing, Richard. 1985. The Defense Program: Buildup or Binge. *Foreign Affairs* 63:848–72.

Suguira, S., and H. Befer. 1962. Kinship Organization of the Saru Ainu. *Ethnology* 1: 287–98.

Sutton, Francis X., et al. 1962. *The American Business Creed*. New York: Schocken.

Swanton, J.R. 1909. Contributions to the Ethnology of the Haida. *Memoirs of the American Museum of Natural History* 8: 1–300.

———. 1928. Social Organization and Social Uses of the Indians of the Creek Confederacy. Annual Report of the Bureau of American Ethnology, 1922–1923. Washington: U.S. Govt. Printing Office.

Taylor, Maxwell D. 1979. Changing Military Priorities. *American Enterprise Institute's Foreign Policy and Defense Review*. 1 (3): 2, 3.

Te Velde, H. 1977. *Seth, God of Confusion*. Leiden: Brill.

Thompson, E. P. 1981. A Letter to America. In *Protest and Survive*. E. P. Thompson and Dan Smith, eds. New York: Monthly Review Press.

———. 1982. *Beyond the Cold War*. New York: Pantheon.

Thompson, E. P., and Dan Smith, eds. 1981. *Protest and Survive*. New York: Monthly Review Press.

Thompson, E. P., et al. 1980. *Exterminism and Cold War*. Edited by New Left Review, Verso.

Thompson, Laura. 1950. *Culture in Crisis*. New York: Russel & Russel.

———. 1951. *Personality and Government*: Findings and Recommendations of the Indian Administration Research. Mexico, D.F.: Instituto Indigenista Interamericano.

Thompson, Laura, and Alice Joseph. 1944. *The Hopi Way*. Chicago: University of Chicago Press.

Thompson, M., M. Warburton, and T. Hatley. 1986. *Uncertainty on a Himalayan Scale*. London: Milton Ash.

Thompson, S. T., and S. H. Schneider. 1986. Nuclear Winter Reappraised. *Foreign Affairs* 64:981–1005.

Thurow, Lester. 1980. The Moral Equivalent of Defeat. *Foreign Policy* (Spring): 114–24.

Timberlake, Lloyd, and Jon Tinker. 1984. Environment and Conflict: Links between Ecological Decay, Environmental Bankruptcy, and Political and Military Instability. Earthscan Briefing Document No. 40. Washington, D.C.: Earthscan/IIED.

Tishkov, V. A. 1983. War and Peace: The View of a Soviet Scholar. Paper presented at the International Congress of Anthropological and Ethnological Science, Vancouver, British Columbia.

Titiev, Mischa. 1944. Old Oraibi, A Study of the Hopi Indians of Third Mesa. Papers of the Peabody Museum, vol. 22.

———. 1951. *Araucian Culture in Transition*. Ann Arbor: University of Michigan Press.

Truman, Harry S. 1955. *Memoirs*. vol. 1. *Year of Decisions*. Garden City, N.Y.: Doubleday.

———. 1956. *Memoirs*. vol. 2. *Years of Trial and Hope*. New York: Doubleday.

Tucker, Robert. 1980. The Purposes of American Power. *Foreign Affairs* 59(2):241–74.

———. 1984. The Nuclear Debate. *Foreign Affairs* 63(1):1–32.

Turco, R. P., et al. 1983. Nuclear Winter: Global Consequences of a Nuclear Exchange. *Science* 222:1283–92.

———. 1984. The Climatic Effects of Nuclear War. *Scientific American* 251:33–43.

Turnbull, Colin M. 1972. *The Mountain People*. New York: Simon & Schuster.

Uberoi Singh, J. P. 1962. *The Politics of the Kula Ring*. Manchester, Eng.: Manchester University Press.

Underhill, Ruth M. 1939. *Social Organization of the Papago Indians*. New York: Columbia University Press.

———. 1940. The Papago Indians of Arizona and Their Relatives the Pima. U.S. Bureau of Indian Affairs, Sherman Pamphlets no. 3.

———. 1946. *Papago Indian Religion*. New York: Columbia University Press.

Van Gennep, Arnold. 1960. *The Rites of Passage*. London: Routledge & Kegan Paul. (First published 1909.)

Von Hippel, Frank. 1983. The Mythos of Edward Teller. *Bulletin of the Atomic Scientists*. March.

Wallerstein, Immanuel. 1980. *The Modern World-System* vol. 2. New York: Academic Press.

Warnke, Paul. 1985. Interviewed on "What About the Russians," an audiotape distributed by The Educational and Video Project, 1529 Josephine Street, Berkeley, CA 94703.

Watanabe, H. 1973. *The Ainu Ecosystem: Environment and Group Structure*. Seattle: University of Washington Press.

Watkins, James D. 1982. The Moral Man in the Modern Military. *Seapower*. December.

Watt, D. C. 1977. Cold War. *Fontana Dictionary of Modern Thought*. London: Collins.

Weinberger, Caspar W. 1985. The Potential Effects of Nuclear War on the Climate. A Report to the United States Congress.

Weisner, Jerome. 1984. Introduction. In *The Counterfeit Ark*. J. Leaning and L. Keys, eds. Cambridge, Mass.: Ballinger.

Weltfish, Gene. 1965. *The Lost Universe, with a Closing Chapter on the Universe Regained*. New York: Basic Books.

Westermann, D. 1912. *The Shilluk People*. Philadelphia: The Board of Foreign Missions of the United Presbyterian Church of North America.

What about the Russians? 1984. Berkeley, Calif.: Educational Film and Video Project.

Willens, Harold. 1984. *The Trimtab Factor—How Business Executives Can Help Solve the Nuclear Crisis.* New York: William Morrow.

Wilson, George C. 1986. Did We Learn Nothing from Vietnam? *Washington Post* National Weekly Edition. April 14.

Wilson, Godfrey. 1938. *The Land Rights of Individuals among the Nyakyusa.* Livingston, Northern Rhodesia: The Rhodes-Livingston Institute.

Wilson, Monica. 1950. Nyakyusa Kinship. In *African Systems of Kinship and Marriage.* A. R. Radcliffe-Brown and M. Fortes, eds. 111–39. London: Oxford University Press.

———. 1951. *Good Company, A Study of Nyakyusa Age-Villages.* London: Oxford University Press.

Winner, Irene P. 1971. *A Slovenian Village: Zerovnica.* Providence, R.I.: Brown University Press.

Winpisinger, William. 1982. Organized Labor and Economic Conversion. In *The Political Economy of Arms Reduction.* Lloyd J. Dumas, ed. 107–11. Boulder, Colo.: Westview Press.

Wolf, Eric. 1973. *Peasant Wars of the Twentieth Century.* New York: Harper Torchbooks.

———. 1982. *Europe and the People without History.* Berkeley, Calif.: University of California Press.

Wolfe, Alan. 1979. *The Rise and Fall of the "Soviet Threat": Domestic Sources of the Cold War Consensus.* Washington, D.C.: Institute for Policy Studies.

Wolfe, Alan, and Jerry Sanders. 1979. Resurgent Cold War Ideology: The Case of the Committee on the Present Danger. In *Capitalism and the State in U.S.-Latin American Relations.* R. Fagen, ed. 41–75. Stanford, Calif.: Stanford University Press.

Worsley, Peter. 1984. *The Three Worlds: Culture and World Development.* Chicago: University of Chicago Press.

——— 1985. Proposals for Anthropology in the Nuclear Age. Newsletter, Commission on the Study of Peace. *International Union of Anthropological and Ethnological Sciences* 3 (3):10, 11.

Wright, James D., Peter H. Rossi, and Kathleen Daly. 1983. *Under the Gun: Weapons, Crime, and Violence in America.* New York: Aldine.

Wyden, Peter. 1984. *Day One: Before Hiroshima and After.* New York: Simon & Schuster.

Yankelovich, Daniel, and John Doble. 1984. The Public Mood: Nuclear Weapons and the U.S.S.R. *Foreign Affairs* 63(1):33–46.

Yarmolinsky, Adam. 1973. The Military Establishment and Social Values. In *National Security and American Society.* Frank N. Trager and Philip S. Kronenberg, eds. 507–15. The National Security Education Program. Lawrence: University Press of Kansas.

Yevtushenko, Yevgeny. 1986. *The Times (of London).* January 4.

Zuckerman, Edward. 1984. *The Day After World War III.* New York: Viking.

Index

Abel, Theodore, 152
Abipone, 16, 18, 24
ABM, 116, 119–21, 124, 125
Abrahamson, Bengt, 26
Abrams, H. L., 104, 106–9
ACDA. *See* Arms Control and
 Disarmament Agency
Adair, James, 19
Adams, Richard, 80, 173
Adversary: automatic suspicion of, 163;
 political, 46; potential, 44, 122, 130,
 134; Romanian cold war, 171; stronger
 than, 129; underestimation of, 40
Advisors, 155
Afghanistan, 6, 39, 49, 125, 162, 164
Africa, 11, 98
Aggressiveness: causes of, 46; emphasis
 on, 33; human characteristic, 147;
 posturing, 45; training, 22; United
 States, 62
Aggressor, 74, 129, 134
Ainu, 16, 17, 23
Air Force Academy, 42
Albania, 6, 11
Algeria, 57
Alliance system, 97
Amazon, 23, 163
American Anthropological Association,
 xiv, 176
American Association for the
 Advancement of Science, 27n
American Rifleman, 137n
Andamanese, 17, 22, 23
Anderson, James, 132, 137n
Anglo-Russian Convention, 96
Anglo-Saxon Protestant, 6
Angola, 101, 163
Annapolis, 42
Anthropologists: American, 162; British,
 167; change in, 155; and cold war, 161,
 166, 167, 172, 176, 178; and conflict
 resolution, 177; contributions of, 46;
 cross-cultural research of, 163; cultural
 relativism of, 175, 176; and culture of
 suspicion, 167; in Eastern Europe, 172;

expertise of, 46; expulsion of, 170;
 foreign, 170; French, 165, 167;
 Hungarian-American, 169; ideas of,
 142; independent-minded, 155;
 "intelligence," 155; involvement of,
 154; insights of, 175; motives of, 167;
 naiveté of, 163; propaganda, 154;
 recruitment of, 155; in Romania, 172;
 Romanian fieldwork, 170; sense of
 otherness of, 175; small communities
 expertise, 177; in socialist society, 172;
 Swiss, 165; Western, 166, 170; West
 German, 165
Anthropologists for Human Survival, 149
Anthropology: access, 166; binary
 opposites, 83; cold war tensions, 172;
 community role, 167; contemporary
 war, 150, 151; contributions of, 147,
 151, 158, 161; course in, 42; data base,
 176; disaster for, 155; discussion, 151;
 ending cold war, 176; as espionage,
 167; findings of, 147; focus of, 174;
 global interactions, 151; goal for, 172;
 inputs for, 149; research, 149, 160–63,
 165–67, 171–73, in Romania, 165
Anthropology Newsletter, 176
Anti-Satellite (ASAT), 119, 120, 124–27
Apache, 16, 19, 21, 24
Apartheid, 11
Arab, 63
Aranda, 23
Argentia, 91–93
Argyres, Andreas, 173n
Armaments, 44, 75, 100, 135, 136n
"Armed Citizen, The," 137n
Armelagos, George, xvi
Arms: control of, 114–17, 119, 121, 126;
 nuclear, 157; possession of, 128, 133;
 sales of to Iran, 63; temptation to use,
 128; use of, 128
Arms Control and Disarmament
 Agency (ACDA), 118, 119
Arms race: cause of war, 128; classical,
 136n; concern with, 85; domestic, 132;
 emphasis on, 85; end of, 135;